Inviting God In

Inviting God In

A Guide to Jewish Prayer

RABBI JEFFREY K. SALKIN

Foreword by Rabbi Dalia Marx, PhD

CCAR
Press

Reform Judaism Publishing, a division of CCAR Press

Central Conference of American Rabbis

5785 NEW YORK 2025

Published by Reform Judaism Publishing, a division of CCAR Press
Central Conference of American Rabbis
New York, NY
(212) 972-3636 | info@ccarpress.org | www.ccarpress.org

Library of Congress Cataloging-in-Publication Data
Names: Salkin, Jeffrey K., 1954-author.
Title: Inviting God in: a guide to Jewish prayer / Rabbi Jeffrey K. Salkin.
Description: First edition. | New York: Reform Judaism Publishing, a
    division of CCAR Press, Central Conference of American Rabbis, 5785 =
    2025. | Summary: "An accessible and engaging primer on Shabbat prayer
    services from a Reform Jewish perspective"—Provided by publisher.
Identifiers: LCCN 2025007846 (print) | LCCN 2025007847 (ebook) | ISBN
    9780881236743 (trade paperback) | ISBN 9780881236750 (ebook)
Subjects: LCSH: Sabbath—Liturgy. | Prayer—Judaism. | Reform
    Judaism—Liturgy.
Classification: LCC BM675.S3 Z7925 2025 (print) | LCC BM675.S3 (ebook) |
    DDC 296.4/5—dc23/eng/20250312
LC record available at https://lccn.loc.gov/2025007846
LC ebook record available at https://lccn.loc.gov/2025007847

Book interior designed and composed by Scott-Martin Kosofsky
    at The Philidor Company, Rhinebeck, NY. www.philidor.com
Cover photograph of Temple Beth-El of Jersey City
    by Rabbi Steven Kushner. Used by permission.
Cover design by Barbara Leff

Printed in USA
10 9 8 7 6 5 4 3 2 1

Contents

FOREWORD   vii
Rabbi Dalia Marx, PhD

ACKNOWLEDGMENTS   xi

INTRODUCTION   1

JEWISH PRAYER: BOOT CAMP   19

MAARIV: EVENING SERVICE   27
    The Preliminary Stuff   27
       Candle Lighting, *Kiddush, Kabbalat Shabbat,*
       Shalom Aleichem, Chatzi Kaddish
    Act One—What We Believe: *Sh'ma Uvirchoteha—*
    Sh'ma and Its Blessings   49
       Bar'chu, Maariv Aravim, Ahavat Olam, Sh'ma,
       V'ahavta, G'ulah (*Emet VeEmunah* and *Mi Chamochah*),
       Hashkiveinu, V'shamru, and *Yism'chu*
    Act Two—What We Need: *T'filah*   63
       Avot V'Imahot, G'vurot, K'dushah, K'dushat HaYom, Avodah,
       Hodaah, Shalom, T'filat HaLev, Magein Avot V'Imahot
    Act Three—What We Learn   79
    Act Four—What We Hope   80
       Aleinu, Kaddish Yatom

SHACHARIT: MORNING SERVICE   89
    The Preliminary Stuff   89
       Birchot HaShachar—Morning Blessings: *Modeh/Modah Ani,*
       Tzitzit, Mah Tovu, Asher Yatzar, Elohai N'shamah, Nisim
       B'chol Yom, Laasok/V'haarev Na, Eilu D'varim, Kaddish
       D'Rabanan
       P'sukei D'Zimrah—Verses of Praise: *Baruch She-amar,*
       Psalm 92, Ashrei, Psalm 150, Nishmat Kol Chai, Yishtabach,
       Chatzi Kaddish

Act One—What We Believe: *Sh'ma Uvirchoteha—*
Sh'ma and Its Blessings   129
   Bar'chu, Yotzeir, El Adon, Ahavah Rabbah, Sh'ma, V'ahavta,
   Vayomer Adonai, G'ulah (Emet V'Yatziv and *Mi Chamochah)*
Act Two—What We Need: *T'filah*   143
   Avot V'Imahot, G'vurot, K'dushah, K'dushat HaYom (Yism'chu/
   V'shamru), Avodah, Hodaah, Shalom, T'filat HaLev
Act Three—What We Learn: *Seder K'riat HaTorah*
L'Shabbat—Reading the Torah on Shabbat   158
   Kabbalat HaTorah, Hakafah and *L'cha Adonai, Birchot HaTo-*
   rah, Mi Shebeirach for *Aliyah, Hagbahah Ug'lilah,*
   Mi Shebeirach for Healing, *Birkat HaGomeil, Haftarah,*
   Hachzarat HaTorah, Prayers for Our Community, *Hallel*
Act Four—What We Hope   207
   Aleinu, Kaddish Yatom

CONCLUSION   213

NOTES   215

ABOUT THE AUTHOR   221

Foreword

Rabbi Dalia Marx, PhD

SHABBAT is unique because it is both a divine innovation and a human formation. According to the Jewish tradition, Shabbat is *sof maaseh b'machshavah t'chilah*, "the last of days for which the first was made," as we sing on Friday night in *L'chah Dodi* (41). Shabbat was God's final act of Creation, intended as both Creation's pinnacle and its purpose. It is also a human formation, because unlike other cycles of time such as the day, the month, and the (solar) year, the cycle of the week is not marked in nature. It is a rather bold decision to mark it, dedicating it as a day apart every seven days. Every Jewish person chooses how to make Shabbat a day of rest, meaningful time with family and loved ones, contemplation, exploration, and prayer (which, in fact, includes them all), whether we are in our homes, outdoors, or in our houses of worship.

Shabbat can be understood through theological, ideological, or halachic (legal) lenses and is marked with many beautiful rituals, prayers, and blessings. For many, the most natural expression of Shabbat for Jews is that of communal and family celebration. Shabbat has a special meaning for us as a people. Asher Ginsberg, known as Achad HaAm and one of the most prominent Jewish thinkers of the twentieth century, argued that "more than the Jewish People has kept Shabbat, Shabbat has kept the Jewish People" (see *Mishkan T'filah*, 163). Throughout the generations, Shabbat has helped us to regroup and recuperate—it has kept us together.

However, today many Jews feel disempowered and puzzled when approaching Shabbat, disenfranchised from the beauty of its worship and liturgy. Many are interested and intrigued by our worship and celebrations but feel robbed of knowledge and experience. Many wish to celebrate Shabbat and observe it but on their own terms, rather than recycling and adopting a ready-made version of it. They want to choose how to approach the sacred nature of our holy day. It is a well-known secret: In order to choose, we must first be informed. If we want to make our own conscious choices about how to observe Shabbat, we need information about it. This is where the unique and tremendously important book by Rabbi Jeffrey K. Salkin offers such valuable help!

Rabbi Salkin—a thoughtful Jewish leader, an experienced writer, a prominent speaker for liberal and progressive Judaism, a columnist and podcaster, and perhaps more than anything else an efficacious and dedicated educator—has created a meaningful tool for understanding Shabbat prayers with his book *Inviting God In: A Guide to Jewish Prayer*. Rabbi Salkin knows that being a liberal and progressive Jew is not about what is sometimes referred to as "the level of observance" (oh, how I find this term disturbing, as if anyone can measure our dedication), but instead about the way we understand and perceive our Jewishness through cognizant choice. His book *Inviting God In* is a wonderful companion for this journey.

Inviting God In is a hands-on book that will guide you through the Shabbat liturgy and serve as a guide to the perplexed, discussing profound and complex concepts in an accessible manner for Jews of all ages—including students preparing for their bet mitzvah, the first prominent rite of passage Jews choose to have. Rabbi Salkin explains in a meaningful and relatable manner not only the "how" of prayer but also the "why." For example, when discussing the blessing over the wine, he explains why we hold the *Kiddush* cup in a different way than we normally hold our regular cup—we hold it in the palm of our hands with our five fingers reaching upward around the cup, resembling, he says, a rose. A rose is a powerful symbol in Judaism because it symbolizes the entire Jewish people. Holding the cup as if we are a rose—a beautiful flower that has a lovely fragrance but also has thorns—brings to mind the joy and the pain that we deal with in this world. "When we hold the *Kiddush* cup this way, the hand must be open as well—the open hand that receives blessing, and the open heart that receives blessing as well" (see page 31). This relatable yet deeply profound explanation of a ritual practice adds extra layers of meaning to our Shabbat rituals.

Throughout his book, Rabbi Salkin invites us to explore the siddur, the prayer book, and discover that between its covers we can find endless topics that will enrich us as Jews and human beings and that will become part of our lives. Another example of this type of discovery comes when he addresses the *Ashrei* prayer (see page 116), which begins with the words "Happy are those who dwell in Your house; they forever praise You!" Rabbi Salkin discusses what happiness really is and the difference between fun and joy. Today, facing our stormy reality, many of us ask ourselves this question, which stands at the core of positive psychology, imbuing it with a Jewish language. These are just two examples of the many questions and topics Rabbi Salkin presents to his readers, grappling with profound concepts in an accessible manner, and inviting readers to explore the endless wealth of the siddur.

Inviting God In addresses matters that are timeless, but in a way that we—Jews of the twenty-first century, living in a time of great uncertainty and anxiety—can relate to. For example, in his discussion of the *Kaddish* prayer, he cites the author Shmuel Yosef Agnon's understanding of the prayer as God mourning for the loss of life, then relates it to the horrors of the massacre of October 7. Rabbi Salkin urges us to find meaning in phrases that one could dismiss as outdated. For example, when discussing the *Hashkiveinu* blessing (see page 59), he shows how the term *dever* (plague)—which many Reform liturgists edited out of prayer books, believing it belonged only to the past—is relevant to our post COVID-19 pandemic times. *Inviting God In* will leave you with enduring questions to ponder by yourself and to discuss with family members and fellow congregants and friends. These thought-provoking questions are not only valuable for bet mitzvah students and people who are in the beginning stages of their Jewish journey but will also prove to be fruitful for people with a solid Jewish background, for Jewish educators, and for clergy. I am sure that everyone who dedicates time to this precious gem, no matter their knowledge and experience, will be tremendously enriched by it.

Rabbi Dalia Marx, PhD, is the Rabbi Aaron D. Panken Professor of Liturgy at Hebrew Union College–Jewish Institute of Religion (HUC-JIR) in Jerusalem. A tenth-generation Jerusalemite, Rabbi Marx earned her doctorate at Hebrew University and her rabbinic ordination at HUC-JIR in Jerusalem and Cincinnati. She is the author of several books and the chief editor of Tefilat Ha-Adam, *the Israeli Reform prayer book (MaRaM, 2020). Her book* From Time to Time: Journeys in the Jewish Calendar *was first published in Israel in 2018 as* Bazman *and has been translated into German, Spanish, and now English. Rabbi Marx and her life partner, Roly Zylbersztein, PhD, live in Jerusalem; they have three children.*

Acknowledgments

The world is sustained by three things:
Torah, worship, and loving deeds.
—Pirkei Avot 1:2

THE ANCIENT SAGES understood Judaism as a threefold path. You could "do Jewish" by studying the sacred words of our tradition, by praying and worshiping God, and by doing acts of *g'milut chasadim* (acts of loving-kindness), the mitzvot that bind us to other people and therefore help us heal society and the world.

Or, my favorite way of putting it: Judaism is the three *H*'s. I learned this from the late Conservative Jewish scholar and teacher Dr. Neil Gillman (Canada and United States, 1933–2017). There is the *head*: learning and study. There is the *heart*: prayer, worship, and spirituality. There is the *hand*: activism through ethical behavior and social justice. Those three things—head/Torah, heart/prayer and worship, and hand/loving deeds—are ideal ways for people to live Jewish lives, act in Jewish ways, and generally be and do Jewish.

This is what I have often believed. While Judaism contains all three, it is extremely rare for any one person to be able to do all three well. Usually, someone "majors" in one *H*, "minors" in a second *H*, and leaves the third *H* for others. No one can pull all three together, which is quite alright, actually—the cool thing about living in a Jewish community is that there is always someone (sometimes a friend or a relative or the person sitting behind you in synagogue) who totally has that missing *H* down. Together we all create Judaism.

This is how it played out for me. I majored in *head*—learning and study. For me, the intellectual part of Judaism resonated strongly, and that is why I devoted so much of my career to being a teacher and a writer. I like helping people think deeply about Judaism. I minored in *heart*—prayer, worship, and spirituality. As for *hand*—activism . . . well, that part of the Jewish tradition was always there for me, but it was never the most important thing.

Recently, however, I changed my mind about this "three-*H* system." I am no longer sure that different people "major" or "minor" or don't do certain parts of the tradition. I now think that people change during their lives—an *H* that was once important can become less important, and an *H* that was less important can become crucial, and even central, to how someone lives their Jewish life. We are all on Jewish journeys, and those journeys change.

That is how it has been for me. Once upon a time, prayer and worship were not that important to me. Let me be clear: As a congregational rabbi, I liked leading services. But as a regular Jew, on a Shabbat when I was not working, or on vacation, or even in retirement, I did not necessarily run to synagogue on a Shabbat or festival for services. And when I did, I always brought my "head" part with me. When I attended services, I let the music and words rush over me, and I would thumb through the prayer book, finding passages that grabbed my mind and made me think.

I have changed, and that *H* of the heart—prayer, worship, and spirituality—is now more important to me than ever. In the final years of my congregational rabbinical career, I dedicated myself, more and more, to helping people find meaning in the prayers of our worship service.

For that reason, I want to give a special shout-out to the members of the congregations I have served. They always pushed me to explain the prayers—when they were written, why they were written, and what those prayers could say to us today. Over the years, I created learning services, introduced special programs called "Praying with Fire," and encouraged questions and answers during services—all with the express desire to lift prayer up to a new level. To some extent, I was trying to treat the worship service the way that many of us had been treating Torah itself—as an opportunity to ask deep questions and to engage our body, mind, and heart.

This was never more true than when I served my most recent congregation, Temple Israel in West Palm Beach, Florida. I landed there at the very beginning of the 2020 pandemic. Services were entirely online. I had to reconstruct the prayer book, engage people from afar, and bring people into what we, as a congregation, needed to do. During that difficult and challenging time, making prayer real became a "realer" project than ever before. In particular, and when we returned in person to the synagogue building, I focused on our young people. I went through the entire service in order—teaching, telling stories, asking questions. Some of those insights have made their way into these pages.

Who were my teachers in all this?

The first, and still the greatest, was Rabbi Lawrence A. Hoffman, PhD, who has taught liturgy at Hebrew Union College–Jewish Institute of Religion for about fifty years. Before Rabbi Hoffman began his career, a liturgy professor was someone who taught about *what* Jews pray—the words of the prayers, their history, their authors, and the historical period and events that birthed them. Rabbi Hoffman was the first Jewish teacher to think about *how* and *why* Jews pray. He taught his students to go beyond the words of the prayer texts, to consider the music, the spaces where we prayed, how people sat, how far away the prayer leaders were from the congregation, and what prayer books looked like. He taught us to think about synagogues not as membership institutions or as "clubs," but as places that create relationships and make life meaningful for people.

Rabbi Larry Hoffman became one of the most creative and crucial thinkers in the Jewish world. Over the decades, he was my teacher and, I am proud to say, my friend. If you are wondering who planted my first seeds of curiosity about the way that we pray and the words that we use, look no further than Rabbi Hoffman.

Second are my years of doctoral study at the Princeton Theological Seminary. There, my "rebbe" (he would smile at the term) was Professor Thomas Long, a professor of homiletics and one of the greatest preachers in the United States. Professor Long invited me to do my thesis with him and mischievously suggested that I look at the problems and possibilities of bar/bat mitzvah (now, as many prefer, bet mitzvah) in America today. Those studies, and our many conversations, led me into a deep dive into the meaning of worship and ritual. It was he who suggested that I turn my thesis into a book, which resulted in *Putting God on the Guest List*. Jethro—Moses's father-in-law and a Midianite priest—was Moses's greatest advisor; Tom Long was my Jethro. Our relationship touched my mind and lifted my soul.

The third major influence on my writing this book is the more than twenty years studying at the Shalom Hartman Institute in Jerusalem. Most of the time, we study about Jewish thought, Israel, and Zionism; only rarely do we study prayer and worship. However, there have been two teachers at the Hartman Institute who have taught about prayer and spirituality, and their insights opened my mind to new vistas of thinking. I think fondly of Melila Hellner-Eshed and Rachel Korazim. They exposed me to the poetry and depth of Jewish spiritual thinking, in ways that I could not have imagined.

Fourth, I would like to thank the folks at CCAR Press who have helped bring this book into existence: Rabbi Hara Person, chief executive of the CCAR; Rafael Chaiken, director of CCAR Press; Rabbi Annie Villarreal-Belford, editor at CCAR Press (I am particularly indebted to her for her keen eye and suggestions that were always on point); Deborah Smilow, CCAR Press operations manager; Raquel Fairweather-Gallie, CCAR Press marketing and sales manager; Debra Hirsch Corman, copyeditor; Michelle Kwitkin, proofreader; Barbara Leff, cover designer; and Scott-Martin Kosofsky, book designer. I am also grateful to the members of the Editorial Advisory Committee, whose insights, ideas, and perspectives helped shape this book.

Finally, I dedicate this book to my children and their growing families: Sam and Kyle; Gabriel and Erica; and my grandchildren, Noah and Amelia. As I look at my young grandchildren and experience the beginnings of their delight in being part of a Jewish community, it is hard for me to imagine what the Jewish community will look like as they get older. It is even harder for me to imagine what meanings prayer will contain for them and how they will experience worship as they grow into maturity. Still, I write this book with love and with the hope that they will, like all of you, find their own meanings; that they—and you—will have their favorite prayers and their favorite melodies; and that, as the years go by, they—and you—will look at this book, along with the other books that have come from my heart, head, and hand, and will see it as a humble offering from their grandfather and as my own investment not only in their Jewish future, but in the Jewish future that their entire generation will create together.

Introduction

I AM A REFORM RABBI. I have been teaching Judaism for many years, to kids and adults. You would think that means that I am pretty smart.

But there is a list of things about which I know very little.

For example (and I am embarrassed to admit this): professional sports. When I was a kid, I used to follow baseball ("Let's go, Mets!"). When I was eight years old, my parents actually let me take the train from our town on Long Island, New York, to a Mets game at the old Polo Grounds at the top of Manhattan in New York City. When you consider that this was more than an hour away, that was pretty cool of them.

But over the years, I became less interested in baseball. I know the names of the major figures, but that's about it. The same thing is true about football. When I watch the Super Bowl with friends, I have no idea what's going on (except I like the commercials and sometimes the halftime show). I don't know the names of the teams; I don't know the names of the players; I have no idea what colors the uniforms are or even why football players wear that little smudge of black stuff under their eyes. When it comes to football, I am hopeless. Second thing: ballet. Nothing. I mean, seriously nothing. I do not know the stories of the major ballets. When I go to the ballet, which is not very often, I admire the talent of the dancers. They are graceful and physically strong. But I have no idea what is going on.

So, let's talk about the whole "clueless" thing.

Sometimes when I go to services or I am leading services, it occurs to me that my fellow worshipers are like me at the Super Bowl or the ballet. They seem to like what is going on, but they don't really get it. This is a shame, because there really is so much going on in the service. It's like sports and ballet. You just have to know what is going on.

So, what could worship services do for us?

When I asked some seventh graders about this, they gave some great answers:

- "Services should wake us up."
- "Services should make us into better people."
- "Services can make us feel more connected to all Jews— whether they are alive or dead or not yet born, and wherever they are."
- "Services can help us talk to God, even if it doesn't seem like God is talking back."
- "When we pray at services, we are actually giving part of our strength to God." (Whoa. You need to think about that for a while.)

When we go to services, it should be like going to a concert of your favorite group or recording artist. You go to the concert, you hear the music, you know all the words, and you are singing along. You feel connected to the artist who is performing. "This is my music," you say to yourself. "This is mine, even though it is not only mine." At the same time, you also feel connected to the other people in the audience. We know this music. We have common memories of this music and what it was like when we first heard this music. This music is part of who we are. We are, at least for a little while, a community.

Or it can be like going to a sports event with your favorite team. "I'm here. I care about this team. I know the rules of this sport. I want my team to win. But, even if they don't win, I know that I am here with my fellow sports fans, and that sense of community feels good."

So, how can those feelings happen in a worship service?

It can happen when people have *kavanah*. That basically means: "I know this prayer. I know something about what this prayer means. I have thought about it. I care. The words mean something to me. I am feeling it, in sort of the same way that I am feeling the love for the rock star or the team."

Not only that. When I pray, it is as if I am standing with the entire Jewish people throughout history. I am in a total Jewish time warp.

There is no past, present, or future.

What is the real meaning of *kavanah*?

The great modern sage Rabbi Chayim Soloveitchik (Belarus, 1853–1918) read the words of the medieval thinker Maimonides (Spain and Egypt, 1138–1204) and taught what Maimonides understood about two types of *kavanah*.

The first type is *peirush hamilot*, understanding the meaning of the words that you are saying. The second type is *da lifnei mi atah omeid*, recognizing that you are praying in the presence of God. Yes, we need to know the meaning of the words. That is what you *know*. We also need to be aware of being in God's presence. That is what you *feel*.

For Maimonides, prayer is *avodah shebalev*, "the service of the heart"—or, "the work that the heart needs to do." Yes, saying the prayers is important, but those prayers are effective only when they come from the heart.

There is also a lot going on "behind the scenes" at a worship service.

Sometimes it is a little bit like seeing a play—or, more accurately, a musical.

What happens when you go to the theater? You watch a performance on a stage—complete with props, choreography, and gestures. The actors know the lines that they have learned from their scripts. The audience is passive and applauds the actors at appropriate times. But what would happen if everyone, including the audience, was involved in the production, instead of it being a passive performance? That's called participatory theater, and it pretty much describes Jewish worship.

> *THE PRODUCTION TEAM.* That would be the rabbi and cantor/cantorial soloist. They are in charge of making sure that the whole "production" is meaningful and flows smoothly. They have help with this, of course, from synagogue musicians, choir, ushers, tech support, building staff, and the other people who help with the service. They all have important roles.

STAGING. Where participants in a service stand is very important. What's the most important place in the synagogue? Right in front of the *aron hakodesh*, the holy ark, which contains the Torah scrolls. Those moments when a bet mitzvah stands before the ark are, up to that moment, probably the holiest moments of that young person's life. ("Bet mitzvah" is a gender-inclusive, catch-all term for the young person undergoing the Jewish coming-of-age ceremony or for the ceremony itself. Many congregations use this term, in addition to "b-mitzvah," "bat mitzvah," "bar mitzvah," and "b'nei mitzvah.")

PROPS. In one sense, the siddur (prayer book) is a prop. So is the Torah scroll. The way we handle those props is very important. They must be handled with tenderness, reverence, and love.

MOVEMENT. At the holiest moments of the service, we stand. We bend our knees. We bow. Some worshipers shake back and forth (shuckling). Some worshipers even go up on their toes at the *K'dushah* prayer, so they can feel as if they are flying up to the heavens.

ACTORS. All of us—the rabbi, the cantor/soloist, and everyone in the congregation—are the actors. We perform a sacred drama that reflects our beliefs, our needs, our dreams, our values.

AUDIENCE. For me, this is the most interesting thing. Sometimes, when I would get ready to lead an Erev Shabbat service in the synagogue, I would need someone to light the candles at the start of the worship experience. Someone would suggest, "Why not ask someone in the *audience* to light the candles?" "Audience!" I would silently scream to myself. "There is no audience! This is a congregation, for God's sake!" Ah . . . so that was it. "For God's sake." *God* is the audience, as well as being the main character in the entire production. In fact, we are doing all this for God.

Script. This is the most important part, and it is the focus of this book. Our script is the siddur, the Jewish prayer book.

The word *siddur* comes from the Hebrew word for "order." Things happen during a service in a certain *order*. The siddur was first compiled during the eighth and ninth centuries CE, though the basic form of the service and many prayers already existed by about 200 CE, and even earlier for others.

But the siddur is not just a script. It is much deeper and holier than that. There is a story about a man who survived the Holocaust. When he entered Auschwitz, he was sure that he would survive, but he was also sure that he would be the last Jew on earth. He also believed that if that were true, it would be his job to rebuild Judaism, from the ground up.

But how would he do that? He decided to memorize the siddur, prayer by prayer, even though he did not have a physical prayer book with him. He would go through it in his head. He would play siddur "memory games" with other Jews in the camp to keep their minds alive. When he got out of the camp, he told his friends and community, "I am a living prayer book." More than that: He was living Judaism. For in a very real sense, the siddur *is* Judaism.

What could the siddur be like for us? The siddur could be like a family photo album. Your parents or grandparents may have these. You may have photos on your phone. The photos are of people and moments that you remember.

The siddur is the Jewish family album that has survived over time. Your job: Find yourself in the Jewish family album, and echo Abraham, Sarah, Isaac, Rebecca, Jacob, Rachel, Leah, Moses, Deborah, and Esther, and every generation between them and you, and say, *Hineini*—"Here I am." This is mine, because this is me.

The siddur could also be like a large seashell. You know how you can find a large shell on the beach and, if you hold it to your ear, you can imagine that you are hearing the ocean? The Jewish prayer book is the same way. If you listen to it, you can hear ancestors, prophets, kings, sages, poets—every kind of Jewish person is there, sharing every kind of Jewish sacred literature.

All you have to do is listen.

The siddur might also be like your social media page. The siddur is the space upon which every generation of Jews has written. To worship with the congregation means to log into your social media, read the messages that previous and current generations have left for you, and write your own as well.

Praying as Reform Jews: How We Got Here

Go to your synagogue library or a used bookstore in a Jewish area, and you are likely to find old prayer books (siddurim) that Reform Jews once used, but no longer use. What are those books, and how do they differ from *Mishkan T'filah*, our current Reform siddur?

Welcome to your whirlwind tour of the history of American Reform Judaism!

Reform Judaism started in Germany in the early 1800s. There were many Jews in Germany and other places in Europe who wanted to enter the modern world—a society that was only then beginning to open up to them. However, they still wanted to be Jewish and to observe Judaism, as they understood it. Many of these German Jews eventually immigrated to America and brought their reforms with them. Let's meet two men who helped create Reform Judaism in America.

The first was Rabbi Isaac Mayer Wise (1819–1900). He was born in Bohemia (now the Czech Republic) and came to the United States as a young man. After serving as a rabbi in Albany, New York, he settled in Cincinnati, Ohio. That was where Rabbi Wise single-handedly founded every major Reform institution. In 1873, he created the Union of American Hebrew Congregations (which is now the Union for Reform Judaism, or URJ), Reform Judaism's congregational organization. Two years later, in 1875, he created Hebrew Union College (which later merged with the Jewish Institute of Religion, becoming Hebrew Union College–Jewish Institute of Religion, or HUC-JIR), which is Reform Judaism's seminary for rabbis, cantors, educators, and communal workers. Four years later, in 1889, he founded the Central Conference of American Rabbis, or CCAR, which is Reform Judaism's rabbinic association. In 1858, Rabbi Wise published his prayer book, *Minhag America*, which translates to

"The American Custom." His prayer book opened from right to left, following the Hebrew—something that would not happen again in Reform Judaism until 1975.

Notice the names of these organizations and siddur. They contain words like "Union," "American," and "Central." Notice what word was missing—"Reform." Rabbi Wise believed that he was creating a new *American* Judaism, not an American *Reform* Judaism.

Then, there was Rabbi David Einhorn (1809–79). He was born in Germany, then came to the United States, where he served congregations in Baltimore, Maryland; Philadelphia, Pennsylvania; and New York City. When he was a rabbi in Baltimore, he preached sermons against slavery, and his life was threatened, so he had to flee across the Mason-Dixon Line to Philadelphia. Rabbi Einhorn was more radical in his reforms than Rabbi Wise. He wanted a prayer book that would reflect his own, relatively nontraditional, principles. That prayer book was *Olat Tamid*, which was also published in 1858. By the 1880s, some Reform congregations were using *Minhag America*, some were using *Olat Tamid*, and some were using their own prayer books created by their rabbis. There was a need for a unified prayer book—something that would represent a "union" between all the different prayer books.

Ultimately, Einhorn's *Olat Tamid* "won"—it ultimately became the *Union Prayer Book*, which was published by the CCAR first in the early 1890s. Different editions and revisions of the *Union Prayer Book* were published in 1924 and in 1940.

That was the Reform prayer book for the next almost eighty years, and its liturgy became what is called classical Reform Judaism. If your great-grandparents were Reform Jews, that was probably the book that they used. In fact, I grew up with that prayer book, and I can still recite some of it by heart!

The *Union Prayer Book* (which we lovingly called "the *UPB*") was mostly in English and opened from left to right, like an English book. In addition, its prayers were labeled "Rabbi" (early editions said: "Minister," which was a common way to describe clergy), "Choir," "Congregation," "Silent Prayer," "Responsive Reading," and so on. The translations of the prayers were highly edited; some people found the English to be somewhat formal or even stilted, while others thought that the English was elegant.

But times change. The *Union Prayer Book* could not have contained any references to the two most important Jewish events of the modern era—the Holocaust and the establishment of the State of Israel. In addition, youth culture was in free swing by the 1960s. In youth groups and summer camps, young people started writing their own creative services. They wanted different ideas, different words, different melodies, and different instruments from what they found in the *Union Prayer Book*. For generations, Reform Jews had grown up listening to the organ in their sanctuaries, but by the 1960s, the organ was out of fashion and the guitar was in. Young people had become accustomed to guitar music in summer camps and the Reform youth movement, and they wanted that in their worship.

Another important change was that by the 1970s, Reform Jews had become more comfortable with traditional practices. More Reform Jews started wearing kippot, and more Hebrew returned to Reform worship. To paraphrase singer-songwriter Bob Dylan (United States, 1941–), "The times they were a-changin'."

That brings us to the next generation of Reform prayer books—*Gates of Prayer*, published in 1975, and its companion volumes for the High Holy Days, home worship, and ritual guidance, published in subsequent years. The old *Union Prayer Book* was thin; *Gates of Prayer* was huge at nearly eight hundred pages long. Why so thick? Because it included ten different services that service leaders and congregations could choose from. Each service had different emphases and themes. One service even avoided mentioning God at all! Most of the services contained more Hebrew, it opened from right to left to follow the Hebrew (though there was an option to open it from left to right), and there was more consciousness of social justice issues.

Skip ahead to our time. Yet another generation had come along who were even more comfortable with Hebrew and ritual.

Welcome, then, to *Mishkan T'filah: A Reform Siddur*, published in

2007, with other accompanying prayer books to follow. Our generation has fully embraced feminism and women's equality; so does our liturgy, with a full inclusion of the Matriarchs in the *Avot V'Imahot* prayer and an absence of gendered language when we refer to God. In fact, the siddur's editor was Rabbi Elyse Frishman (United States, 1954–), which marks the first time that a woman edited a Reform Movement prayer book.

This new generation was also much more accustomed to having choices in life. Just go into a Starbucks and see how many choices of beverage there are! That consideration is part of *Mishkan T'filah*'s unique format. Each prayer is spread across two pages that open before you. On the right side, there is the Hebrew and a faithful translation (those are the prayers that we will focus on in this book). On the left side, there are several poetic interpretations of the prayers. At the bottom of the page, there is commentary, so you can learn a little bit about the prayers. You can choose which prayers you want to pray, whether in Hebrew or English. No two services need be alike. And, for those who do not know Hebrew or are learning Hebrew, there is a full Hebrew transliteration right on the page.

When it comes to worship customs, no two congregations do the same exact thing. So, *Mishkan T'filah* does not include any cues for who does what. Congregations can choose whether the rabbi or prayer leader reads a prayer, whether the cantor or soloist or choir sings a prayer, or whether prayers will be read together, individually, responsively, or silently. Each congregation can choose when to rise or be seated.

Mishkan T'filah also includes diverse customs, many previously unknown or rare in Reform Jewish worship. On Erev Shabbat, at the end of *L'chah Dodi*, the congregation is invited to rise for the Shabbat bride (page 21); this practice had become more common in Reform synagogues, but this is the first time a prayer book includes the instruction. (Note, however, that the instruction is at the bottom of the page, so that congregations can still choose whether or not to observe it.) In the Torah service, we find the Sephardic greeting "May God be with you" and the congregational response "May

God bless you" (page 250), which affirms the importance of non-Ashkenazic practices.

So, that is your sweeping, very quick tour of the history of American Reform prayer books. Who knows what the next generation of prayer books will look like? Maybe they won't be books at all. In fact, many congregations are using Visual *T'filah*, projecting the prayers on overhead screens in the sanctuary. During the COVID pandemic, congregations held remote, online worship, and congregations had to figure out how to create Power Point worship services and other online programs so that people could pray from home using various technologies (and applause to the CCAR for making that possible!).

What will happen in the future? I can imagine congregations getting rid of books entirely. I hope this won't happen; more than a thousand years ago, it was Muslims who first called Jews "a people of the book." There is something powerful in holding a book in your hand.

Even still, I can imagine congregations having iPads (or whatever it will be in coming years) in the pews; people might be able to navigate between various prayer books, watch videos, or listen to different melodies. Who knows? Perhaps the next prayer books will be written by ChatGPT (but I hope not).

One thing is for sure: Every generation of Jews has figured out its own way to serve God and to join together in community, from ancient sacrifices to prayer books to whatever comes next. Our tradition is in our hands. The future lies before us.

The Acts of the Script

So, we have a script—the siddur. The script tells the story of the way we Jewish people view the world. Every play is broken into "acts." The siddur has acts too. These are the traditional sections of the worship service.

This book is going to focus on both the Erev Shabbat service and the Shabbat morning service. So, here is what you can expect:

PRELIMINARY STUFF

These are the "warm-up" sections. In the Erev Shabbat service, this is the *Kabbalat Shabbat* (Welcoming Shabbat) section. It includes candle lighting, *Kiddush*, songs, and psalms. In the Shabbat morning service, this section is *Birchot HaShachar*, "the Morning Blessings," and the *P'sukei D'zimrah*, "the Chapters of Song." They lay out some of the basic themes of Jewish worship and spirituality.

ACT ONE—WHAT WE BELIEVE

This section is the *Sh'ma* and Its Blessings. After the *Bar'chu*, we get a lesson in basic Jewish beliefs: God creates the world (through the symbolism of darkness, which was present before God created the world, and light, God's first creation); God demonstrates love for the Jewish people through Torah; God redeemed the Jewish people from Egypt.

ACT TWO—WHAT WE NEED

This section is *T'filah*, or "Prayer." It is also known as the *Sh'moneh Esreih* (the "eighteen" prayers. . . or maybe nineteen—the math is a little weird here) or the *Amidah* (the "standing" prayer), because it is traditionally recited while we stand. This is the part of the service where we ask God for things for ourselves and for our people.

Our needs include to be linked to our ancestors; to believe that God's power is eternal; to feel part of God's holiness; to know that God needs and accepts our prayers; to give thanks; to find fulfillment and shalom (peace).

If you ever attend services on a weekday, you will notice that this section is much longer. That is because there are many more requests in the daily *T'filah*—pleas for healing, sustenance, forgiveness, and the restoration of Jerusalem.

Why is this section shorter during the Shabbat service? One kid told me, "God deserves a rest as well. On Shabbat, let's not bother God too much with what we need." This is a great answer, but there is a deeper reason why our list of requests is shorter on Shabbat. Shabbat is like a coming attraction of the messianic age. In the messianic age, we will not need much of anything.

This is why I love Shabbat in Jerusalem—there is almost total peace, with very few cars on the roads and most businesses closed. It is about being—just pure being, rather than doing.

ACT THREE—WHAT WE LEARN

This section is the Torah reading. It takes place on Mondays, Thursdays, festivals, Rosh Chodesh (the first day of the Jewish month), and of course Shabbat. During this section of the service on Shabbat mornings, we also read the haftarah (a section of the historical and prophetic books of the Hebrew Bible). While some synagogues do read Torah on Friday night, in this book you will find the Torah service only in the Shabbat morning section.

ACT FOUR—WHAT WE HOPE

We are coming to the end! This section contains *Aleinu* and *Kaddish*, prayers during which we say that someday everyone will understand that God is one and that someday there will be perfection and peace, God's sovereignty on earth.

Now, any good director will tell actors that they need to learn the script—not only how to read the words in the script, but to really engage with them, think about them, understand them, and perhaps even argue with them. This book is designed to help you do all of that.

How You (Whoever You Are) Can Use This Book

This book is intended to be used as a companion to *Mishkan T'filah*. The order of the book follows the order of *Mishkan T'filah*'s Shabbat worship, and the page numbers of the prayers in *Mishkan T'filah: Weekdays, Shabbat, Festivals and Other Occasions of Public Worship* (which correspond to the blue, bracketed page numbers in *Mishkan T'filah: Shabbat*) are indicated in parentheses next to the corresponding title of the prayer. Read the prayer in English translation in *Mishkan T'filah*, then read the teachings about that prayer contained in this book. Or you can do the opposite! There are questions for discussion following each prayer.

While this book was written with bet mitzvah students in mind, its material is engaging and insightful for any reader. Students can read the book as they learn the prayers of the service. In addition, they can write their responses to the questions in *Mishkan T'filah: Journal Edition*. Parents can read the book, with their children or on their own, so that they can become familiar with the worship service itself. A group of parents whose children will become bet mitzvah together can form a book club to study the book.

Rabbis, cantors, and teachers can use the book to teach young people the prayers necessary for communal worship or to create *iyunei t'filah* (study of prayers) that introduce and explain prayers during the worship service. In addition, rabbis, cantors, and educators might want to use the book as a springboard for adult education programs.

Congregational leaders might want to put copies of the book in the pews for people to read during services, or use the book at board meetings so that leaders can become more literate in the liturgy. Worship/ritual committee members might want to use the book as a study project to more fully understand what is happening in synagogue worship. I hope you see how many ways this book can be used to make your worship experience more meaningful and personal.

Words from the Heart

One of the times that prayer became extra meaningful to me was after the horrible events of October 7, 2023. The Hamas attack on Israel, the many deaths, the taking of hostages—it was the worst day in Jewish history since 1945, when the Holocaust ended. Throughout those terrible days and weeks that followed the attack, the words of our traditional Jewish prayers provided comfort and inspiration to countless numbers of Jews. Our prayers seem to always become more meaningful and important in times of sorrow, fear, and need. It is important to remember, however, that prayer is important in other times too—when we feel grateful or when we have something to celebrate. Whatever we are feeling, the words of our prayers can remind us of our common past, our common dreams, and our common hopes.

Many years ago, I was listening to a sermon in which the rabbi was saying wonderful things about "our traditional Jewish *lethargy*." The rabbi meant "liturgy." Ouch.

"Lethargy" is a good vocabulary word. It might even appear in a future SAT exam.

Here is a dictionary definition: "a lack of energy and enthusiasm." Bear in mind: "Enthusiasm" is derived from the Latin words for "God within us."

No, we should not approach the liturgy with lethargy. We should approach it with energy, enthusiasm, interest—at the very least, some curiosity about it and what it could mean to us.

This raises a question for many young people (and not just young people): What if I have problems with the whole God thing? Let's think about that.

Jews have always struggled with God. This struggle goes all the way back to the beginnings of Jewish history. When God wanted to destroy Sodom and Gomorrah for their sinfulness, Abraham challenged God to do justice for the innocent people in those cities: "Abraham then came forward and said, 'Will You indeed sweep away the innocent along with the wicked?" (Genesis 18:23).

When the Israelites built the Golden Calf, God wanted to destroy the Jewish people, but Moses demanded that God spare them: "But Moses implored the Eternal his God, saying, 'Let not Your anger, Eternal One, blaze forth against Your people, whom You delivered from the land of Egypt with great power and with a mighty hand. Let not the Egyptians say, 'It was with evil intent that he delivered them, only to kill them off in the mountains and annihilate them from the face of the earth.' Turn from Your blazing anger, and renounce the plan to punish Your people" (Exodus 32:11–12).

When God tested Job by causing him to lose all that was precious to him—his children, his home, and his health—Job demanded justice from God as well:

> Indeed, I would speak to the Almighty;
> I insist on arguing with God. . . .
> Hear now my arguments,
> Listen to my pleading. . . .
> I may well be slain; I may have no hope;
> Yet I will argue my case before [God]. (Job 13:3, 6, 15)

Elisha ben Avuyah, a rebellious sage from the second century CE, lost his faith in God when he saw a child die. The child had obeyed his father, who had told him to climb a tree to take eggs from a bird's nest, but to shoo away the mother bird before taking them. That child was fulfilling two mitzvot—to honor a parent and to send away the mother bird from the nest—for which the Torah promises a long life as a reward. Yet, that child fell from the tree and died. Elisha wondered where the divine justice was in that death and lost his faith as a result (Babylonian Talmud, *Kiddushin* 39b).

In the musical *Fiddler on the Roof,* Tevye the Dairyman, tired of persecutions by Russian soldiers, says to God, "I know that we're the chosen people. But could You please choose some other people for a change?"[1]

And let us not forget Jacob. On the banks of the Jabbok River, Jacob wrestled with a nameless stranger, who might have been a divine being or even God. "The other said to [Jacob], 'What is your name?' and he said, 'Jacob.' 'No more shall you be called Jacob, but Israel,' said the other, 'for you have struggled with God and with human beings, and you have prevailed'" (Genesis 32:28–29). Jacob limped away from the encounter wounded, transformed, and with a new name: Yisrael, "the one who struggles with God."

That's us. We are Yisrael. We are the children of Israel—the children of Jacob, who was the God Wrestler. I know of no other religion that encourages its people to constantly question both God and the meaning of that religion itself. This is totally Jewish, and it is uniquely Jewish.

Or perhaps you are not sure that you believe in God. Let me ask: Which God don't you believe in? Because there is a pretty good chance that other people don't believe in that God either. Are we talking about the God who has a starring role on Rosh HaShanah or Yom Kippur—the God who sits on a throne in heaven, going through the Book of Life, deciding who will live and die? Yes, many Jews have problems with that understanding of God, and I think that this is why many Jews have retreated from God-belief.

I think that part of the problem is that we use only a small fraction of the images and ideas about God that Judaism offers us. That is sad, because there are so many, and many of them show up in the traditional prayer book.

So, here is a short list of some of those prayer book images, na
mes, and descriptions of God. Yes, of course, there's *Adonai, Elohim,
Melech haolam* (Sovereign of the universe), but also:

- *Shechinah* (Divine Presence; understood by Jewish
  mystics as the feminine aspect of God)
- *Tzur Yisheinu* (our Rock and Deliverer)
- *Tzur Yisrael* (Rock of Israel)
- *Tzaddik b'chol hadorot* (Righteous One of all generations)
- *HaTov* (Good One)
- *Shomreinu* (our Guardian)
- *HaMakom* (The Place; meaning that the world is located
  within God, making God "the place" of thc world)
- *Magein Avraham v'Ezrat Sarah* (Abraham's Shield,
  Sarah's Helper)
- *Melech malchei ham'lachim* (the One who is sovereign
  over all)
- *She-amar v'hayah haolam* (the One who spoke and the
  world came to be)
- *Avinu* (literally, "our Father," but also "our Parent" and
  "our Source")
- *Av harachamim* (Source of mercy)[2]

That is just a few ways our prayer book describes God—the tip of
the proverbial theological iceberg. If you were to delve into even more
Jewish literature—the Hebrew Bible, Rabbinic literature, medieval
philosophy, Jewish mysticism, and various modern Jewish theolo-
gies including feminist Jewish thought, queer Jewish thought—you
could make a much longer list of all the terms that Jews have used
for God and the ways that they have imagined God.

When people tell me they don't believe in God, I sometimes
encourage them to think more deeply and widely about how Judaism imagines God and to explore some of those other names of God.
Sometimes they find a Jewish way of thinking and a name for God
that appeals to them. This book will teach you many ways of thinking about God and speaking to God. You might find something you
like. As my teacher Melilah Helner-Eshed (Israel) taught some years
ago: It might be that the search for God is itself a godly act.[3]

Finally, you might just say, "No, I just don't believe in God. I am an agnostic [someone who doesn't know whether there is a God]. I am an atheist [someone who doesn't believe in God]. Should I even become bet mitzvah?"

To answer this question, let me digress a moment. I have watched almost every movie in which a kid goes through the bet mitzvah process. I have discovered an interesting trend. In almost every single movie, the kid goes through some kind of crisis in which they struggle over what they believe and how they can understand the words of prayers that they are saying. They rebel. They decide that they don't want to go through the bet mitzvah. In some movies, they actually run away. So, if you are feeling rebellious (and if you are considering running away, which I do not recommend)—once again, you are in good company.

So, should you even do it if you are not on board with the whole "God thing"? In short, my answer is "Yes."

Perhaps you can think about the prayers in a different way. Imagine that the prayers are the inherited literature of the Jewish people. In your ceremony, you can present those prayers to proclaim that you are connected to the Jewish people and its history. And remember—our people has always included those who have issues with God.

How is it possible to do this if you don't believe in the words that you are saying? Remember that the Jews are not the "Jewish belief club." We are a *religion* that has a people and a culture, and we are also a *people* that has a religion and culture. This is your opportunity to stand up and say: I am part of this people.

There is another reason to have this ceremony. At the age of thirteen, you have certain beliefs and questions. But your ideas about God might change as you get older. In fact, if you ask most people if their ideas about God have changed during their lives, they will almost always answer yes. Don't let your current ideas deprive you of what will be a wonderful experience with your family, friends, and Jewish community.

Years later, you will look back on this experience with lovely memories. You will probably not remember much of what you said or read during your bet mitzvah day. Most of your memories will probably be of the people who were there with you. Never waste the opportunity to create a good memory.

Finally, if you are struggling with the God stuff—congratulations. That means that you are taking this more seriously than if you were just doing it by rote or getting ChatGPT to do it for you. It means that you are putting the time and energy into really thinking about it.

A contemporary Israeli poet named Rabbi Dov Singer wrote:

> The printed, set prayer book
> Can cause our prayer to become rote.
> But if we smooth its pages, ponder the spaces between the words,
> We will sense how each prayer was written in a moment of inspiration, of Divine guidance.
> Each word in the prayer book is a word that comes from the heart
> And reaches the heart of the world.[4]

Each of the prayer book's words was born in a moment of connection, rising up from within the heart. Welcome to your script—a script created by great souls and great hearts and which will go straight to your own heart.

Jewish Prayer: Boot Camp

E VEN BEFORE WE START, let's address one of the most common
questions about prayer: "Why do I need a synagogue? I can
pray at home." How many times have rabbis, cantors, educators, and
Jewish leaders heard that over the years?

Those who ask that question may be on to something—at least
partially. You *can* pray at home, or in a field, or at the beach, or while
taking a walk on a mountain. No doubt about it—you can pray anywhere. You can even pray the words that are in your heart instead
of relying on a siddur (prayer book). The Hebrew Bible is filled with
stories about people who prayed spontaneously. The shortest prayer
in the entire Hebrew Bible came from the lips of Moses, who prayed
for his sister, Miriam, to be healed of a particularly nasty skin disease: "O God, pray heal her!" (Numbers 12:13).

In Biblical times, that was the way prayer was: I feel it; I need it; I
say it. That is the way prayer still is with many people. Think about
the number of students who, sitting down for an exam, have said
silent and sincere prayers: "O God, please let me pass this test!"

It is only later in Jewish history that Jews moved away from spon-
taneous prayer. Yes, of course people continue to pray spontaneously.
But over the course of many centuries, gifted rabbis, sages, and poets
wrote the fixed prayers that we pray to this day. There was a certain
amount of flexibility and fluidity in how they addressed the deeply
felt needs of the Jewish people. In some periods of Jewish history,
there was a great deal of liturgical openness and creativity.

Eventually, the Rabbis decided that the whole "pray whenever you
feel like it" thing in the Bible was not going to work long-term. In
the ancient Temple in Jerusalem, there had been regular sacrifices at
set times. But then the Temples were destroyed. As an act of remem-
brance, the Rabbis made the times for Jewish worship coincide with

the times of the sacrifices in the ancient Temple: morning (*shacharit*), afternoon (*minchah*), and evening (*maariv* or *aravit*).

You might be saying, "What if I am not feeling the words that are in the siddur?" Maybe you will someday. Perhaps this book will help you figure out some of those meanings. Perhaps you will understand that the purpose of the siddur—of all Jewish worship—is not necessarily to coincide with the deep needs of any individual worshiper. That would be impossible. Instead, it is possible that the purpose of the prayers in the siddur is not necessarily for us to say what we value right now, but rather to recognize what we have valued across time.

Jews know something else. True, you can pray alone. But it is even better to worship with a community, because the community represents the entire Jewish people—past, present, and future—and unites us wherever Jews might live. When a Jew in St. Petersburg, Florida, prays, it is as if she is praying along with a Jew in St. Petersburg, Russia.

So, how many Jews do you need in order to have a community for worship? Traditionally, you need ten adult Jews—called a minyan— to participate in a service that has the *Bar'chu* (the call to worship), *T'filah*, *K'dushah*, Torah and haftarah readings, and *Kaddish* for mourners. (Consider how different this is from meditation. You can meditate alone; in fact, many people prefer to do precisely that.) But why ten?

Take your choice of explanations. First explanation: When Abraham confronted God over God's intended destruction of the wicked cities of Sodom and Gomorrah (Genesis 18), Abraham tried to convince God to spare the cities if there were innocent people there. Abraham bargains with God: Would God spare the cities if there were fifty innocent people? What about forty? Thirty? Twenty? Abraham bargains God all the way down to ten. Unfortunately, there weren't even ten innocent people in those cities, and you probably know the rest of the story. God destroyed the cities of Sodom and Gomorrah. That's the point: Ten innocent people—a minyan of people—could have saved Sodom.

Second explanation: Moses sent spies to scout out the Land of Israel, to see if the Israelites would be able to conquer the land (Numbers 13). There were twelve spies in all, one representing each of the twelve tribes of Israel. Ten spies brought back discouraging reports; two spies—Joshua and Caleb—believed that the land was conquerable and that the Israelites should move forward. So, ten scouts—a minyan—had discouraging reports.

I admit that I never understood those explanations. Remembering that there weren't even ten decent people in those cities? "Rewarding" the ten spies who delivered negative reports? It just doesn't seem right.

My favorite interpretation of the minyan comes from Rabbi Elyse Frishman (United States, 1954–), who first heard it from the late Rabbi Zalman Schachter-Shalomi (Poland and United States, 1924–2014). In Jewish mysticism, there are ten s'firot, or emanations of God, each one representing a different aspect of the divine personality. Therefore, each of the ten people who come to worship represents an aspect of God. God only becomes "whole" when there are ten people praying.

What's the lesson here? It is huge. We like to say that we need God. It turns out that God also needs us—our presence, our voices, our prayers—to become whole. To become, as we will learn about later, one—echad.

Before we start with the worship service, let's talk about those words that begin most Jewish prayers: Baruch atah, Adonai Eloheinu, Melech haolam. Our siddur translates these words as: "Blessed are You, Adonai our God, Sovereign of the universe. . . ." This formula is quite ancient, though not every prayer starts that way. This phrase might seem pretty basic, but the reality is that these words create a whole journey for the person who is praying—a six-word journey. Because you are going to be encountering this opening formula so often, let's figure out what it really means.

Let's start with Baruch atah—"Blessed are You." We start by speaking directly to God in the second person. We are calling God "You," in almost the same way as we would speak to someone we know and care about. Notice that we are not talking about whether we think that there is a God. We assume that God is there, and we assume that we can talk to God, which can also mean: "I am angry with God," "I am disappointed with God," "I wish that God. . . ." This is sort of how we deal with our parents or other loved ones. They can make us happy, or sad, or angry, or disappoint us, but we know that they are there.

This whole thing about people blessing God might be a little confusing. In the Hebrew Bible, it is God who blesses people. However, as time went on, the tables are turned, especially in the period after the Bible. Then, it is people who bless God. People take a much more active role in religious life, and perhaps God "needs" our blessing. I think that the best understanding of *Baruch* in the opening formula is that God is the Source of blessing; in fact, some writers of Jewish prayers actually translate *Baruch* just that way.

Adonai Eloheinu—"*Adonai* our God." What is God's name? According to Jewish tradition, God has many names, perhaps a hundred. The siddur itself refers to God in many different ways, which means that at any given time we can always find a name for God or a way of thinking about God that makes sense or means something to us. But most of the time, the siddur calls God by the name *Adonai*. How do we translate that? Sometimes we understand *Adonai* as "Lord," but that doesn't tell the whole story. In fact, *Adonai* is not really how we pronounce God's name. That is more of a mystery. In ancient times, the High Priest would enter the Holy of Holies in the ancient Temple in Jerusalem on Yom Kippur and say the sacred four-letter name of God: *yod-hei-vav-hei*. What does this name mean? We simply do not know. It might be a crazy simultaneous way of putting the Hebrew word for "to be" into its past, present, and future tenses. That means that God's ancient name was something like ISWASWILLBE, but all said at the same time. Do not try this. You will make yourself crazy. Maybe this is part of the reason why some Jews call God *HaShem*, which simply means "The Name."

Unfortunately, at a certain time in ancient Jewish history, our ancestors forgot how to pronounce that four-letter name of God, and they replaced it with the word *Adonai*. So, how do we *really* translate *Adonai*? That's the point. We don't. *Adonai* is simply God's name. But here is the deal: *Adonai Eloheinu*—"*Adonai* is *our* God." We started with having an individual relationship with God—You to me, God to person. We then move to having a relationship with God as part of the Jewish people.

Next is *Melech haolam*, "Sovereign of the universe." We don't think all that much about kings these days, but our ancestors certainly did. Ancient Israelites had kings and queens until the Romans destroyed Judean independence. For them, the biggest symbol of power was the king, or the sovereign. So, at a certain point in history, our ancestors began to imagine that *Adonai* is not only a God with whom you could have a personal relationship, and not only a God who is the God of the Jewish people, but also a God who is in charge of the entire universe.

Not everyone loves the symbol of God as "king," and they wonder what kinds of symbolic language will replace the older terms and how those new words will change how prayers will look like and feel like.

Let's try a little thought experiment: Think of God as the internet. Where is the internet? Actually, it is everywhere. And just like some of us imagine God, the internet seems to see all and to know all. How do you access the internet? Sometimes it's simply open; sometimes you need a password.

Every religion has its own "password" to God/Internet. You can consider those six opening words of Jewish prayer sort of like a Jewish password into the world of prayer. These six words opening our prayers imagine that we have a personal relationship with God, a Jewish communal relationship with God, and that the entire universe is under God's authority.

Six words that we say all the time, and so much meaning in them. One last thing about those words. Whenever we do a sacred act—a mitzvah, something that connects us to God and to other Jews past, present, and future, we add the following words to those opening six words: *asher kid'shanu b'mitzvotav v'tzivanu*, "who hallows us with mitzvot, commanding us. . . ."

"Hallow" means "to make holy, to set aside as special, to bring us into a relationship." It is our way of saying that what we do is not simply something nice, or even traditional—but that it is part of being Jewish.

B'mitzvotav—we are hallowed, made holy, set aside as special, brought into a relationship through God's commandments. *Mitzvah* is a key word in Judaism—perhaps, even, *the* key word. What does it mean? It depends on how you pronounce it.

A few years ago, I landed in Israel at Ben Gurion Airport, and I immediately lost my suitcase. It is a crazy story, but all you really need to know is that my cabdriver helped find it and returned it to me.

"Ah, yes," you would say, "he did you a *mitzveh*." One small vowel change; one large change in worldview. When we pronounce the word as *mitzveh*, we are speaking in Yiddish. *Mitzveh* is the Yiddish word for "a nice thing to do." And the driver definitely did a nice thing for me.

However, when I offered to give him an additional tip for doing that, he became angry at me. "There is no tip for this!" he said to me in Hebrew. And then, he proceeded to quote to me, from memory, the two teachings in the Torah about how you are obligated to return lost objects to their rightful owners. "We are responsible!" he said to me, quite loudly.

You see, my cabdriver did not do what he did because he was doing a *mitzveh*. He did not do what he *wanted* to do because he was nice. Instead, he did a *mitzvah*. He did what he was *obligated* to do—because he is a Jew.

That is the way it is with *mitzvah*. It means (take your pick): a commandment, an obligation of Jewish living, an opportunity to do something Jewish.

Here's something else about that word "mitzvah." Yes, it means "commandment," but the Hebrew root (*tzadi-vav-hei*) can also mean "to connect." I happen to love that interpretation—mitzvah as connection.

When we do mitzvot, we are connected to (take your pick): God, other Jews, living or dead or not even born yet; all people. Mitzvot connect us through ritual acts, prayer, worship, ethical actions, acts of justice, and acts of kindness.

However you choose to translate "mitzvah," it is definitely the connective tissue that ties Jews to each other, to God, and to our history. When we do mitzvot, we become part of that great tapestry of Jewish striving, history, association, feeling, love, and more.

It is simply that big.

QUESTIONS:
1. When have you felt a personal connection to God?
2. When have you felt a connection to God as part of the Jewish people?
3. When have you felt a sense that God is the ruler of the entire universe?
4. How do you translate the word *mitzvah*?
5. What mitzvot make you feel particularly holy?
6. What do you think of the idea of minyan—of needing a quorum for prayer? Is it necessary?
7. What do you think of having fixed prayers and texts for prayers? Are they necessary?

Maariv: Evening Service

The Preliminary Stuff

CANDLE LIGHTING (120)

"**B**LESSED ARE YOU, Adonai our God, Sovereign of the universe, who hallows us with mitzvot, commanding us to kindle the light of Shabbat."

When I close my eyes, I can still see and hear my mother, of blessed memory, lighting the Shabbat candles at our table on Friday evenings. In the midrash it is taught that the light of a person's face during the weekdays is different from the light of their face on Shabbat (*B'reishit Rabbah* 11:2). I believe it, because I remember my late mother's face. It is a sacred memory, and many Jews have that memory. Maybe you have one too.

Wait a moment—our service is just getting started, and we already have a problem.

When did God command us to kindle the light of Shabbat? To start to find an answer, it might help to think of the Jewish worship service—in fact, all of Judaism—like lasagna. It has many layers, and they all taste good.

Let's think of the layers of Judaism and how Judaism developed. The first layer is Abraham, Sarah, and the rest of our ancestors in the Book of Genesis. What was their "Judaism"? Basically, it was following one mitzvah—*b'rit milah*, circumcision. They were a tribe, a people, a group, but there was nothing "religious" (at least, the way that we imagine religion today) about them—no rituals or belief.

The second layer of our lasagna is the covenant that Moses and the Jewish people made at Mount Sinai. According to tradition, that covenant resulted in 613 mitzvot for the Jewish people—the beginning of "Judaism."

The third layer is the Rabbis who lived after the time of the Torah. They realized that the mitzvot of the Torah were not always clear, and they needed to interpret those laws and expand upon them. Sometimes they created new laws as well. For example, the Torah says that you should not work on Shabbat, but what is "work"? (Clue: It's not your job or your career.) What kind of physical effort is permissible on Shabbat? What are the rules? The Sages and Rabbis debated that question and many more. Not only that: When the Romans destroyed the Jerusalem Temple in the year 70 CE (the Common Era), many of the laws of Judaism that were based on the sacrifices at the Temple instantly became irrelevant. So the Rabbis needed to reinvent and expand the mitzvot—and with that, Judaism itself.

During the fourth layer, the Middle Ages (1000–1600 CE), great thinkers like Maimonides thought about the mitzvot, especially the reasons for doing them. During this period, the Jewish mystics also thought about God and mitzvot, and they invented new mitzvot and came up with new reasons for older mitzvot. Once again, Judaism expanded.

The fifth layer is modern through contemporary times (1800 CE–now). Modern Jews wanted to be both modern and Jewish; that is how Reform Judaism started. They needed to look at the mitzvot differently. Some of those mitzvot seemed to no longer make sense; they were outmoded and inappropriate for Jews who wanted to be modern. So the Reformers set those mitzvot aside. If they saw mitzvot that excluded women, they changed those mitzvot to be more inclusive. They changed the worship service. They included prayers in the language of their country, as well as in Hebrew; they added instrumental and choral music; they encouraged men, women, and families to sit together, rather than sending women off to their own section in the synagogue. More recently, we have made changes to ensure inclusion of LGBTQ+ people. Once again, Judaism expanded.

There will probably be more layers in this delicious lasagna, but we don't know what they are yet!

Let's return to the question that got this whole thing started: How is it possible for our candlelighting prayer to say that God "commanded us to kindle the light of Shabbat?" Did God *really* command us to kindle that light?

If you interpret "command" to mean that God spoke to us, directly, in what we might imagine was a loud, booming voice—then, no. God did not "command" us. Remember, though, that Judaism is constantly expanding. That means that every generation reimagines what God wants from us. In that sense, every generation adds its own layer to the "cheese lasagna" of Judaism. So even though God did not explicitly command the Jewish people to light Shabbat candles, one layer of the lasagna decided Shabbat candle lighting was part of the expanding Judaism that brings Jews into relationship with God. In every generation, Jews have had to figure out what it means to live Jewishly and to respond to the Divine Presence. Each generation creates its own layer of meaning and mitzvah in that "sacred lasagna."

QUESTIONS:
1. What are some other examples of mitzvot that came after Torah times?
2. What are some mitzvot that you would want to add to Judaism right now?
3. What are some mitzvot that you would want to remove from Judaism?

Let's continue to think about the light of Shabbat. The prayer says that God commanded us to kindle the "light" of Shabbat (*l'hadlik ner shel Shabbat*), when, in fact, we light not one light, but usually two lights. Why? Let's talk about light.

Every Jewish holiday, including Shabbat (which is our weekly holiday), begins at sundown, and with that, every Jewish holiday begins with the lighting of candles. This is because every Jewish holiday brings us back not to the beginnings of Judaism or the Jewish people, but to the very beginning of time, back to Creation itself.

Before the creation of the world, what was there? Darkness and chaos. What was the very first thing that God creates? The Torah says: "God said, 'Let there be light!'—and there was light. And when God saw how good the light was, God divided the light from the darkness; God then called the light Day, and called the darkness Night, and there was evening and there was morning, [the] first day" (Genesis 1:3–5). As for the light that God created on the first day, we don't know what it was. Some Jewish mystics believe that it was the light of the individual soul. We do know that it was not the sun, because on the fourth day, "God made the two great lights: the greater light to govern the day, and the lesser light to govern the night and the stars" (Genesis 1:16). One of those two great lights was the sun, and the other was the moon.

That is why we light two candles on Shabbat and holidays. (Some people light even more.) When we light those two candles, we imagine that the two candles—those two lights—symbolize the sun and the moon. We imagine that our hands are actually creating the sun and the moon! This means we imagine that we are imitating God. This is one of the most powerful ideas in all of Judaism—and in some other religions as well. People can imitate what God does.

The Babylonian Talmud discusses an interesting problem with this idea. Deuteronomy 4:24 refers to God as "a consuming fire." On the other hand, Deuteronomy 13:5 says that you should "follow God" and "hold fast to God." How is that possible? Wouldn't the fire of God's presence burn you up if you tried to hold fast to God? To solve this contradiction, the Rabbis reinterpreted the meanings of "follow God" and "hold fast to God." They understood this to mean that you should follow God by imitating what God does in the world: "Just as God clothed Adam and Eve when they were naked, we must supply clothes for the naked poor. Just as God visited Abraham when he was healing from his circumcision, we should visit the sick. Just as God buried Moses, we must bury the dead. Just as God comforted Isaac after the death of his mother, Sarah, we should comfort mourners" (Babylonian Talmud, *Sotah* 14a).[1]

We can add to that list. Just as God creates, we can be creative. Just as God heals the sick, we can heal the sick. Just as God brought the Israelites out of slavery in Egypt, we can help free those who are enslaved and in trouble. So, when we light those two candles on Erev Shabbat, those are not just our hands. Those are also the hands of God.

QUESTIONS:
1. Make a list of the times that we use candles in Jewish ritual. What does each light symbolize?
2. What are some things that God does in the Torah? How do you, in your life, imitate what God did?

KIDDUSH (122–23)

Traditionally, the *Kiddush*—the sanctification of the wine for Shabbat—begins with a description of how God rested after the work of Creation: "The heaven and the earth were finished, and all their array. On the seventh day God finished the work that God had been doing, and God ceased on the seventh day from all the work that God had done" (Genesis 2:1–2). That makes sense when you remember that Shabbat is based on two things—a memory of how God rested after six days of labor to create the world, and a memory of how God freed the Israelites from slavery in Egypt. In both cases, it's about ceasing from work—God's creative work, and the work that Pharaoh imposed on the Israelites. Consider this teaching from the Babylonian Talmud (*Shabbat* 119b):

> Rava said, and some say it was Rabbi Y'hoshua ben Levi who said: Even an individual who prays on Shabbat evening must recite the passage: "And the heavens and the earth were finished [*vay'chulu*]" (Genesis 2:1–3), as Rav Hamnuna said: Anyone who prays on Shabbat evening and recites the passage of *vay'chulu*, the verse credits that person as if they became a partner with God in the act of Creation. As it is stated: "And the heavens and the earth were finished [*vay'chulu*]." Do not read it as: Were finished [*vay'chulu*]; rather, as: They finished [*vach-alu*]. It is as if God and the individual who says this become partners and completed the work together.[2]

With this teaching, the ancient Rabbis get really creative. They imagine that when you recite *Kiddush* and you proclaim the holiness of Shabbat, that act is so powerful that you—a mortal creature—participate in the act of Creation itself!

My own interpretation is that it is not as if the *Kiddush*-sayer participates in the creation of the world. That would be . . . a lot. Too much, maybe. However, the *Kiddush*-sayer does participate in something almost as good—the creation of Shabbat itself, right then and there!

One last thing about the way that we hold the *Kiddush* cup. We do not hold the *Kiddush* cup the same way that we would hold a regular cup, glass, or mug. Rather, the tradition is to hold the cup in the palm of our hands, with our fingers spread open. What does our hand resemble? A rose with five petals that parallel the five fingers of the human hand. The rose is a powerful Jewish symbol, especially when you realize that roses also have thorns—it is a symbol of beauty, mixed with pain. And when we hold the *Kiddush* cup this way, the hand must be open as well—the open hand that receives blessing, and the open heart that receives blessing as well. There is a world of meaning, even in how we hold the cup!

QUESTIONS:
1. To what extent do you agree with the Biblical account of Creation? Do you prefer the scientific version? Can the two versions be understood together, yet differently?
2. In what ways are you and other individuals partners with God in finishing the work of Creation?
3. What are your hands open to?
4. What is your heart open to?
5. Do you agree that the person who says *Kiddush* is a partner with God in Creation?

KABBALAT SHABBAT—WELCOMING SHABBAT

Our prayer book translates *Kabbalat Shabbat* as "welcoming Shabbat." That is a pretty good translation, because that is what we are doing in this first part of the Shabbat evening service. But a better translation would be "receiving or accepting Shabbat."

What does it mean to "receive" and "accept" Shabbat? When you receive a gift, it is not enough to merely take the gift. You need to see it as a gift, and you need to accept it for what it is—a token of affection or love. Ideally, you would also express your gratitude for such an amazing, almost overwhelming, gift.

That is what Shabbat is for the Jews—a once-every-seven-days gift from God, with the intention to make our lives richer, deeper, and better.

THE PSALMS OF EREV SHABBAT (130–37)

A "psalm" is a sacred song, usually about God or addressed to God, that is often part of a worship service. Many of the psalms are titled *mizmor*, which means "a song sung to a stringed instrument," because our ancestors played stringed instruments, as well as wind and percussion instruments, in the ancient Temple.

In fact, many of the ancient psalms in the Book of Psalms in the Hebrew Bible were part of the service in the ancient Temple in Jerusalem. Many of those psalms indicate that their author was King David, the greatest of the ancient kings of Israel. Scholars are pretty sure that King David did not write most of those psalms, but he was so important that people liked to imagine that he did. These psalms serve as the passageway into the *Kabbalat Shabbat* section of the service. Here is what those psalms are saying:

Perhaps, for the last six days of the week, we have been ignoring God.

Not today. Even though God has always been there, perhaps we have not been paying as much attention as we should. That changes when Shabbat comes, and we really can feel the Divine Presence.

On Shabbat, we remember that God rules. God is "Sovereign."

Here is a word that you might know but need to learn now: "metaphor." A metaphor is a word that symbolizes something else. If you have a friend who is a "night owl," it doesn't mean that your friend is really a bird that flies at night. It simply means that they like doing things at night. If you say your parent has a "heart of gold," it doesn't mean that the heart is really made of gold; it simply means that your parent is kind. Both of these are metaphors.

When it comes to God, we have so many metaphors that we can barely count them. You already know some of them: "King" and "Father" are among the most common, though many people prefer "Ruler" or "Parent." You could even, as I said before, refer to God as the "Internet"—all around us, invisible, and something we can connect with.

Or, perhaps, something bigger and deeper.

Jewish mystics like to imagine that there are two aspects to God: the masculine *Kadosh Baruch Hu*, "the Holy One, blessed be He" (with emphasis on "He"); and the feminine *Shechinah*, the "Indwelling Presence." Think of it as "Dad" and "Mom," combined in one God. The great modern Jewish mystic Hillel Zeitlin (1871–1942), who lived and taught in Warsaw, Poland, and who died in the Holocaust, taught, "The *Shechinah* is the mother of all Creation. She is the mother of the world, married to *Adonai*. She is the mother of Israel and the mother of all individuals—the loving mother, the compassionate mother, the supernal mother."[3] Maybe this idea of God as *Shechinah*, a maternal presence, appeals to you.

There is no shortage of metaphors for God. Contemporary musician Paul Simon (United States, 1941–), one of rock music's greatest singer-songwriters, wrote about God in a song titled "The Lord." In the song, he imagines God as an engineer, a forest, music, and "a meal for the poorest of the poor, a welcome door to the stranger."[4]

This is the point: There is no shortage of ways to think about and imagine the Divine Presence in our lives. Some are ancient, some are modern, some are very creative—and all are possible.

PSALM 95 (130). Welcome to another metaphor for God: "Rock." Judaism often uses the "rock" metaphor. The famous Chanukah song "Maoz Tzur" is translated as "Rock of Ages." In the silent meditation, we speak of God as *Tzuri v'Go-ali*, "my Rock and my Redeemer." For many people, "rock" symbolizes something that is strong, solid, and unchanging. (Of course, water can wear rock away, but it takes a very long time.)

Here is the most famous, and most interesting, use of the "rock" metaphor in Jewish history. When the creators of the modern State of Israel were writing *M'gillat HaAtzma-ut*—the "Scroll of Independence," Israel's Declaration of Independence—some of the authors were observant Jews. They wanted the Declaration to mention God. In fact, earlier versions of the Declaration said, ". . . and placing our trust in the Almighty." Some observant Jews wanted the Declaration to say, "God of Israel."

There were other founders of the State of Israel who were secular Jews. They cared a lot about the Jewish people, about Judaism and its traditions, but they didn't care that much about God. So, what did they do? They did what Jews have often done: They compromised. They put these words at the very end, right above their signatures: "Placing our trust in the Rock of Israel."

What was the "Rock of Israel"? It depended on whom you asked. Those signers who believed in God believed that the "Rock of Israel" was, in fact, God—because there are many prayers that refer to God precisely that way. Those signers who were not so sure about God or did not believe in God had any number of ways of interpreting "Rock of Israel." They might believe that the "Rock of Israel" was the Land of Israel, or the people of Israel, or the historic strength of the people of Israel. It could mean almost whatever you wanted and needed it to mean.

David Ben-Gurion, who would become the first prime minister of the State of Israel, said, "Each of us, in his own way, believes in the 'Rock of Israel' as he understands it."[5] And, so it was—the phrase was adopted.

QUESTIONS:
1. What does "Rock of Israel" mean to you?
2. What are some of your favorite metaphors for God?
3. What are some new metaphors that you would want a
   future prayer book to include?

PSALM 96 (131). You probably know many songs. Some are old songs; some are more recent. One thing you can always expect is that there is always a new song coming.

Here is an interesting theme that keeps returning in these psalms.

We are called upon to *shiru l'Adonai shir chadash*, "sing to Adonai a new song." There are many songs in the Torah and the rest of the Hebrew Bible. The Book of Psalms is nothing but sacred songs to and about God. One book of the Hebrew Bible is *Shir HaShirim*, the Song of Songs, filled with love poetry and songs.

What does it mean to sing a new song to God? We find the first mention of singing a new song to God in Isaiah 42:10:

> Sing to the Eternal a new song,
> Praise from the ends of the earth—
> You who sail the sea and you creatures in it,
> You coastlands and their inhabitants!

Those are the words of an anonymous prophet called Second Isaiah. He preached during the time when the Judeans expected to return to the Land of Israel after exile in Babylonia (modern-day Iraq). What was that "new song" that this prophet was imagining? We were living in exile, in the foreign land of Babylonia; we were about to come home to the Land of Israel. This "new song" was a song of homecoming.

It is like that for the week as well. Just as we came home to our sacred land, we come home to our sacred day—Shabbat—when we sing a new song to God.

QUESTIONS:
1. What are some of your favorite songs?
2. What was the last new song that you learned?
3. What makes that song different from earlier songs that you have enjoyed?
4. How is Shabbat different from the rest of the days of the week?

PSALM 97 (132–33). God is coming, and God will rule. There will be justice, and tyranny will end. Will we all get to see that new realm of justice? Maybe. Or, perhaps, only some people will have that opportunity.

Psalm 97 says, "Light is sown for the righteous, radiance for the upright." Do only the righteous get to see that light? Remember when we were learning about the light of Shabbat and how the first light of Creation is sort of mysterious? We know it is not the sun, because that was created on the fourth day (Genesis 1:14–18). Could the first light of Creation be connected to the light for the righteous in this psalm?

Some Jewish mystics believe that this first light was a different kind of light. Rabbi Lawrence Kushner (United States, 1943–) teaches that according to the *Zohar*, the medieval book that is a main source of Jewish mysticism, "The first light of creation was not optical, but spiritual, the light of consciousness. Thus, consciousness comes before everything, a primordial awareness preceded creation. This is the 'hidden light.'"[6]

You know how cartoons will sometimes show a light bulb going off to signify that someone has a great idea? Or maybe you know that expression "Now, I see the light," which means "Now, I get it." The mystics believed that the hidden light, the light of the first day of Creation, was the light of consciousness—that light bulb over your head type of light. They also believed that light was the light of the soul—the individual soul, the soul of the world, the soul of the universe. According to this understanding, the psalm is saying that the righteous get a glimpse of that hidden light of the first day of Creation. It is stored away for them, and sometimes they get to see it.

QUESTIONS:
1. What do you think the light of the first day was?
2. When have you said or felt, "I see the light"?
3. What are some things that people might have to do in order to get that gift of light?

PSALM 98 (133–34). That new song that we are singing? It is getting better—now, that "new song" has some instruments to accompany it.

The author of Psalm 98 had visited the ancient Temple in Jerusalem. In the ancient Temple, there was an orchestra of Levites who played instruments to accompany the sacrificial offerings.

Let's "listen" to that ancient orchestra. First, there was the *kinor*, the lyre. The lyre was an ancient stringed instrument; it may have been like a harp. When you go to synagogue and you hear someone playing the guitar to accompany the prayers, the guitar is a "descendant" of the ancient lyre.

There were also two kinds of wind instruments—*chatzotz'rot* (regular brass trumpets) and shofar (the ram's horn). What is the difference between those two instruments? The regular brass trumpets were entirely made by human beings. But the shofar comes from nature itself—from an animal, like a ram (a male sheep) or a goat. To use the shofar, we don't simply remove the horn from the slaughtered ram. We must hollow it out and prepare it by hand so that it can bring forth its notes. In other words, we have to take what nature gave us and "improve" upon it.

The music of the regular brass trumpets must have sounded wonderful; if you have heard an orchestra or a band perform, or if you are part of an orchestra or a band, you have heard the trumpet. It sounds glorious. The shofar, not so much. The sound of the shofar is raw, ancient, and rough.

We need both sounds—the raw sounds of the shofar and the melodious sound of the trumpet—especially because the brass trumpet would sound its notes whenever it was time for the ancient tribes of Israel to march forward in their journey through the wilderness. The psalm reminds us, though, that the instruments are not enough. Nature itself becomes the orchestra. Once again, God is coming to judge the earth. As Jewish scholar Ellen Frankel (United States, 1951–) writes, "The recurrent themes of God's power, military triumph, and love for Israel appear in this psalm as in previous ones. The new imagery introduced here is orchestral, conjuring up music produced by human beings (harps, trumpets, horn, and song) but also the natural sounds of the world: the sea, the earth, and all their creatures."[7]

It is all part of God's song.

QUESTIONS:
1. Do you play an instrument? What kind? How hard do you have to work to produce its sounds?
2. Why do you think we need both the beautiful sounds

from the brass trumpet and the rough sounds from the
shofar?
3. What sounds serve as a way to push you forward in the
tasks that you need to accomplish every day?
4. How does nature itself become an "orchestra" for God?
What sounds in nature move you deeply?

PSALM 99 (135). God is our Sovereign. God rules. This is the last
psalm in the *Kabbalat Shabbat* section of the service that will mention that. The psalm also says, "Adonai enthroned on cherubim, is
sovereign." Who—or what—were the cherubim?

The cherubim were winged creatures, usually depicted with the
faces of children. (It is sort of like the way we imagine Cupid, the
ancient Roman god of love.) The cherubim make various appear-
ances in the Hebrew Bible. We first meet them in Genesis, where
they guard the Tree of Life in the Garden of Eden (Genesis 3:24).
We then meet them in the Book of Exodus, where we read that they
adorn the cover of the Holy Ark (Exodus 25:18–20). They even carry
God's throne (Psalm 18:11) and then appear again here in Psalm 99.

Where did our ancestors get the idea for the cherubim? The origins
of the cherubim are probably buried somewhere in ancient Middle
Eastern mythology. Winged creatures stood guard outside the gates
of ancient Assyrian and Babylonian temples, so it was natural for
our ancestors to imagine that our God and our Temple were not all
that different.

Surprised? Don't be. Throughout our long history, Jews have used
symbols and stories from surrounding cultures, and we have made
those symbols and stories our own.

This psalm says that "Adonai is great in Zion." To be sure, I (and
many others) uniquely experience God in Zion—in Jerusalem and
the entire Land of Israel. But, ultimately, that experience of God's
greatness in Zion is not just for Jews. One day, *all* the nations will
praise God. All the nations of the world, and not just the Jews, will
someday make their own sacred journey to the Temple in Jerusalem.
One day, they will all know that Adonai is God.

What will that mean? Will it mean that all people will become Jews? Not really. In some ways, it is even better than that. One day, all people will live good and just lives. That will be the real sign of believing in God.

QUESTIONS:
1. What do you think of the inclusion of the cherubim in the Torah? Do they have a place in our story?
2. What does "all the nations coming to Jerusalem" mean to you?
3. What would be some universal ethical laws that you'd like to see instituted?

PSALM 29 (136–37), Have you ever been in a storm—a really big storm? It is easy to understand how our ancestors must have imagined a storm like that. Yes, of course, they believed that God's presence could be found in the ancient Temple. More than that, they understood that God was present in nature itself—and in particular, in the midst of a big storm.

What is going on in Psalm 29, which also appears in the Torah service? The psalm says, "The voice of Adonai is over the waters; the God of glory thunders, Adonai, over the mighty waters." This paints a picture of a rainstorm filled with thunder. The Psalmist is saying that above it all—above the mighty waters that are in the atmosphere and will soon be hitting the ground—God is in charge.

Let's talk a little bit about how the ancient Israelites understood thunder. They imagined that the thunder was the voice of God. "The voice of Adonai is power; the voice of Adonai is majesty"—so powerful that "the voice of Adonai breaks cedars; Adonai shatters the cedars of Lebanon." Our grandparents and great-grandparents knew all about the "cedars of Lebanon." When American Jews built hospitals, many of them were called "Cedars of Lebanon." Many of those names have simply been abbreviated to "Cedars." Why were hospitals called "Cedars of Lebanon"?

When King Solomon built the First Temple in Jerusalem, he used the wood of trees that had come from Phoenicia to the north of the

Land of Israel, which today is Lebanon. They were very strong trees that produced great wood. In various places in the Bible, the term "cedars of Lebanon" simply means strength and power.

It is a big deal to say that "Adonai shatters the cedars of Lebanon." It would mean that God's voice—thunder—was very loud and very strong. It would mean that God is powerful—so powerful that God could make "Lebanon skip like a calf"—actually uprooting Mount Lebanon! God is so powerful that God could make the constellation Sirion leap "like a young wild ox"! God's voice—again, thunder and lightning—could set the wilderness on fire, "cause hinds to calve" (to give birth), and "strip forests bare." So, yes—we can experience God in the forces of nature.

Back here on earth: "In God's Temple all say 'Glory!'" That word "glory" (*kavod*) is a tricky word. Yes, in Modern Hebrew *kavod* means "glory, respect, and honor." But in Biblical times, it also meant the presence of God. So, we feel God in the ancient Temple, in nature, and particularly during the ancient Flood. During the Flood, God ruled. God made divine law known at that time. That is where God's power ultimately lies. We want a little bit of that strength for ourselves, but ultimately God gives us peace and well-being.

Fun fact: The phrase *kol Adonai* (the voice of Adonai) occurs seven times in this psalm—one for every day of the week.

> QUESTIONS:
> 1. Have you ever been in a powerful storm? What were your feelings at that time?
> 2. When have you experienced God's presence in nature?
> 3. When have you experienced calm and a feeling of well-being after a storm?

L'CHAH DODI (138–39)

If Shlomo Halevi Alkabetz had been a rock star, there would have been no one like him. He was a mystic and a poet, and his most famous poem was *L'chah Dodi*. How many melodies are there for *L'chah Dodi*? No one really knows. Hundreds, at least. Every Jewish community—American Jews, Western European Jews, Central

European Jews, Eastern European Jews, Chasidim, Sephardic Jews, Jews of various Arab lands, and on and on—all have their favorite melodies to this beautiful, poetic hymn.

Where does *L'chah Dodi* come from? And how did this song become so famous and so beloved? Let's go back in time to 1492. Yes, that was the year that Columbus "discovered" America. Interesting fact: Columbus had Jews on board his ships, because King Ferdinand and Queen Isabella of Spain had expelled the Jews from Spain. The Hebrew word for "Spain" is "Sepharad," and the descendants of those expelled Spanish Jews are called Sephardic Jews today. The Jews went from Spain to neighboring Portugal. Several years later, Portugal expelled them as well. From there, they went in every direction. North—to the Netherlands and Germany. West—to the Americas. South—to North Africa. And east—to Italy, Greece, Turkey, and as far as the Land of Israel, to the small town of Safed, in the north of Israel.

There weren't that many Jews in Safed; in the early 1500s, there may have been perhaps three hundred Jewish households. But never doubt what a small community of Jews can accomplish! The Jews of Safed were mystics. They believed in secret, hidden truths. They believed in secret, hidden interpretations of Jewish texts and ideas. They believed that there were hidden aspects of God. Their biggest teaching: God had both typically masculine and typically feminine qualities—the masculine *Kadosh Baruch Hu* (the Holy and Blessed One) and the feminine *Shechinah*.

The Jewish mystics believed that the feminine presence of God—*Shechinah*—showed up every week. On Shabbat, she would "disguise" herself as the Shabbat Bride or the Shabbat Queen. The Shabbat Bride would then prepare to meet her "husband," the masculine part of God. That would be like a wedding.

How did the Jews of Safed dress for a wedding? They would dress in white clothing. They would go out into the fields surrounding Safed, and they would welcome the Shabbat Bride. They would sing, "Beloved, come to meet the bride; beloved, come to greet Shabbat."

There is so much magic in this song, beginning with the opening letter of each verse.

Each verse begins with a different letter of the Hebrew alphabet—*shin, lamed, mem, hei* (combined, those letters spell "Shlomo," the first name of the composer). The next four verses begin with *hei, lamed, vav, yod* (that spells "Halevi"). The last verse begins with *bet*—nothing special there.

Each verse contains a major teaching:

- Verse 1: There are two commandments regarding Shabbat—*shamor v'zachor*. We must "keep" (*shamor*) Shabbat, and we must also "remember" (*zachor*) Shabbat. Some Jews do well at observing and guarding the traditional laws of Shabbat. Some Jews do better at remembering that it is Shabbat, doing wonderful, holy things in its honor. Either way—it is a mitzvah to pay attention to Shabbat.
- Verse 2: Shabbat is "the last of days, for which the first was made." The entire purpose of Creation was for God to rest. When we rest and rejuvenate our souls, we imitate God. All creation leads to Shabbat, and Shabbat leads to re-creation.
- Verse 3: Even though the songwriter is in Safed, he is thinking of Jerusalem. So should we: "royal shrine, city of kings" Jerusalem of the 1500s was not doing well; it was poor and often distressed. But the poet-composer had faith that the holy city would rise again: "You have dwelt long enough in the valley of tears." It is as if he is saying to Jerusalem: You have cried long enough. Life will get better. He was saying this not only to Jerusalem, but to the entire Jewish people.
- Verse 4: What does it mean for life to get better? "At hand is Bethlehem's David." This is a reference to King David, who was born in Bethlehem. The Jewish tradition imagines that King David is the ancestor of the Messiah, who will bring in an age of peace and prosperity for all.
- Verse 5: God's "light has come . . . upon you." Light, Shabbat candles, joy, warmth—that is what Shabbat is all about!
- Verse 6: Jerusalem will be rebuilt—"the city renewed upon its ancient ruins." Jerusalem is a tel, an archaeological mound in which new truths are revealed, layer by layer. Like Judaism, and like life.

- Verse 7: "The scavengers are scattered, your devourers have fled." The poet-composer is referring to the enemies of the Jews, who had scattered them. If only that idea had become irrelevant! Sadly, it has stayed relevant. After the devastating things that have befallen Jews and Israel in recent years, we welcome a time when, in fact, "the scavengers are scattered."
- Verse 8: "Await the promised one"—literally, "the one who is descended from Peretz." Who is Peretz? In the Book of Genesis, Jacob's son Judah has a son named Peretz with Tamar. Peretz is the direct ancestor of King David, who is the ancestor of the Messiah.
- Verse 9: Shabbat is the "crown of your husband." We rise for the Shabbat bride, turn toward the sanctuary entrance, and bow—as if we were rising for the bride at a wedding. *Shechinah*, the feminine presence of God, is reunited with the masculine presence of God. God is whole, the world is whole, and we are whole.

A question remains. Who is *dodi*, the "beloved" to whom the song is addressed? It could be that *dodi* is the masculine part of God, and we are encouraging the *dodi* to embrace and unite with the *Shechinah*—the Shabbat Bride or Queen.

It could be that *dodi*, the "beloved," is your friend, the person with whom you pray, the people who make up your Jewish community.

It could be that *dodi* is your own soul. The Jewish tradition speaks of the *n'shamah y'teirah*, the "extra soul," that every person receives on Shabbat. Perhaps during the week, we don't really think about that extra soul. But when Shabbat comes, that soul can come out of hiding and say, "Wow! Look at me! I am here!"

The phrase *l'chah dodi* does not really mean "beloved, come." It really means "beloved, *go*." Go forth, my beloved inner soul. I have imprisoned you too long.

QUESTIONS:
1. What other songs do you know that have multiple versions?
2. What does Shabbat mean to you and your family? How

do you *observe* Shabbat? How do you *remember* Shabbat?

3. What do you do to help your own soul to run free? What gives you joy? What is fun for you?

4. In Reform Judaism, we don't often speak about the Messiah as a person. We prefer to speak of a messianic age, when everything will finally be good for everyone. What would be on your wish list for a messianic age?

PSALM 92 (140)

Psalm 92 clearly states that it is intended for Shabbat. It mentions the joy of worship and the music of the ancient Temple—"a ten-stringed harp, with voice and lyre together," stringed musical instruments that combined beautifully with singing voices. "The righteous bloom like a date-palm, they thrive like a cedar in Lebanon; planted in the house of Adonai, they flourish in the courts of our God. In old age they still produce fruit; they are full of sap and freshness, attesting that Adonai is upright, my Rock, in whom there is no wrong."

Remember that a "cedar in Lebanon" symbolizes great strength. So this means that righteous people are like sturdy, strong trees. Even when they age, righteous people are still productive. Their lives testify to the fact that God is just.

QUESTIONS:
1. In what ways do righteous people bloom?
2. In what ways do righteous people exhibit strength?
3. Give examples of righteous people who still "produce fruit"—are still productive—even in old age.

PSALM 93 (141)

Psalm 93 is the final psalm in the *Kabbalat Shabbat* service. Once again, we find the theme of God's sovereignty. Once again, we find the image that God is present, even above and beyond nature.

What does the psalm mean by "Your [God's] decrees are indeed enduring"? These are not legal decrees that God issued. Rather, as we are about to leave this section of the service, we are affirming that God's decrees are, in fact, the forces of nature themselves.

SHALOM ALEICHEM (142)

Shalom Aleichem, like Shabbat candle lighting, holds so many memories for so many Jews. Customarily, Jews sang this song not in the synagogue, but rather around the Shabbat dinner table at home. To this day, its melody fills my mind and my soul with memories. My fondest memories of Erev Shabbat in Jerusalem are leaving synagogue just as the sun was setting, walking through the streets, heading to Shabbat dinner at the home of a friend, smelling the wonderful Shabbat dishes that had been prepared, and hearing people singing this song that welcomes the angels of Shabbat.

This is one of the most common questions that rabbis, cantors, and Jewish educators hear: Do Jews believe in angels? Well, yes. Sort of.

First, we encounter cherubim, angelic figures, who stand guard over the gates of the Garden of Eden. Those cherubim make another appearance, standing guard over the ancient Ark, and also appear in a *Kabbalat Shabbat* psalm (see page 39). Their Biblical "cousins," the seraphim—fiery angels—stood guard over God in the ancient Temple in Jerusalem. The prophet Isaiah had a very clear view of them: "Seraphs stood in attendance, each with six wings—two covering the face, two covering the body, and two to fly with. And one would call to the other, 'Holy, holy, holy! Adonai of Hosts—whose presence fills all the earth!'" (Isaiah 6:2–3).

The Torah is filled with angels (*malachim*). When Hagar and her son Ishmael were near death in the wilderness, an angel appeared to her and offered her comfort (Genesis 16, 21). Angels came to announce that Sarah will have a child (Genesis 18); another set of angels came to visit Lot in the city of Sodom (Genesis 19). When Abraham was about to sacrifice his son Isaac, an angel of God came and stopped him from doing so (Genesis 22). Jacob dreamed of a ladder of angels (Genesis 28). Moses encountered an angel at the Burning Bush (Exodus 3). Much later in the Bible, in the Book of Daniel, those angels get names: Gabriel, Michael, Raphael. To this day, some Jews pray that when they go to sleep, those angels will surround their beds and offer them protection, comfort, and a good night's sleep.

None of this answers the question: What are angels? Do they have robes, harps, wings, and halos, as they are frequently depicted in art? I do not think so.

That first group of angels—the cherubim and the seraphim—are "leftovers" from ancient Middle Eastern mythology. Apparently, ancient Jews knew about those mythical figures, liked them, and incorporated them into their writings. Beyond that, Judaism considers these angels as messengers of God. They are like avatars of God, or as I heard in a lecture, they are "aspects of God on one minimission."[8]

In Aryeh Lev Stollman's (United States, 1954–) book *The Far Euphrates*, a rabbi's son named Alexander visits one of his classmates—a girl who is very sick. His father said to him, "Alexander, you did the most wonderful kindness when you went to visit your friend. And this kindness, which forms the true substance of angels, will escort you and protect you, as all your good deeds do, every day of your life."[9] In other words, angels don't wear robes or play harps. They probably look just like you and me.

One last thing. When you consider that we have just welcomed the Shabbat bride and that we are now welcoming the Shabbat angels, you would think that Jews have imaginary friends who come to visit them on that holiest of evenings. And you would be right!

Judaism is filled with "imaginary friends" and visitors. The prophet Elijah makes an "appearance" at every covenantal ceremony for an infant, at the *Havdalah* service that ends Shabbat, and at the end of the Pesach seder. On Sukkot, figures from the Jewish past visit us in the sukkah in a ritual called *ushpizin*.

Judaism is many things, and it is also an act of the imagination.

QUESTIONS:
1. Who have been angels for you?
2. What actions have you performed that created angels?
3. How do you use your own imagination as a Jew?
4. Imagine that there are angels—divine emissaries—sitting next to you. What would they say to you?

CHATZI KADDISH (144)

A group of Reform Jewish teens went on a trip and visited a traditional Orthodox synagogue for Shabbat services. At various times in the service, they heard the words of *Kaddish*, the traditional prayer for the dead, which they recognized. After the service, one teen asked, "Why are there so many *Kaddish*es in the service?"

Another teen responded, "Maybe it is because we have so many losses in our lives, and so many things die for us, that we have to say *Kaddish* even more than we had thought."

This is a wonderful, sensitive answer. It is not quite right. While we tend to think that *Kaddish* is a prayer for the dead, in reality that is not how this prayer always functions in the worship service. Quite often, we say a version of *Kaddish* as a way of creating a mental and spiritual space between the sections of the service. Think of it as being like a YouTube ad that separates two parts of a video. However, all those versions of *Kaddish* have some things in common.

First, they are all in the language of Aramaic, which is a "sister" language to Hebrew and Arabic. Aramaic is a very ancient language—the everyday language that Jews spoke in ancient times. Just as the *Kaddish* is in Aramaic, so is the Talmud, the major work of Jewish law and lore. The Pesach song "Chad Gadya" ("An Only Kid") is in Aramaic. So is *Kol Nidrei*, the famous statement that opens Yom Kippur. So is the *ketubah*, the traditional wedding document, and the *get*, the traditional divorce document.

Second, each *Kaddish* is an expression of faith, specifically the belief that "God's great name" will be "exalted and hallowed." In other words, the prayer expresses the hope that God's great name will become even mightier and holier.

It's not a bad thing to say as one part of the service ends and another begins. This particular *Kaddish* is unique because it is a little bit shorter than the other versions of *Kaddish*. *Chatzi* means "half," and that is why this is called the *Chatzi*—Half—*Kaddish*.

QUESTIONS:
1. What kinds of things do you do that create a space between two kinds of experiences?
2. When have you felt faith in God? When have you questioned your faith in God?

Act One
What We Believe: *Sh'ma Uvirchoteha—Sh'ma* and Its Blessings

What do Jews actually believe? That is a question that many Jews ask. Is there a list of "approved" Jewish beliefs?

Over the centuries, great Jewish thinkers (like Maimonides, in the Middle Ages) have tried to come up with a core list of Jewish beliefs, similar to what some Christians would call a catechism. You will not be surprised to learn that whenever a Jewish thinker came up with a list of beliefs, other Jews would say, "No, that's not right. You left out . . ." or "No, that's not right. No one believes this. . . ."

However, if you were to ask me for some basic Jewish beliefs, that short list would be right here—in this section of our worship.

The first belief is that God created the world—and with it, God created the cycles of time that are predictable and unchanging.

The second belief is that God loves the Jewish people, and the sign of that love is the gift of Torah. For Jews, the Torah is not a burden; it is an opportunity to live as part of a larger story and to do mitzvot. We reciprocate that love when we declare that "God is One," the essential unity of all being, and when we act in certain ways that demonstrate that love.

The final belief is that God brings us out of Egypt. Notice the present tense: That long-ago, mythic event is the blueprint for all other redemptive moments in history, including through today.

All of that in just one act!

BAR'CHU (146)

You are at a rock concert, and a band has been warming up the crowd. They play some good music, including some songs that you recognize. But, through it all, you are waiting for the "main show" to begin. You are waiting for the featured performers to take the stage and really make the event come alive.

Then, the lead singer of the featured band comes on and says, "Good evening, Detroit [or whatever city you are in]! Are you ready to rock?" Everyone in the crowd bursts into cheers and applause, because they are ready to rock.

The *Bar'chu* is sometimes called the "call to worship," and because of that, everyone who is capable of doing so stands up for it—just like you might jump to your feet to greet that lead singer. The *Bar'chu* is basically saying, "Okay, you've been warming up. We have done some nice prayers—mostly old psalms—the oldies collection. But are you ready to really speak to God?" The answer must be: "Yes. Bring it on."

> QUESTIONS:
> 1. What things do you do that require warm-up and preparation?
> 2. Can you describe the excitement that exists before a concert or a game?
> 3. How is that excitement similar to what happens before a worship service? How is it different?

MAARIV ARAVIM (148)

When you were very young, you were probably afraid of the dark. There is no reason to be embarrassed. Most people have been afraid of the dark.

In fact, think of this: Before Thomas A. Edison invented the light bulb in 1879, when it was night—it was really night. It was really dark, unless you walked around carrying a torch. There were no restaurants or stores that were open at night. It was just totally dark.

Our fear of the dark is so basic that almost every little kid's room has a night-light installed in the wall. So, as we come to the evening prayers of the service, here is what you need to know. The basic theme of the evening prayers is: How do I get over my fear of the night? It starts with *Maariv Aravim*, the prayer to God, who brings on the evening.

Read the Hebrew, and you will understand:

> . . . *asher bidvaro maariv aravim,*
> *b'chochmah potei-ach sh'arim*
> *uvitvunah m'shaneh itim*
> *umachalif et haz'manim,*
> *umsadeir et hakochavim*
> *b'mishm'roteihem barakia kirtzono.*

This is lovely poetry, even if you prefer a strictly scientific explanation of the cycles of time. There is a message in the way the words sound in Hebrew. Notice how the words line up—in tidy groups of two or three. Each line invites us to believe that there is a rhythm in the world and in Creation and that we can depend on it. The words are almost a rocking motion, as if a parent were rocking an infant to sleep.

Now, check out the English:

> . . . who speaks the evening into being,
> skillfully opens the gates,
> thoughtfully alters the time
> and changes the seasons,
> and arranges the stars
> in their heavenly courses according to plan.

These words are based on a very ancient view of the universe—the idea that when day becomes night, it is because God opens gates in the heavens. This might be confusing, because usually when we open something, we shed light; when we close something, we make things dark. This is switched here, because of the ancient mythic view of how light and darkness came into the world—God manages those passages.

As the contemporary songwriter Rabbi Noam Katz (United States, 1978–) puts it in his song "Roll into Dark":[10]

Roll into dark.
Roll into light.
Night becomes day.
Day turns to night.

Then, notice the second half of the prayer:

... *goleil or mip'nei choshech,*
v'choshech mip'nei or.
Umaavir yom umeivi lailah,
umavdil bein yom uvein lailah.
... rolling light away from darkness
and darkness from light,
transforming day into night
and distinguishing one from the other.

Again, there is a rhythm to the Hebrew. Each line of the prayer contains two sets of phrases. Those groups of words are there to make us remember the eternal rhythm that will always be there—as surely as day flows into night and night flows again into day.

Why does the prayer insist on reminding us that it is God who creates the night? In the ancient world, people believed that nighttime was the realm of demons and scary monsters. No, the prayer tells us—there are no demons and monsters out there. It is just God.

Notice one more thing—the sound of the Hebrew:

maariv aravim
sh'arim
m'shaneh itim
umachalif et haz'manim
b'mishm'roteihem

Contemporary professor Reuven Kimelman (United States, 1944–) invites us to read those Hebrew words and to notice and hear the *mem* letters—the *m* sound.[11] *Mmm.*

That *m* sound—*mmm*—is the sound of comfort and consolation. In many languages, the word for "mother" starts with the *m* sound. It is almost like the prayer is saying, "Yes, the night is here, but *mmm*—don't worry. Do not fear."

QUESTIONS:
1. Ask a parent or an adult in your life: When you were young, were you afraid of the dark?
2. Did you have a nightlight when you were growing up?
3. What are some things that frighten you now?
4. When you are afraid, what gives you courage and comfort?

AHAVAT OLAM (150)

Ahavat Olam begins with the words "Everlasting love You offered Your people Israel." The evening prayer flows seamlessly into the prayer for God's love of the people Israel—*Ahavat Olam*.

There's that *mmm* sound, again—this time, in the word *olam*, which means "everlasting" or "eternal." Why is there another *m* sound? Because once again, we need comfort and reassurance.

As I said before, once upon a time, people really believed that night was a time of monsters and demons. Many little kids still believe it. They are sure that the monsters and demons are right there, in their rooms—underneath the bed! Hiding in the closet! Therefore, we need God's love most intensely at night, when we might imagine that the monsters and demons are there.

"When we lie down and when we rise up" from the bed, we sense the presence of God.

Rabbi Shai Held (United States, 1971–) teaches the words of the Chasidic master Rav Zadok HaKohen (Poland, 1823–1900) of Lublin: "There are different kinds of love in the morning and the evening. Morning is a time of passionate hope and open-ended possibility. Evening, in contrast, is a time of anxiety and apprehension. Therefore, in the evening, we speak of 'everlasting love,' the kind of love that remains indestructible even during the night and the darkness of troubles."[12] The Torah, which comes from light and which is light, is our nightlight.

One last thing. We have *Ahavat Olam*, which speaks of God's love for us. We have *V'ahavta*, which speaks of our reciprocal love for God. And the *Sh'ma* is in the middle.

The *Sh'ma* is a love sandwich.

Seriously.

QUESTIONS:

1. Do you believe that God's love is everlasting? What makes you believe that? Do you ever doubt it?

2. How is God's love different from human love? What would help humanity love more like God?

3. This prayer says that one way God shows God's love is by giving us the Torah. What other ways do you think God shows love to us?

SH'MA (152–53)

It is the most important sentence in the Torah. Okay, make that in the entire Hebrew Bible. Come to think of it—make that in all of Judaism.

We are talking about the *Sh'ma*, of course—six Hebrew words that are sometimes referred to as "the watchword of the Jewish faith," or what the ancient Sages called *kabbalat ol hashamayim* (the acceptance of the yoke of heaven). Farm animals would wear yokes to help them carry loads. That is how our ancient Rabbis understood mitzvot; yes, they could be a burden, but they help us bear the burdens of life. It is right there in the Torah—Deuteronomy 6:4—written in large ink, so that it stands out.

The second line of the prayer, *Baruch shem k'vod malchuto l'olam va-ed*, "Blessed is God's glorious majesty forever and forever," is an add-on. It is not part of the Torah, which is why in some congregations this line is said or sung in a softer voice. In fact, we are not even sure if this is the correct translation. Literally, it translates as "Blessed is the name of God's presence of God's majesty forever and ever." This seems sloppy; some ancient writer needed a good editor.

So, what could it mean? Let's add some missing punctuation.

- *Baruch shem!* "Blessed is the name [of God]!" Some Jews still say something like this; ask them, "How are you?" and they are likely to say, *"Baruch HaShem!"*—"Blessed is The Name!" which means "Blessed is God!" Since we do not really know how to pronounce God's name (see page 22), many Jews refer to God simply as *HaShem*, "The Name."

- *K'vod malchuto l'olam va-ed*, "The glorious majesty of God's kingdom is forever and ever." Just imagine that there is God's kingdom—a realm where ethics, justice, mercy, and holiness prevail—and that it is our role to bring that kingdom down to earth and to make it real in our lives.

The *Sh'ma* is the first sentence in Hebrew that a Jewish child learns. When Jews pray, we say it at morning worship (*Shacharit*) and at evening worship (*Maariv*). We sing it as part of the Torah service. We say it at the end of Yom Kippur. Many of us say it when we wake up and right before we go to sleep.

Just as the *Sh'ma* is the first Hebrew sentence that a child learns, it is also the last Hebrew sentence that a Jew says, if they can. It is part of the *Vidui*, the deathbed confession, which sometimes another person will say on behalf of the person who is dying.

Many people believe that the entire purpose of the *Sh'ma* is to teach the idea of monotheism—that there is only one God. In fact, the ancient Israelites were probably not strict monotheists. They recognized that other nations had their gods and goddesses but that *Adonai*, the God of the Israelites, was the "best" of the gods. Centuries later, prophets would come to believe that *Adonai* was, in fact, the only God.

You might wonder why monotheism—the belief in one God—is a good thing. A number of years ago, I was talking to a little kid about Greek mythology. That little kid said to me, "I like all those stories of those gods, but Judaism is better."

"Why? I asked.

"Because," he said, "the Jews just have one God."

"Yes, so?" I asked.

"Well," he continued, "if you have too many gods, then the service is too long because you have to pray to all of them."

"That is certainly true," I said, smiling to myself.

"And then," he continued, "if each one of those gods gives a different Torah, then there is too much to read and too many people to call up to do blessings over those different Torahs."

"Whoa," I said. I had just met the youngest Jewish thinker in the world, because he had figured some things out.

First, the service should not get too long. Jewish law actually prohibits a service from being too long. This would be an unnecessary burden on the people, something called *tircha d'tzibura*. If a service goes on too long, or if people have to stand for long periods of time during the service…well, no one wants that. Probably not even God.

Second, he had hit on the most basic understanding of monotheism—the belief in one God.

We are all children of that God and therefore equal.

Because there is only one God, there can be only one true ethical code. Not everyone believes that, of course. Some people like to say, "You do you." Or, "Whatever." While that might be true about matters of taste (I like ice cream; you like cake), it gets more difficult when we start talking about ethics and how we treat other people.

Is it okay for some cultures to permit extreme violence? Is it okay for some cultures to allow stealing? If it was, the world would descend into chaos, and Judaism would say, "No. These behaviors are not okay." That is the basic truth of the *Sh'ma*: one God, one humanity, one moral law that all people might aspire to follow.

QUESTIONS:
1. What do you think are some of the benefits of monotheism?
2. What do you think are some of the benefits of polytheism (the belief in many gods)?
3. Why do you think that Judaism has always believed in monotheism?
4. What do you think should be some basic ethical laws of humanity?

V'AHAVTA (154)

Just as day follows night, the *V'ahavta* follows the *Sh'ma*—often in the worship service, and certainly in the Torah itself. The *V'ahavta* is also called *kabbalat ol mitzvot* (the acceptance of the yoke of the mitzvot). The *V'ahavta* tells us that it's not enough to know that there is a God. That knowledge must be manifest in specific actions. What actions are listed in the *V'ahavta*?

- "Recite them when you stay at home and when you are away, when you lie down and when you get up." It does not say, "Recite them in the synagogue." Judaism does not just "live" in the synagogue. Judaism begins at home. More than that: You can take Judaism into the world with you. Imagine how Judaism affects the way you treat your parents, your teachers, or other kids.

- "Teach them [the words of the *Sh'ma*] to your children." You are learning Judaism. While it might be very hard to even imagine this, someday you might have children. Make sure you teach them Judaism as well. That is the meaning of Jewish continuity. In the words of Fania Oz-Salzberger (Israel, 1960–), "The great story and its imperatives passed from generation to generation on tablets, parchment and paper. As I check my references on an iPad, I realize that we have come full circle: from tablet to tablet, from scroll to scroll."[13]

- "Bind them as a sign on your hand and let them serve as a symbol on your forehead." This is why many Jews wear *t'fillin* (leather boxes containing words of Torah that are worn on the forearm and forehead during weekday morning worship). We wear *t'fillin* on our forehead so that they help us think; they rest between our eyes so that Torah becomes our way of seeing the world. We wear them on our arms so that Torah teaches us how to act in the world. The *t'fillin* on the arm faces the heart so that Torah will be inside our hearts.

- "Inscribe them on the doorposts of your house and on your gates." This is the reason for the mezuzah that marks the doorposts of the Jewish home.

Right now, you're probably thinking: How can the Torah tell us to love God? Isn't love an emotion? How can you command an emotion? To answer this excellent question, we need to learn from archaeologists of the ancient Middle East. They tell us that when ancient kings made treaties (or covenants) with their underlings, the underlings were commanded to "love" the more powerful king. Love wasn't an emotional thing; the word "love" was used to symbolize loyalty. Our prayers are a way for us to demonstrate our loyalty to God.

Finally, why does *V'ahavta* remind us to remember that God took us out of Egypt?

We were not powerful. We were slaves. When we remember where we come from and who we once were, we remember who we are.

QUESTIONS:
1. How do you bring Judaism into your home? How do you bring Judaism into your life?
2. How does Judaism affect the way that you see the world? The way that you think about the world? The way that you feel about things?
3. When have you loved God? When have you not been so sure that you love God?
4. How do you demonstrate loyalty to God?

G'ULAH (*EMET VEEMUNAH* and *MI CHAMOCHAH*) (156–58)

You go to the swimming pool and you get ready to jump in. Here is something that you never consider, because you have never had to consider it: Every time you jump into a swimming pool, you have faith that since the last time you jumped into the pool, the laws of physics have not changed.

Or, how about this: Every time you board an airplane, the same thing happens. You have faith that the pilot knows how to fly the plane, that the laws of aerodynamics have not changed since the last time you boarded a plane, and that airplanes can still fly through the air.

Of course, both of these examples are about things that already happened in the past. I swam last week; I am swimming again. I traveled in an airplane last year; I am flying in a plane again. Our past experiences help us have total faith that everything is the way it is supposed to be, based on the way it was. What about those things that you have not yet encountered or experienced? Would you have the same kind of faith?

This question is precisely what challenged the Israelites when they got to the shores of the Sea of Reeds. The Egyptians were behind them. The sea was in front of them. Either way they turned, there was the probability of death—either by the sword or by drowning. What would they do?

What happened at the edge of the water? Some ancient sages said that each tribe demanded the privilege of going in first. Others said quite the opposite: Each tribe demanded that the others go in first. In this Torah portion, it would seem that the Israelites discovered the fine art of complaining—and some say, that is what they all did at the shores of the sea.

Except for one man. "When Israel stood by the sea, the tribes stood arguing with each other, one saying, 'I will go in first,' and the other saying, 'I will go in first.' At that moment, Nachshon ben Aminadav of the tribe of Judah jumped into the waves of the sea" (Babylonian Talmud, *Sotah* 36b–37a).[14] When Nachshon jumped into the sea, the waters parted, and the people were able to walk through to safety and freedom.

This is what we sometimes call a "leap of faith." Nachshon chose not to be afraid. Because Nachshon jumped, our tradition says that he would be the ancestor of King David and would have the honor of being the first person to bring an offering at the dedication of the Tabernacle.

QUESTIONS:
1. What are some things that happen in life that simply require faith?
2. What are some things that happen in life that you take for granted, that you believe will never change?
3. When have you experienced Nachshon-type behavior in others and in yourself?

HASHKIVEINU (160)

Many parents and children have their own nighttime rituals—reading stories, singing songs, or saying prayers. (I know one family where they sing old Beatles songs at bedtime.) Why do families do that? Because, like we said earlier, nighttime can be scary. The darkness is scary. That is what this prayer does for us—it provides us with yet another "nightlight."

"Grant, O God, that we lie down in peace, and raise us up, our Guardian, to life renewed." Think of that: Yes, we are going to sleep, and we will be unconscious for eight hours. When we wake up, we will have the opportunity to experience the world anew. Since it is nighttime, there are things that might frighten us. The prayer lists them.

"Defend us against enemies, illness, war, famine, and sorrow." Do those things still exist? Absolutely.

"Enemies": Just think of the date October 7. You don't even have to explain what that means to people. It is like saying "the Fourth of July." Everyone knows what happened on the Fourth of July (a very good thing). Everyone knows what happened on October 7 (a very bad thing—the Hamas terror attack on Israel, which killed more Jews on a single day since the Holocaust and resulted in the taking of hostages, followed by a prolonged war). On top of that, there were so many antisemitic acts that took place all over the world in the weeks and months following. So, yes: The Jews still have enemies.

"Illness": The Hebrew word for illness is *dever*, which actually means "pestilence" or "plague." If we ever thought that *dever* had gone out of business, COVID-19 made us realize that this is sadly not the case. So, yes: We still have illness, *dever*.

"War": The Hebrew word used for war here is *cherev*, which actually means "sword." To be sure, most armies do not fight with swords anymore; their weapons are more sophisticated and, tragically, more violent. So, yes: We still have war, *cherev*.

"Famine": The Hebrew word for famine is *raav*, a shortage of food. In the Book of Genesis, there was a famine in the Land of Israel. That famine brought Jacob's eleven sons down to Egypt in search of grain. The twelfth son, Joseph, was already living in Egypt and had taught the Egyptians to store their grain so they would not go hungry. Famine is the reason the Israelites wound up in Egypt in the first place. In ancient times, famine was an ever-present danger, but it is not as if famine ever goes away. Sadly, famines still take a massive toll throughout the world—not only in impoverished countries, but also in the seemingly prosperous United States. Many people in the United States live with food insecurity. In major cities, there are entire neighborhoods where there are no grocery stores, where people do not have access to healthy foods. This is called a food desert. So, yes: There is still famine, *raav*.

"Sorrow": The Hebrew word used for sorrow is *yagon*. This entire list—"enemies, illness, war, and famine"—can be sources of sorrow. However, there are many other sources of sorrow, and this prayer wants us to be protected from those as well.

Notice something important about this prayer. "Enemies, illness, war, famine, and sorrow"—these are generally external things that impact us. They come from external sources—enemies cause a war, or a natural disaster causes famine. What about other kinds of dangers? The prayer talks about those as well.

"Distance us from wrongdoing"—from *pesha*. *Pesha* is an interesting word for wrongdoing. We know various words for sin and moral failure—like the word *chet*, which has a "starring role" on Yom Kippur. Believe it or not, *pesha* is somewhat worse than that. It actually means something that breaks trust in a relationship. For example, when a nation breaks a treaty with another nation, that is a *pesha*. As sins go, it is pretty up there—or, down there. Therefore, we need protection not only from external forces; we need protection from ourselves as well.

QUESTIONS:
1. What examples can you offer of the enemies that Jews face? That others face?
2. What illnesses are particularly difficult that people would need protection from? Are there ways to protect from those illnesses?
3. What are some wars that are happening in the world today?
4. What are examples of famine in the world? In your country? In your community?

5. What are some things that bring you sorrow?
6. Have you ever broken trust with someone? Has someone broken trust with you?
7. What are some examples of things within ourselves that we may need protection from?
8. What else would you add to this prayer's list of things we need protection from?

V'SHAMRU AND YISM'CHU (162)

Shabbat is holy, right? It wasn't always that way. Back in the ancient Middle East, some religious cultures believed that the seventh day was actually cursed—that any work done on that day would lead to failure. The seventh day was taboo.

The ancient Jews turned it around. They said that the seventh day was not cursed, but rather it was blessed. It was no longer taboo; it was holy. Jews bequeathed that notion of sacred time to her daughter religions—Christianity and Islam—and yes, even to modern secular culture, in which we sense that some days are more important and holier than others, such as national holidays.

Nothing is more central to Judaism than Shabbat. But figuring out exactly how we celebrate and honor Shabbat can be a little tricky. In *L'chah Dodi*, we already encountered the two verbs of Shabbat—*shamor v'zachor*, "keep and remember."

Let's focus on just the first one, *shamor*. People who keep Shabbat are called *shomeir Shabbat*. One of my favorite films is *The Big Lebowski*. A character, Walter, is in a bowling league. He has joined the Jewish people through conversion. He makes it very clear to his fellow bowlers, "I don't roll on *Shabbos* [the Yiddish word for Shabbat]!" and announces that he is "*shomeir Shabbos*!"

Maybe Walter knew that those who keep Shabbat will rejoice in God's realm. He was willing to keep Shabbat. It is a pretty good idea for us all to at least try to keep Shabbat. After all, there is a difference between Wednesday and Shabbat, and there is even a difference between "Saturday" and Shabbat. Walter knew that, and so do I. No doubt about it: I love Shabbat. I love the festive dinner, candles, wine, and blessing children and grandchildren. It is magic.

But as much as I love and teach the rituals of Shabbat, the most important thing about Shabbat is what it can mean to us in our lives. Ask anyone, and they will tell you that the Sabbath is a "day of rest." It is, but it is also a day when we can "give it a rest."

"Give it a rest." Maybe young people understand this better than anyone else, but not every day has to be productive. We don't have to do stuff all the time. There is a time when we can allow the playful spirit that is within us to emerge. There is a day wherein we don't have to worry about schedules, lists, being busy, responsibilities. Shabbat is that day, and it can make us more fully human.

QUESTIONS:
1. What do you do to keep Shabbat?
2. What would you like to be able to do?
3. Why do you think so many Jews love Shabbat?
4. What are the challenges to observing Shabbat?

Act Two—What We Need: *T'filah* (164)

Act Two is made up of a section of our prayerbook called *T'filah*, or "Prayer." The ancient Rabbis believed that it was the essential prayer—an *Amidah*, a "standing" before God, as one would have stood before an ancient (or even modern) monarch. You identify who you are (a descendant of the Patriarchs and the Matriarchs); you praise the Monarch; and then you make your requests. At least, that is sometimes how it goes.

At this point in the service, people rise and take three steps forward—as if approaching royalty.

"God, I have a sore throat. Make my throat feel better," or "God, I am about to compete in a swim meet. Make my arms, legs, and lungs work well," or even, "God, I have the math final soon. Make my brain work adequately."

The prayers in *T'filah* are different from those types of prayers. You are about to pray *to* God.

Wait! You mean we haven't been praying to God all along? Well, yes, we have. But through this point in our worship, we have been mostly speaking words that are *about* God. With *T'filah*, we are speaking directly *to* God.

We are about to open up our mouths to speak personal words to God. I should just be able to do it—to open my mouth, speak to God, and be done with it.

Not so fast.

"Adonai, open up my lips, that my mouth may declare Your praise." Why do we need to ask God to "open my lips"? Perhaps, because we have stubbornly closed them. We do not want to say these words. Perhaps we think that they don't speak for us or to us.

If we feel that way, it is quite okay. If that should happen, let God open our lips.

QUESTIONS:

1. Have you ever felt the need to pray to God for help with a particular part of your body?
2. Have you ever had difficulty praying? Why? What helped (or didn't help)?

AVOT V'IMAHOT (166)

It is true that this prayer is called *Avot V'Imahot*, which we usually translate as "Fathers and Mothers." The word *av*, "father," can also mean "source." But *avot* doesn't really mean "fathers." The word for fathers should really be *avim*, using Hebrew's standard masculine plural form.

I learned this from my late colleague and teacher Rabbi Martin Rozenberg (Latvia and United States, 1928–2023), who taught Bible at Hebrew Union College–Jewish Institute of Religion. He taught that *avot* means "ancestors"—but, even deeper, it means (this is an awkward term) "ancestorness"—the fact of having ancestors.

When we pray *Avot V'Imahot*, we are praying not *to* our ancestors, but *with* our ancestors. Imagine someone who has two parents. That person will have four grandparents, eight great-grandparents. Go back ten generations, and that brings us to 4,096 great-grandparents to the tenth degree. You carry something within you that is connected to them. Not just genes. Not just traits. You carry their experiences, as well. And for Jews, this includes the experiences of our ancestors stretching back to Biblical times:

- Abraham and Sarah leave their homeland, and they have the greatest adventure in history—going to a place they don't even know and creating a future for themselves, for their family, and for the entire Jewish people.
- Sarah is an inventor. When she learns that she is about to be pregnant, at a rather advanced age, what does she do? She laughs. According to the Torah, no one had ever laughed before. Sarah, therefore, invents laughter.
- Isaac doesn't really go anywhere. He stays in the Land of Israel. He re-digs the wells that his father, Abraham, dug.
- Rebecca knows that Jacob will make a better inheritor of the covenant than Esau does. She makes it happen. She is tough and determined. She can see the implications of things far better than anyone else can.
- Jacob has huge ambitions. He dreamed of a ladder of angels. But his life did not work out the way he thought it would. He learns some hard lessons about those ambitions.
- Rachel takes the idols of her father, Laban, out of his house. She gets him off the idolatry thing.
- Leah gives birth to the most important ancestors of the Jewish people, the heads of the most powerful tribes. She had to share Jacob with her sister, Rachel, and knew Jacob loved Rachel more. It could not have been easy, but she endures.

The ancient Rabbis put it this way: "The actions of the Patriarchs and Matriarchs are like a blueprint for their descendants" (*Midrash Tanchuma, Lech L'cha* 9:3). In other words, their actions become part of the DNA of the Jewish people (even, and perhaps especially, of those who join the Jewish people through conversion).

In *Hachsharat HaAvreichim*, a work of Chasidic educational philosophy written by Rabbi Kalonymus Kalman Shapira (Poland, 1889–1943), who died in the Holocaust, we read this advice to the learner of the Hebrew Bible: "When you learn the *Tanach*, try to be so involved in the holy events that happened to the extent where you feel as if you were there when they were happening. Join Abraham and Isaac on their way to the *Akeidah* [the Binding of Isaac], and feel Jacob's distress at the moment when he prayed to God, 'Please save me from the hand of my brother, from the hand of Esau, for I fear him.'"[15]

QUESTIONS:
1. How are you like Abraham or Sarah? Have you ever left a place to go to another place—not knowing what to expect? Have you ever invented something original?
2. How are you like Isaac? He re-dug his father's wells. What do you think you might do that will reflect or repeat what your parents have done?
3. How are you like Rebecca? Have you ever made your mind up about something and pursued it no matter what?
4. How are you like Jacob? What are your ambitions?
5. How are you like Rachel? Have you rebelled against your parents?
6. How are you like Leah? Have you had to tolerate situations that are barely tolerable?

G'VUROT (168)

M'chayeih meitim—"You revive the dead." Just two little Hebrew words and so much controversy!

For centuries, the traditional Hebrew prayer praised God as the One who "revives the dead." That is still the only version that is found in traditional prayer books, though our Reform prayer book offers an option to say either these original words or "You give life to all."

Let's talk about how Judaism views life after death. Judaism has always believed in some kind of life after death. In the Bible, we read about Sheol, a dark pit where the dead go to reside. At a certain point in Jewish history, Jews began to believe that the dead would reside with God in *olam haba*, "the world-to-come," or in a heavenly *Gan Eden*, Garden of Eden. (People always tell me that this sounds Christian. It might, but then again—where do you think Christianity got this belief from? Islam also believes in an afterlife. In fact, of the three faiths that come from Abraham—Judaism, Christianity, and Islam—the one that makes the least big deal about the afterlife is Judaism. Jews are very focused on this world instead of the next world.)

Now, let's talk about the whole "reviving the dead" thing. Some Jews believe that in the messianic age, the dead will come back to life and be "resurrected." This was a major belief throughout much of Jewish history. The great medieval philosopher Maimonides was so sure that this was true that he made it one of his thirteen articles of Jewish faith. He thought that a Jew must believe this! That is one reason why, for example, some Jews frown on autopsies—they don't want anything to happen that would violate the body of the dead person, because it might affect their body's resurrection.

When Reform Judaism started in Germany in the early 1800s, many Reformers did not like the idea of life after death or the resurrection of the dead. They thought that it did not make sense and that it was unscientific. As a result, they got rid of the idea by erasing all references to resurrection from their prayer books. That is why Reform siddurim speak of God as the One "who gives life to all."

In recent decades, Reform Jews have adopted more historical practices and beliefs. If you were to go back in time to a Reform synagogue—even fifty years ago— you would not have seen Reform Jewish worshipers wearing kippot or tallitot. The service would have had less Hebrew. Over time, and for many reasons, Reform Jews became more comfortable with traditional aspects of Judaism. Reform reformed itself, and it keeps reforming itself.

Reform Jews have not only adopted more traditional practices and rituals. They have also adopted more traditional ideas, including "reviving the dead." Sometimes, there are good reasons to do so. I had the honor of conducting High Holy Day services for the Progressive (Reform) congregation in Warsaw, Poland. Polish Jewry had suffered incalculable losses during the Holocaust. The congregation met in a building that had once been within the walls of the Warsaw Ghetto. Some of the Jews in the congregation were the grandchildren of Holocaust survivors or of people who hid their Jewish identity out of fear.

As I looked into the eyes of the worshipers there, I found myself praying the words *m'chayeih meitim*—"You revive the dead." I really felt it, and I really believed it.

What does this idea of reviving the dead really mean? God has given us the power to hope that something nonphysical and beyond our bodies lives forever. We call that nonphysical "something" the soul. Because we have souls, we are endowed with eternal worth and eternal hope.

Perhaps it is not that the dead will be resurrected. Perhaps it is simply that the soul—the good part of us, the part that strives for the highest, the part that is godly—is immortal. Perhaps when we say that the soul is immortal it means that all the good things that we did will survive forever.

I feel that way about some of my teachers and rabbis: They may be dead, but what they taught me will live forever. Maybe you have a grandparent or another close family member who has died. If so, you probably sense that they are still "with" you in many ways.

QUESTIONS:
1. Do you believe in life after death? Why or why not?
2. What people who have died are still "with" you?
3. What changes in Jewish practices have you observed in your synagogue? Your family? What is your opinion of them?
4. How does Reform Judaism keep reforming itself?
5. What gives you hope?

K'DUSHAH (170)

What does it mean to be holy? It means many things—special, set apart, touched by God, and more. In ancient Jerusalem, it meant something really big.

Sometimes I find myself really missing the ancient Temple in Jerusalem. Not because I have any real longing to see domesticated animals sacrificed on an altar, but because I envy the High Priest of old. When you compare his Yom Kippur responsibilities with those of modern rabbis and cantors, it seems to me that he got off rather easy.

This was the High Priest's job description for Yom Kippur: He would go into the Temple and enter the *Kodesh HaKodashim*, the Holy of Holies, the place that contained both the tablets of the Law and the Divine Presence. The ancient Sages believed that it was the very center of the world. Once the High Priest entered the Holy of Holies, he would pronounce the unpronounceable four-letter name of God, *yod-hei-vav-hei*, which we now pronounce *Adonai* (see page 22). By pronouncing that name, the High Priest would gain atonement—first, for himself, then for his family, and finally for the entire Jewish people. (By the way, this is a good lesson on how responsibility works: You start with yourself, then the people closest to you, and ultimately, your entire people.)

To sum this all up, the holiest person of the Jewish people would go into the holiest place in the holiest building in the holiest city in the holiest land on the holiest day saying the holiest word in the holiest language.

That is pretty big stuff. You put all those dimensions of holiness together and who knows what could happen? Rabbi Lawrence Kushner teaches, "There are worlds more real than this one. Shabbat is more real than Wednesday. Jerusalem is more real than Chicago. The *sukkah* is more real than a garage. *Tzedakah* is more real than income tax."[16] Judaism wants to take that moment of sanctification in the Holy of Holies and make it real all the time. Judaism wants to sanctify all life.

QUESTIONS:
1. What places, times, people, and ideas are holy in your life?
2. How can you sanctify life?
3. How are you responsible for yourself, your family, and your people?

K'DUSHAT HAYOM (172)

"You set aside the seventh day for Your name, the pinnacle of Creation; and You blessed it above all other days, more sacred than all Festival times." What does it mean to set Shabbat aside for "Your name," meaning the name of God? What does it mean to feel the Divine Presence on Shabbat? Consider how the Ten Commandments teaches us about Shabbat: "Remember the Sabbath day and keep it holy. Six days you shall labor and do all your work, but the seventh day is a Sabbath of the Eternal your God: you shall not do any work" (Exodus 20:8–10).

This is how Blu Greenberg (United States, 1936–), an Orthodox Jewish feminist, rephrases the Biblical commandment:

> Six days shall you be a workaholic; on the seventh day, you shall join the serene company of human beings. Six days shall you take orders from your boss; on the seventh day, you shall be master/mistress of your own life. Six days shall you create, drive, invent, push; on the seventh day, you shall reflect. Six days shall you be the perfect success; on the seventh day, you shall remember that not everything is in your power. Six days shall you be a miserable failure; on the seventh day, you shall be on top of the world. Six days shall you enjoy the blessings of work; on the seventh day, you shall understand that being is as important as doing.[17]

That is the living reality of Shabbat—a day of personal renewal.

QUESTIONS:
1. How have you made Shabbat a holy time?
2. In what way could the "Shabbat you" be different from the "weekday you"?

AVODAH (174)

Sometimes we refer to this prayer by its first word, *R'tzei*, though its formal name is *Avodah*, "divine worship." It focuses our attention on a distant part of our history—the sacrificial offerings in the ancient Temple in Jerusalem.

Although we no longer have a Temple, every Jewish home is a *mikdash m'at* (miniature sanctuary) in which we can transform the ordinary into the sacred. For example, dinner on Thursday night might be a simple take-out pizza, eaten on paper plates. But on Shabbat, the table can be set with good china, and dinner can be special and holy.

"Let our eyes behold Your loving return to Zion. Blessed are You, Adonai, whose Presence returns to Zion." This is one of my favorite lines in all Jewish liturgy. My own translation is "Blessed is *Adonai*, who returns the wandering Feminine Presence of God to Zion."

What is "the wandering Feminine Presence of God"? Let us return to a topic that we addressed earlier (see page 42). Jewish mystics believe that there are two aspects of God—the masculine *Kadosh Baruch Hu* (the Holy One, blessed be God) and the feminine *Shechinah*. *Shechinah*, they believed, was that aspect of God that was present with and for the Jews in their wanderings in the world. It is a beautiful, poetic idea.

A personal aside: Whenever I travel to Israel and I first see Israel's shoreline, I say that prayer. We live in a time when Jews have come home to Israel. In coming home to Israel, we have learned that God has not abandoned our people. Some sages say that the Divine Presence was in exile with us. If that is true, then God has returned with us to Zion, the Land of Israel.

Some years ago, I visited the so-called model ghetto of Theresienstadt in the Czech Republic. In one of the barracks, these same words are inscribed on the walls—"Let our eyes behold Your loving return to Zion. Blessed are You, Adonai, whose Presence returns to Zion." This is evidence of how powerful that hope, that longing for Zion, is.

We are talking about holy space, especially the Land of Israel. But since we are on the subject of holiness, let us remember holy times as well. At this point in the service, we would add certain prayers for special days, such as Rosh Chodesh (the first day of the Jewish month), Pesach, and Sukkot.

HODAAH (176)

Remember that whole thing about observing, keeping, and guarding Shabbat? There are many aspects to that observance. Some Jews do not use electricity, drive, or write (all forbidden actions according to halachah, Jewish law).

Here is another one: Many Jews don't go shopping on Shabbat.

There are several reasons for this. First, Jewish law says that it is forbidden to spend money on Shabbat; it is even forbidden to carry money on Shabbat.

Let us go deeper than a mere prohibition. Why might Jews refrain from shopping on Shabbat? It might be time for Jews to reclaim the idea of Shabbat as *protest*—a one-day protest against the way that the world functions for the other six days of the week. One of those acts of protest is to say this: Six days a week, I am a consumer. I want, and I buy. On Shabbat, however, I recognize that I have enough.

Our siddur shares the words of Rabbi Abraham Joshua Heschel (Poland and United States, 1907–72): "A thought has blown the market place away. There is a song on the wind and joy in the trees. Shabbat arrives in the world, scattering a song in the silence of the night: Eternity utters a day."[18]

What is the thought that "has blown the market place away"? The thought of Shabbat, of holiness, of sacred values. These values often stand in contrast with the values of the marketplace.

I love the play *Cat on a Hot Tin Roof* by Tennessee Williams (United States, 1911–83). It is a drama about family issues. In the play, Harvey "Big Daddy" Pollitt and his son, Brick, are discussing their wife/mother's outrageous spending habits:

Brick Pollitt: Why'd you let Mama buy all this stuff?
Harvey "Big Daddy" Pollitt: The human animal is a beast that must die. If he's got money, he buys and buys and buys everything he can, in the crazy hope one of those things will be life-everlasting, which it can never be.[19]

The *Hodaah* prayer asks us to remember to be thankful for what we have. Because it is Shabbat, there is little that we ask of God. Shabbat is a dress rehearsal for messianic times, the time when the Messiah will come, giving us the opportunity to imagine what life would be like without asking for anything, to have all our needs satisfied. We give thanks for all that we have, for all that we might have, and even for the ability to give thanks.

QUESTIONS:
1. What do you think of the mitzvah of not shopping on Shabbat? Do you think that this is something you or members of your family could do?
2. What are you grateful for?
3. What do you still need?

SHALOM (178)

What do we mean by *shalom*, "peace"? Some people might define peace as "no war." And certainly, in our time, that is a valid hope. I think of an Israeli song, "HaMilchamah HaAchronah," "The Last War." It was written by the Israeli popular music star Yehoram Gaon (1929–). The singer imagines that the Yom Kippur War of 1973 would be the last war: "I promise you, my little girl, that this will be the last war."
If only.

Perhaps the vision is not just an end to war for Israel and the Arab countries. Perhaps it means that *all* wars will end. Isaiah 2:2–4 offers this vision of peace:

> In the days to come,
> The Mount of the Eternal's House
> Shall stand firm above the mountains
> And tower above the hills;

And all the nations
Shall gaze on it with joy.
And the many peoples shall go and say:
"Come,
Let us go up to the Mount of the Eternal,
To the House of the God of Jacob;
That we may be instructed in God's ways,
And that we may walk in God's paths."
For instruction shall come forth from Zion,
The word of the Eternal from Jerusalem.
Thus [God] will judge among the nations
And arbitrate for the many peoples,
And they shall beat their swords into plowshares
And their spears into pruning hooks:
Nation shall not take up
Sword against nation;
They shall never again know war.

The prophet Isaiah imagines a kind of United Nations—all the nations of the world coming to Jerusalem (more precisely, to the site of the ancient Temple). (As a matter of fact, you can see the words "They shall beat their swords into plowshares, and their spears into pruning hooks; nation shall not lift up sword against nation, neither shall they learn war any more" on the so-called Isaiah Wall at the United Nations headquarters in New York City.) God will hear all their complaints and claims, and God will judge which of those complaints and claims are valid. And then, war will end—all war.

There is a third possibility of what peace could look like. Once again, we turn to the prophet Isaiah: "The wolf shall dwell with the lamb, the leopard lie down with the kid; the calf, the beast of prey, and the fatling together, with a little child to herd them" (11:6). In this vision, there would be peace—not only between human beings, not only between nations, but between *all* living things. Even animal species that are hostile to each other will make peace with each other. Not bad. Most of us would settle for any of these visions of peace.

QUESTIONS:
1. Which of these visions of peace do you prefer?
2. What would be necessary to make them possible?
3. Do you have any role in making those visions real?
4. Do you have another vision of what peace means?

T'FILAT HALEV (180)

Many years ago I attended a lecture given by the late Holocaust survivor, author, and activist Elie Wiesel (Romania and United States, 1928–2016). Someone asked, "Is there a Jewish tradition of silence?" To which he responded, "Yes, but we don't talk about it." It is time for us to embrace the great Jewish ideal of silence.

First, silence means that you don't have to say everything that you are thinking. The Talmud says that even though everyone knows what a couple might do on their wedding night, if someone talks about it in an obscene way, they will get seventy years of misery (Babylonian Talmud, *Shabbat* 33a). (In other words—don't be a jerk, respect other people's privacy, and don't turn intimacy into something obscene.) The Vilna Gaon, the spiritual leader of eighteenth-century Eastern European Jewry, wrote, "For every moment that one holds one's tongue in this world, one merits as a result a hidden light that no angel or creation can ever imagine."[20]

Second, silence means that you don't have to say everything you know. In the Bible, the young future king David and his friend Jonathan, the son of King Saul, had great affection for each other. When Saul and Jonathan died in battle, David eulogized them. He said that his love for Jonathan was even more powerful than his love for women. But the Bible never says why Jonathan loved David so much. This is what the late French writer André Neher (France and Israel, 1914–88) teaches about this love.[21] David first makes his appearance at the court of King Saul because the king was struggling with depression. David's job was to play the harp for Saul, in order to make him feel better. Later, after the young David killed the Philistine giant Goliath, King Saul called him over and asked out loud, "Who is this young man?" Think of how David could have responded.

"What do you mean—'Who is this young man?' It's me, David. David—the Judean shepherd who's been playing harp for you all these nights. I'm your music therapist! I am the shepherd boy whose duty it has been to heal your depression!" But that is not what David said. In fact, he said nothing.

If David had said what was on his mind, the people would have known that Saul was mentally ill, and they would have demanded that he abdicate the throne. David stayed silent. That is why Saul's son, Jonathan, loved him.

And finally, silence means that when words are inadequate, you don't have to say anything. Sometimes, it is simply enough to be quiet.

There is a tradition that teaches that whoever visits a house of mourning must remain silent until the mourner speaks first. Why? If you start speaking before the mourner, you are speaking out of your own need to be heard rather than from a desire to support the person in mourning. Give mourners time and space to address their own needs. Your "job" at the house of mourning is to respond to those needs. When we are silent, we can hear things that cannot usually be heard.

One of the greatest Jewish mystics was Isaac Luria (circa 1532–72), who lived and taught in Safed in the Land of Israel in the 1500s. While Luria was born in Jerusalem, he grew up in Egypt. He would walk along the banks of the Nile, listening intently. One of his companions asked him, "What are you listening for?"

"I am listening for the cries of the infant Moses. Moses drifted down this river when he was an infant. If you ask me why I am listening for the cries of the infant Moses, it is for this and for this alone: Only the one who hears the cries of the infant Moses is capable of teaching the Torah of the adult Moses."[22]

QUESTIONS:
1. When do you think that silence is useful?
2. When have you been silent?
3. What did you learn from those experiences?

Magein Avot V'Imahot (183)

Magein Avot V'Imahot is a quick summary of many of the prayers in the *T'filah* section—it's all of those prayers scrunched together. It repeats many of the words and phrases used in this section. However, we find in this condensed prayer a term for God that is very rare: *El Elyon, koneih shamayim vaaretz*, which means "God transcendent, Maker of heaven and earth."

What is the source of this description of God? There is a story, of course.

At the very beginning of Jewish history, Abram (whose name will be changed to Abraham) had to engage in battle (Genesis 14). A coalition of kings had taken his nephew, Lot, as a hostage. (This was the first hostage crisis in history.)

Abram pursued that opposing army, traveling as far north as Damascus, which is the capital of modern-day Syria, and rescued Lot. Right after that battle, when Abram returned to what was probably the area of what would someday be the city of Jerusalem, something happens. He has a very odd encounter:

> The king of Sodom came out to meet him [Abram] after his return to the Valley of Shaveh (that is, the King's Valley) from fighting Chedarlaomer and his allied kings. Now Melchizedek king of Salem brought out bread and wine—he was a priest of God Most High [*v'hu chohein l'El Elyon*]—and blessed him, saying, 'Blessed be Abram by God Most High [*baruch Avram l'El Elyon*], maker of heaven and earth [*koneih shamayim vaaretz*], and blessed is God Most High, who has given your foes into your hands.' Then he [Abram] gave him a tenth of everything. (Genesis 14:17–20)

Whoever he was, Melchizedek was a good person. He was an ally of Abram, and it is good to have allies. The question is: Which God did Melchizedek invoke?

Easy answer, you might think. *El* is one of the names for the God that Jews worship—like *Elohim*. That might be right, but it might be more complicated than that. *El* just happens to be the name of the chief Canaanite god. This would make total sense; Melchizedek was a Canaanite, a member of the ancient peoples who lived in the Land of Israel even before the Israelites entered.

It gets even more complicated. *Elyon* (the transcendent) is the name of yet another Canaanite god. In several texts, those two names occur simultaneously, and we get *El Elyon*—"*El* [or, God] transcendent."

It is not as if we haven't "met" *El Elyon* already; that phrase for God shows up in the *Avot V'Imahot* prayer. The thing is, we don't know if Melchizedek was speaking of *El* the God of the ancient Hebrews or *El* the god of the ancient Canaanites. It is the same word; scholars disagree on whether it was the same god.

Regardless, this is what you need to know: We have already said that Melchizedek was a good person, an ally. We now know that he blessed Abram using either the name of his god or the name of Abram's god. Or maybe it was the same god.

Melchizedek doesn't stop, however, with just the words *El Elyon*. Melchizedek added the phrase about the God who was "maker of heaven and earth" (*koneih shamayim vaaretz*), which certainly sounds Jewish. Using this phrase, though, is a theological jump for Melchizedek.

In his Torah commentary *Maaseh Adonai*, Eliezer Ashkenazi, a sixteenth-century commentator, suggests that Melchizedek believed in God, but not in a God who was capable of having a personal relationship with people—that is, until he witnessed the miracle performed for Abram in his military victory.[23]

Maybe you are wondering about the source of *El Elyon, koneih shamayim vaaretz* in our liturgy. Rabbi Achai of Shabcha, an eighth-century Babylonian authority, wondered this too. He wrote that Abraham first used this term after hearing it when Melchizedek blessed him with these words (Genesis 14:18). In other words, a king who was not Jewish introduced this term for God. In a wonderful act of liturgical hospitality, our ancestors incorporated Melchizedek's piety into its own.[24]

Sometimes, people talk about "kumbaya moments," when it seems that people can simply get along. When we use this ancient term for God, and we realize that we are borrowing it from an ancient Canaanite priest-king . . . well, *that* is a "kumbaya moment."

QUESTIONS:
1. Have you ever been involved in an interfaith worship experience? How did it feel?
2. Have you met people like Melchizedek, who are simply good and decent people?
3. What do you think of the spirit of inclusion, which allowed Jews to use Melchizedek's term for God?

Act Three—What We Learn

Right around this time in the service (though it could happen at other times), you will probably hear the rabbi, cantor, another service leader, or a member of the congregation share a teaching from the bimah. You know it as the sermon, though in Hebrew it can be called a *d'var Torah* (a word of Torah) or a *d'rashah* (a "seeking out" of the meaning of a text).

Jewish teachers have been giving formal sermons for hundreds of years, both in Hebrew and in the vernacular. The *d'var Torah* or *d'rashah* is much older. It might go back to when the Judeans returned from exile in Babylon, and their leader Ezra read the Torah to them for the first time in the re-built Temple.

Is there any real difference between a sermon, *d'var Torah*, or *d'rashah*? Sort of. A sermon is likely to be on a broad theme of relevance to the congregation or the world—usually, on some matter of contemporary concern. A *d'var Torah* or *d'rashah*, however, will usually be a shorter teaching about a verse in the Torah or haftarah reading or another Jewish sacred text.

Remember: It is not just grownups who get to teach from the pulpit. Young people do it as well, especially when they celebrate becoming bet mitzvah. Offering this kind of teaching is a sacred opportunity to make sure that the ancient words are still relevant. It is not always easy to find that relevance, but like most things, the effort really does pay off.

Traditionally, the Torah is read only in the morning service. Many Reform synagogues do, in fact, read Torah on Friday evening during the Erev Shabbat service. If this is the custom in your synagogue, please refer to Act Three in the morning service (page 158).

Act Four—What We Hope

ALEINU (586–91)

If there was a contest for most popular Jewish prayer, I am not so sure how *Aleinu* would do. Some people just don't like *Aleinu*.

While it is true that our prayer book translates the beginning of the prayer as "Let us now praise," in fact *aleinu*, the first word of the prayer, means "it is on us." It is our responsibility. For the sake of comparison, the English-Hebrew edition of the current prayer book of the Israeli Reform Movement, *Tefilat Ha-Adam*, translates the word *aleinu* as "it is incumbent upon us." It is on us. We must do this. Still, some Jews don't like the idea of responsibility for praising God. On top of that, over the last few centuries, there have been Jews who don't like the line "who has set us apart from the other families of the earth, giving us a destiny unique among the nations." For many of them, this phrase is at least better than the more accurate translation of *shelo asanu k'goyei haaratzot*, that "God has not made us like the nations of the world."

In fact, so many people did not like this line that Reform Jews created their own version of this prayer, which is offered as an alternative *Aleinu* (top of page 587). There is nothing in that version that speaks of God choosing the Jews, or setting the Jews apart, or making the Jews unlike the nations of the world. That version is just about "the Creator whose unity we are charged to declare." Another version of *Aleinu* (bottom of page 587) speaks about God who "spread out the heavens and established the earth, whose glory is revealed in the heavens above, and whose greatness is manifest throughout the world."

Let's return to that troublesome phrase—"God has not made us like the nations of the world." This is probably the most misunderstood verse in Jewish prayer. In the late Middle Ages, some gentile rulers forbade Jews from singing it in their synagogues, believing that it insulted Christians. In fact, there were other phrases in that prayer that Jews, and others, did not like. The traditional wording of the prayer contains this phrase: "For they bow down to emptiness and folly"—this was about ancient idols, but some people thought that it referred to Jesus. Some printers actually censored that phrase from the prayer book. They went right into the text and crossed it out!

In reality, the phrase "who has not made us like the nations of the world" means that God chose us for a unique task—to teach Torah to the world and to bring the world closer to a belief in the one God.

How do we do that? The prayer tells us: *l'takein olam b'malchut Shaddai*, "perfecting the world under the rule of God." The word *l'takein*—which has the same Hebrew root as the common phrase for social justice, *tikkun olam*—actually means to *repair* the world, not necessarily to perfect it. ("Perfecting" the world seems like a lot to do.) By repairing the world, we bring the world closer to how we sense God wants it to be. Our tools for doing this are the mitzvot.

There is one other reason why some people may not like this phrase in the *Aleinu* prayer. They are afraid that saying "who has not made us like other nations" makes the Jews too exclusive. They might not like highlighting the fact that throughout their history, Jews have been different.

Is there a way out of this problem? Is there a better way to understand what it means for Jews to be different? I think there is. We can find a solution in the current Conservative prayer book, *Lev Shalem*. The editors of that prayer book translate this troublesome phrase as "who has not made us merely a nation, nor formed us as all earthly families, nor given us an ordinary destiny."[25] I like this translation, because this is what it is saying:

- As important as peoplehood is to the Jews, the Jews are not merely and only a nation, not merely and only a people. Neither are the Jews merely and only a religion. They are a mixture of those two essential elements.
- While it is true that the Jews have been formed like all

earthly families, the Jews are different because Judaism makes them different. Jews have a different sense of *time*, since we sanctify certain days (like Shabbat and other holy days) and certain seasons (like the days of repentance that lead up to Rosh HaShanah and Yom Kippur). Jews have a different sense of *place*, since certain places, like the home (and even more specifically, the table upon which we dine), the synagogue, and the Land of Israel are holy. Jews have a different sense of *eating*, with various forms of kashrut and other dietary restrictions and customs.

• Finally, it is also true that Jews do not have "an ordinary destiny." Jewish history has not been like the histories of other peoples. In some ways, Jewish history is a collection of mysteries. How did this people manage to preserve its identity for centuries, without a land or political institutions, and being allowed to practice its religion in peace? How is it that this small people has had such a large voice and such overarching influence in religion, morality, philosophy, social institutions, political ideas, art, science, drama, technology, and medicine? Why has this people attracted all the impulses of hatred that are available to humanity? Finally, how has the Jewish people come to symbolize resilience and renewal? The State of Israel is the only country that upholds the same faith, speaks the same tongue, and inhabits the same land as it did three thousand years ago. If our ancient prophets were to attend a Jewish worship service, they would understand large pieces of our liturgy, and almost none of its ideas would be foreign to them—though they would probably miss the sacrifices.

No matter how you choose to express it, Jews are different, because Judaism is different.

KADDISH YATOM (598)

This may be the most popular prayer in Judaism. Not the *Sh'ma*, and not even *Kol Nidrei*, a liturgical statement that is chanted on the evening of Yom Kippur. No—it's *Kaddish Yatom*, the Mourner's *Kaddish*. Almost nothing defines Jewish identity more than this prayer. The reason is clear: It, and almost it alone, links Jews to their parents and their ancestors.

That being said, there is a small translation problem in our prayer book. This prayer is not really the "Mourner's *Kaddish*." To this day, Jews will sometimes refer to their child as their *kaddish* or, in Yiddish, their *kaddishl*—the person who will someday have the solemn responsibility for saying this prayer on their behalf.

Kaddish Yatom literally means "*Kaddish* for Orphans." To further complicate matters, the Biblical *yatom* is not really an orphan the way we think of it today—as someone whose parents have both died. Its official meaning is someone whose *father* died, because in the ancient world, someone without a father was particularly vulnerable, economically and otherwise (the same is true today). We also say *Kaddish Yatom* for siblings, cousins, friends, and—tragically—children. *Kaddish* includes a much bigger group of people than just our parents and grandparents.

That being said, *Kaddish* does not mention death and originally had nothing to do with mourning. There are other forms of *Kaddish*, such as the *Chatzi Kaddish* (see page 48) and the *Kaddish D'Rabanan*, which is said after Torah study (see page 111). They are all very similar in their wording.

When did this statement of faith become a prayer for mourners?

Sadly, it was because of one of many tragedies in Jewish history. In 635 (or 638) CE, the Muslim Caliph Umar captured the city of Jerusalem. Jerusalem would become one of Islam's sacred cities, and it was already sacred to both Jews and Christians. The Christian rulers of Europe waged a series of wars to regain control of the Land of Israel. Those wars were the Crusades, which started with the First Crusade in 1096.

As the Crusaders marched through Europe on the way to the Land of Israel, they took advantage of the opportunity to loot Jewish communities and slaughtered many of the Jews they encountered. There were an overwhelming number of Jewish casualties and deaths—so much so, that it was often impossible to mourn each death when it occurred. As a result, Jews would join together to remember their common dead. Many of our best-known customs around death emerged or became popular during the period of the Crusades—most significantly, the *Yizkor* (memorial) prayers that are part of festival services.

Still, the question remains: Why say *Kaddish* in the first place? There are many answers. First, it is a Jewish tradition, and for many Jews, that is sufficient reason to say *Kaddish*. Second, it is a mitzvah. Especially when we say *Kaddish* for our parents who have died, it is an extension of the fifth commandment, which teaches us to honor our parents. Third, it helps us remember the dead and to symbolically stand in their presence. Henrietta Szold (1860–1945), the American founder of Hadassah, once described *Kaddish* as a way for survivors to say that they "wish and intend to assume the relation to the Jewish community which the parent had."[26]

Today, we say that *Kaddish* helps us remember the dead, but once upon a time it was believed to have great power—over the dead themselves! What kind of power?

As we have explored before, Judaism has always believed in some kind of life after death (see page 66). People sometimes ask, "Does Judaism believe in hell?" The answer is not really. Judaism does have a belief in *Geihinom*, or Gehenna, a place where really bad sinners go after death to become purified of their sins. Sinners would go there for up to twelve months, and then they would "graduate" from *Geihinom* and go on to *olam haba*, "the world-to-come"—what many people call "heaven."

There is one caveat. Jewish folklore said that if someone had been a sinner and sent to *Geihinom*, one thing could get that person out. What was that one thing? If their child said *Kaddish* for them.

In the early Middle Ages, a legend about the famous Rabbi Akiva (Land of Israel, circa 50–135), perhaps the greatest sage of early Judaism, appears in *Machzor Vitry*, Laws of Shabbat 144. He was wandering in a cemetery late at night, and he met a man who was carrying a ridiculously heavy pile of wood.

"What have you done, that you deserve such a punishment?" The man answered, "I was a tax collector, and I created policies that favored the rich over the poor." Notice the man's sin: It was not a failure of personal ethical behavior. He did a reverse Robin Hood— he stole from the poor to favor the rich. It was a failure of social justice. "Is there anything that you can do that will save you from such a punishment?" Akiva asked him.

"Yes," he said. "Find my son; teach him how to say *Kaddish* for me, and I will be saved from this painful fate." By being spared this painful fate, the man would go on to *olam haba*.

All because of that one prayer—*Kaddish*. That is one reason why *Kaddish* became so important and crucial to the lives of so many Jews. Jews wanted someone to say *Kaddish* for them, and if they had no children, they would sometimes hire someone, even a stranger, to do so! Years ago, there was even a toll-free number that you could call to arrange for someone to say *Kaddish*! For many Jews, it is simply that important. It's about immortality.

What if you don't believe in Sheol, or *olam haba*, or *Gan Eden*, or *Geihinom*? There are many paths to immortality:

- We live on through our children. Perhaps you are named, in English or in Hebrew, for a relative who has died. Your parents gave you that name to honor that relative and in the hopes that you will embody the good things that relative did. You are part of that person's immortality.

- We live on through our work. People hope that something they do will live on after they die. In the Middle Ages, Jewish artisans used to chisel the insignias of the professions of the deceased on their tombstones. The doctor who saves a life is immortal. The lawyer who wins a case that saves a life or recreates a life is immortal. The architect who designs a building is immortal. The administrative assistant who devises an efficient and lasting filing system is immortal. Someday, in your work, you will do things that will survive you.
- We live on through the good things that we do. Call it the immortality of influence. Every time a Black person votes in this country, that act is a living, ongoing *Kaddish* for Rev. Dr. Martin Luther King Jr. and all the other activists who worked to codify the Civil Rights Act. When a Jew lands in Israel, that act is a living, ongoing *Kaddish* for Theodor Herzl and the other early Zionists.
- We live on through what we teach. I recall a *Yizkor* service many years ago in a congregation I served. I asked people in the congregation to name their departed teachers. In the pews that morning was the founding rabbi of the congregation, the late Rabbi Eugene Borowitz, PhD (United States, 1924–2016), the greatest American Jewish theologian of our time, the man who was my greatest mentor. When my gaze met his, he called out the name of his teacher Professor Samuel Cohon. Cohon to Borowitz . . . and Borowitz to me . . . and me to my students. At that moment, I felt eternity. The Talmud says that when we quote a dead teacher, their lips move in the grave (Babylonian Talmud, *Y'vamot* 97a). No word that I have ever uttered in any classroom or from any pulpit has ever died. I live with the faith that it sends forth a spark and that it lives within the hearts and lives of receptive and responsible students.
- We live on through our stories. Remember that thing about hiring someone to say *Kaddish* for you? My late father had a second cousin who had never married or had any children.

When he got older, he contracted with a man named Mr. Schwartz to say *Kaddish* for him when he died. Two weeks later, the cousin wrote a note to someone in the family: "Cancel contract with Schwartz. I was in synagogue with him today. I heard him chant the prayers. He stinks." There is no one left alive who remembers this second cousin, but everyone remembers the story.

You might ask: What if someone has no children, or no useful work, or never taught anyone, or has no stories? Are they, well . . . just totally and cosmically out of luck, totally dead? Are they then like a picture or file that gets deleted from the cloud and disappears? I believe that God, the Soul of the universe, takes care of human souls and that the soul abides with God forever.

That is precisely the way that Reform prayer books put it in the translation of the prayer for the dead, *El Malei Rachamim*:

> Merciful God, God Most High: Let there be perfect rest for the souls of our loved ones who have gone into eternity. May they find shelter in Your presence among the holy and pure whose light shines like the radiance of heaven. Compassionate God, hold them close to You forever. May their souls be bound up in the bond of life eternal. May they find a home in You. And may they rest in peace."[27]

I believe those words, as have generations of my ancestors. In that sense, I have inherited their faith.

The greatest Jewish invention is a four-letter word—a four-letter word both in English, and in Hebrew—a four-letter word that is the national anthem of the Jewish people: hope, *tikvah*. I believe that Jews invented the idea of hope—that tomorrow might be better than today; that history is moving forward; that a messianic age will come, if we help bring it to fruition; that the return of Jews to sovereignty in the land of their ancestors is the summation of Jewish hope in history; and, yes—that the soul lives on.

QUESTIONS:
1. Have you ever said *Kaddish* for a loved one? Why did saying it matter to you?
2. How do you believe a person makes the most impact—through their family, their actions, their teachings, or their stories?
3. What gives you hope for the future?

Shacharit: Morning Service

To pray the morning liturgy is to encounter what the late Jewish thinker and activist Rabbi Abraham Joshua Heschel called "radical awareness." The entire purpose of the morning liturgy is to awaken us again to an ever-renewing sense of wonder at God's presence in the world and in our lives.

The operative word in the morning liturgy comes pretty early in the service. It is *mah*, "how," which rhymes with "wow!" *Mah tovu ohalecha, Yaakov* is the beginning of one of the first prayers of our service—"How fair are your tents, O Jacob!"

Mah keeps coming. It shows up a few prayers later in *Elohai N'shaMAH* and even later in the morning *Yotzeir* prayer with the words *Mah rabu maasecha, Adonai*—"How numerous are Your works, Adonai!"

It's not only *mah* that fills our worship. It is also the *ah* sound—as in *Hal'lu Yah* (Praise God) and *Ahavah rabbah* (How deeply You have loved us).

The evening prayers repeat the *m* sound for us—a maternal sound of comfort. The morning prayers have *ah* as their essential vocal element—the *ah* of gratitude, of awe.

The Preliminary Stuff

Birchot HaShachar—Morning Blessings

The morning service begins with *Birchot HaShachar*, the Morning Blessings. Yet, you would expect that if this section was really the "Morning Blessings," it would be *Birchot HaBoker*, as in *boker tov* (good morning). *Birchot HaShachar* really translates to "Blessings of Dawn," which are prayers that people would say when they first woke up. You would expect people to say them at home. In fact, they once did, but at a certain point, people stopped saying them at home, and their recital moved to the synagogue service.

If you have ever woken up early enough to see the sunrise, you know why these prayers are called *Birchot HaShachar* instead of *Birchot HaBoker*. Morning is one thing; dawn is quite another. I had the blessing of living in a dwelling overlooking the Atlantic Ocean that offered me a view to the east, which means that I got to see some pretty spectacular sunrises. For a while, I would photograph those sunrises on a daily basis. I began to notice that while every morning is pretty much the same, every sunrise is different. If you were to paint them every day, your color options would be infinite. As Rabbi Sandy Sasso wrote (United States, 1947–), that is evidence of "God's paintbrush."[1]

It is not just the beauty of the dawn—it is what the dawn awakens within us. Just as the dawn is the way that the world wakes up, our ability to see the dawn is what wakes us up. I heard a story about Rabbi Abraham Joshua Heschel, whom I mentioned above. He used to open his classes for rabbinical students by saying, "Do you all know that a great miracle occurred today?"

The students would ask, "What?! What miracle occurred today?" He would answer, "The sun rose."

The sun rising is a blessing. It is always a blessing, a miracle—even though it happens every day. It is a blessing to see the dawn.

The second mishnah of *B'rachot*, the section of the Mishnah and Talmud that deals with blessings, brings us into the dawn by asking a question about Jewish prayer practice: "From when does one recite *Sh'ma* in the morning?" (*Mishnah B'rachot* 1:2).[2] This is really another way of asking, "When has the night ended, and when does the morning begin?"

For us, that question would be a no-brainer. We look at the clock, and we know when one day ends and the next day begins—at 12:01 a.m. That is not how our ancient Rabbis understood the boundary between night and morning. Let us learn the answers of the Sages.

"Rabbi Eliezer says: From when one can distinguish between sky-blue and leek-green" (*Mishnah B'rachot* 1:2). Where would you see those kinds of colors? By looking at the sea. When you can gaze into the sea and are able to see those colors clearly, that is when you know that night has ended and day has begun—at least according to Rabbi Eliezer.

"Rabbi Meir says: The day begins when one can distinguish between two similar animals, such as a wolf and a dog" (Babylonian Talmud, *B'rachot* 9b).[3] A wolf and a dog look very similar. In fact, biologically, they are part of the same genus. They are "cousin" animals. The main difference between a wolf and a dog is in how they behave: A dog is domesticated—one of the first animals to have been domesticated. A wolf, however, is wild. That is the only real difference between a wolf and a dog. The other difference is that it is very difficult to tame wolves and relatively easy to tame dogs. In daylight, you are able see how a wolf behaves, and you would know immediately it is a wolf and not a dog. (This is especially true if the dog happens to be, say, a poodle or a dachshund. There is no way of mistaking a French poodle for a wolf.)

"Rabbi Akiva says: The day begins when there is sufficient light to distinguish between a [domesticated] donkey and a wild donkey" (Babylonian Talmud, *B'rachot* 9b). Rabbi Akiva is making this even harder. Maybe we can understand the dog and wolf example, but the difference between a domesticated donkey and a wild donkey? No—you would have to spend a little bit of time looking at those animals. At first glance, you would not see the difference between a domesticated donkey and a wild donkey. You would not be able to make snap judgments. To really see the difference, you would need time and patience—and plenty of light.

The text concludes with this wonderful teaching: "*Acherim* say: The day begins when you can see another person who is merely an acquaintance from a distance of four cubits and recognize them" (Babylonian Talmud, *B'rachot* 9b). Who are *acherim*? The "others." *Acherim* say that the day begins when you can recognize the face of a friend. When you know that that person is not a stranger. When you know that that person is someone with whom you live in relationship. When you know that that person is someone toward whom you have an obligation.

Let's talk about cubits for a moment. A cubit was a Biblical measurement. How long was a cubit? About eighteen inches. So, four cubits is seventy-two inches—exactly six feet. That really isn't that far, is it? That means you have to get relatively close to that person to recognize them.

There is a difference between an acquaintance and a friend, and many people have forgotten that difference. Social media has completely changed our sense of what it means to have relationships. On social media, it is easy to collect "friends." However, these "friends" might not even be acquaintances! You may never have met them in person!

The late French Jewish thinker Emmanuel Levinas (1906–95) taught that our societal obligations begin the moment we see someone else's face. The mere act of living in community constitutes obligation. When you know that, you know that the dawn has come.

QUESTIONS:
1. How do you feel at sunrise? Is it different from how you feel at other times of the day?
2. What other colors and animals are difficult to tell apart?
3. How would you need to treat someone to know that that person is a friend? How would you need to be treated?
4. What do you think the difference is between a friend, an acquaintance, and a social media "friend" you have never met in person? How many true friends do you have?

MODEH/MODAH ANI (186). You might remember Yoda in *Star Wars*. He had a rather odd way of forming sentences. He would put verbs and adjectives before nouns, or he would put the direct object of the sentence even before the subject: "Soccer I play"; "Services I attend." Scholars of Jewish liturgy now believe that Yoda was responsible for the first words that Jews say in their morning prayers. Not really, but look at the beginning of the prayer: *Modeh/modah ani*. The exact translation: "Thanks I give." It definitely sounds like Yoda!

There is an echo of this sentiment in the *T'filah* section (see page 72): *Modim anachnu lach*, which our prayer book translates as "We acknowledge with thanks," but which would translate literally as the rather awkward "Acknowledge with thanks we do to You."

Why *modeh/modah ani*, and not *ani modeh/modah*? *Ani* means "I." The first word in the worship service should not be "I." This teaches humility. When we express gratitude, the gratitude comes first. "Thanks" comes before "I," because in the act of giving gratitude, you are actually putting the "I" second.

The prayer continues with the words "ever-living Sovereign." The Hebrew is *Melech chai v'kayam*, which translates literally as "the Ruler that lives and endures." Why would we say this in the morning? Because, as we discussed when we looked at the evening service, the night is a scary time. The imaginary demons could have taken over. An ancient sage said that "sleep is one-sixtieth of death" (Babylonian Talmud, *B'rachot* 57b). In the "old days," people really believed that you died during the night, and then when you awoke you came back to life. Some thought that while you may not die when you sleep, your soul went on a journey overnight and then came back in the morning. Sleep was a frightening and fascinating realm. The morning gives us the opportunity to say that God is alive and still working. I am grateful that this "ever-living Sovereign" has "restored my soul to me in mercy," and hope you are too.

The Bible has much to say about sleep time:

- God put Adam to sleep and then took one of his ribs and created Eve (Genesis 2:21–22).
- Abram, whose name would be changed to Abraham, fell into a deep sleep and had a mysterious dream about how Jewish history would unfold (Genesis 15:12–16).
- Jacob slept and dreamed of a ladder of angels (Genesis 28:12).
- Joseph slept and dreamed of superiority over his brothers (Genesis 37:5–10) and later interpreted the dreams of his fellow prisoners in Egypt (Genesis 40:5–13) and of Pharaoh (Genesis 41:15–32).

That is just a short list of examples of sleep and dreams in the Hebrew Bible.

The Hebrew Bible also talks about one major difference between human beings and God. Psalm 121:4 says, "Behold, the Sentinel of Israel does not doze and does not sleep." At least, this is our hope; we want God's constant presence. I think that is why this prayer calls God *Melech chai v'kayam,* "ever-living Sovereign." When we go to sleep at night, we want to awaken to the God who is still very much alive and working.

The ancient Rabbis understood that dreams could contain powerful messages (there are pages upon pages about this in the Talmud). The founder of psychology, Sigmund Freud (Austria and England, 1856–1939), devoted much of his work to the interpretation of dreams. Modern psychologists know that dreams can be powerful as well.

Today, we need not believe that sleep is the same as death. Still, we might choose to live our lives mindful that every day there is the possibility that something will restore our souls and help us feel closer both to God and to ourselves.

The prayer continues with the words *rabbah emunatecha,* "how great is Your trust." The word for "trust" is *emunah,* which can also mean "belief," "steadfastness," and "faith."

But wait a second! Aren't we the ones who are supposed to have *emunah* in God? Why does the prayer say that God has *emunah* in us? What is the nature of that *emunah*—trust, belief, steadfastness, and faith? It turns out that *emunah* is reciprocal. We have faith in God, and God has faith in us. God has faith that when we find ourselves renewed after (hopefully) a good night's sleep, we will awaken to the possibility of living this day with virtue and value.

That is the main message of this prayer: I wake up every day, and this day contains the possibility of something marvelous for me, and in some small way, I can make the world better.

QUESTIONS:
1. For what are you particularly grateful in your life?
2. When have you felt gratitude?
3. When have you felt humility?

4. Have you ever felt that something deep inside of you—
your soul—came alive again?
5. What can you do, on any given day, to make the world
better?

TZITZIT (190). It is time for you to forget all the science that you
know. Well, not exactly *all* the science that you know. But a good deal
of it. Or, at the very least, it is time to set it aside for a few moments.
Consider this your opportunity to put yourself back into the place of
a Jew who lived two thousand years ago.

You would have had an entirely different, poetic way of understanding both God and the sunrise. You might have literally believed
that God wore several garments: "glory," "majesty," and "light." You
would have imagined that when the sun rose in the morning, it was
because God put on that garment of light—and when the sun set in
the evening, it would have been because God took off that garment
of light.

This is partially why we wear a tallit in the morning. You have
to be able to see the tzitzit, the special knots on the corners of the
tallit. In ancient times, the only available light with which to see was
during the day. It is also as if we are reenacting the act of God putting
on that garment of light and making the sunrise happen. The only
time worshipers wear a tallit at night is on the eve of Yom Kippur or
if they are leading prayer.

You might be saying to yourself, "Oh, come on! How can they
expect us to say this when we pray? It simply isn't true." You would
be right. However, it might surprise you that the prayer texts we say
and sing do not have to be either historically or scientifically accurate. They need only be poetic and contain poetic truths and images
that make us use our imaginations.

That is a pretty good definition of prayer—using your Jewish
imagination.

Mah Tovu (192) What are the first words that Jews traditionally say when they enter a synagogue? Words that are part of the *Mah Tovu* prayer: "How fair are your tents, O Jacob, your dwellings, O Israel!" (Numbers 24:5).

It's an interesting choice. The words of this prayer were first uttered by a non-Jew, a Moabite soothsayer named Balaam, who had intended them to be a curse and which God transformed into blessing.

And yet, look where the ancient editors of the prayer book put it: right at the beginning of the morning service. It is as if they were saying, "The prayer of a non-Jew is worthy in our eyes. Not only that—this is someone who tried to curse us, and instead, blessings came out of his mouth. If only that would always happen—that haters might become lovers."

But there is another reason why we say (or, more likely, sing) those words as we enter the synagogue. Balaam praised the "tents" (*ohalecha*) of the Jewish people. It is as if he saw into the future and saw that the tents of the ancient Israelites would become synagogues and study places. In the prayer itself, Balaam's opening words transition into the words of the Psalms, praising the beauty of the ancient Temple and the feelings of awe that those who entered it would have experienced.

If the "tents" are the synagogues, the "dwellings" (*mishk'notecha*) are Jewish homes. Synagogues represent the Jew in public spaces; homes represent the Jew in private spaces. Some people believe that you only need one, but not the other. Some people say, "Why do I need the synagogue? I can pray in my home."

People might say that, and it would be great if they did, in fact, pray in their homes, but they probably don't. Why is it likely that they don't, in fact, pray at home? Here's a way of thinking about it—a lesson that comes from the world of the gym.

Let's say that you are trying to get into shape or training for an athletic competition. Sure, you can work out on your own, but you are more likely to have success if you do it with others. That's how Jewish communities work as well. Jews need each other to be Jews. Many religious traditions have stories about hermits—people who have decided to live apart from other people. As far as I know, Jews have no stories about religious heroes who are hermits. "Do not separate yourself from the community!"—those are the words of the sage Hillel (*Pirkei Avot* 2:5).

Which is more important—the home or the synagogue? They are equally important. However, this prayer makes it clear that the synagogue is the place for worship, study, and simply hanging out with other Jews. It is very important that young people find a place in our synagogues.

A midrash teaches, "All the nations came to Balaam and asked, 'Can we take on this nation of Israel in battle?' He replied, 'Go and circulate among their synagogues and study halls; if you find children there crying out, you will not be able to confront them'" (*B'reishit Rabbah* 65:20). The strength of the Jewish people lies not in its weapons, but in its children and the words we teach.

Ever since the Romans destroyed the Second Temple in the year 70 CE, Jews have lacked a Temple. Today we believe that God is as present in the synagogue as God was in the ancient Temple. The destruction could not end that sense of immediate contact with God. That is the lesson of Jewish survival.

There is one more important lesson about *ohalecha*, "tents," and the interpretation that those tents represent the future synagogues and study places of the Jews. If you have ever gone camping, then you know you put up a tent, sleep in it, and then take it down. A tent is, by definition, a temporary dwelling. (I walk along my street and I see people experiencing homelessness living in "tents" that they have constructed out of old coats and sleeping bags. Those "tents" are their homes.) So, why call a synagogue a "tent"?

Because the Jews are a wandering people. That notion of wandering continues even today. In many communities where we lived, Jews established synagogues and schools. Then those neighborhoods changed, people moved away, and they reestablished their synagogues and schools in new neighborhoods.

In other words, we Jews still live in tents.

QUESTIONS:
1. What are some things that have happened to you that seemed bad, but that turned out to be blessings?
2. What would you hope that every Jewish home would contain?
3. What would you hope that every synagogue would contain?
4. What Jewish communities have changed, necessitating Jews to move elsewhere and to reestablish their synagogues and communities?

ASHER YATZAR (194). Yuck alert! This prayer is about poop and urine—or whatever you want to call those unpleasant products of the human body.

So, let's talk about going to the bathroom. We have many euphemisms for that private place: bathroom (even if there is no bath in it), toilet, lavatory, the facilities, powder room, john. In England, they have their share as well: the WC (water closet), loo, or "the gents" for men. Apparently, British Jews use the euphemism "the asher yatzar room"—the place where someone might say the prayer Asher Yatzar. That's because this prayer is recited after someone uses the bathroom (or loo or toilet).

However, this prayer is really not about elimination. It is much more elegant than that. The prayer says that our bodies have various holes, which are one way that we experience the outside world—the stuff that goes in, and the stuff that goes out. It is what makes us human. Our bodies also have passageways within them—veins, arteries, passageways for air. The whole system is necessary for us to live. If that system were to break down—if a hole or passageway that should be open were to be closed or one that should be closed were to be open—we would be in big trouble.

As we learned above, the Shabbat morning service opens with the hymn *Mah Tovu*. The verses begin with entering the ancient Temple in Jerusalem: "I, through Your abundant love, enter Your house." The Temple was holy, and so is the human body. The Temple had entrances and exits, and so does the human body. The ancient Temple was *where* we served God, and our bodies are *how* we serve God, which means that we should have as much reverence for our bodies as we would have for a sacred site. We are made in the divine image; taking care of ourselves is the least we can do. Some people care more about their mobile phone not working than their bodies not working. They will rush to a repair shop if their phone screen cracks. With their bodies, though—not so much. Some people ignore a sore throat until they are hospitalized with scarlet fever or walk around on a broken ankle until someone forces them to see the doctor! Many of us notice our bodies not when they are working great, but when we are feeling terrible.

Think about it: The human body is a pretty remarkable "machine." That it works so well and for so many people (until it doesn't, when we get sick or age) is somewhat miraculous. The design of the human body is a reflection of divine wisdom—what we call *chochmah*. God created our bodies in such a way that all of those holes and passageways need to be working correctly, in harmony, or we would be in big trouble. Our bodies have many entrances, exits, and passageways. Your skin is a pathway to, and from, the outside world. You have lungs, which are gateways to the world so many times a day that you don't even notice them. Well, most of the time. Take your sinuses, for example. Remember the last time you had a head cold? Whether you were aware of it or not, you were probably praying that those entrances and exits would work properly and that your congestion would clear up. Ask anyone who has been on a ventilator and recovered how grateful they are that their passageways are working well.

So, what is this prayer saying to us? If you are looking for evidence of God's wisdom, look at the human body. In fact, it really is a wonder that it works well, when you think about it!

QUESTIONS:
1. When have you felt that your body was working great?
2. When have you felt that your body wasn't working so well?
3. What do you do to take care of your body?
4. Recall a time when you had been ill and then recovered. What did you feel?

ELOHAI N'SHAMAH (196). Up to this point in our service we have learned some important lessons:

- We experience God in holy places—the ancient Temple, the modern synagogue, and our homes.
- We experience God through what is going on in our bodies.

And now, *Elohai N'shamah* tells us that God is in our souls, because that is the "place" within us where we experience God most intensely.

You are born with both a body and a soul. Your soul is in mint condition when you get it—"shrink wrapped," if you will. We try to keep our souls pure and committed to achieving the highest of our goals. As Israeli Reform rabbi Dalia Marx (1966–) teaches, "The words 'the soul You have given me is pure' are a declaration before God—and no less before ourselves—that we are fundamentally good. . . . We may do something bad, but at the most basic level we are good. Moreover, even if we have done something bad or strayed from the path, we are able to set things right. Every morning we are given the full potential to do good. A fresh new page is spread before us, even if yesterday's page is stained and creased."[4]

Not every religion believes this. Some religions believe that people are, by nature, deeply flawed—that our "default setting" is one of sinfulness and shame. Judaism sees life differently. Judaism believes that human beings have the capacity to do great good and great evil. Ultimately, our actions affect how our souls will develop.

There is another message in this prayer, hidden in the way that we hear the words. Look at how many times the Hebrew letter *hei* appears in the prayer. It makes the sound *hah* and *ah*. It is the sound of the exhaling of breath. As a matter of fact, the word *n'shamah* (soul) is related to the word *n'shimah*, which means "breath."

Just stop for a moment and listen to yourself breathing. We are not often aware of our breath unless we are sick and our breathing becomes difficult. This prayer is saying to us: Be aware.

Why should we be aware of our breath? Because it is the foundation of our humanity. God breathes the soul into Adam, and he becomes a living being (Genesis 2:7). On Rosh HaShanah, we remember that this is how we came to life. By blowing into the shofar, it is as if we are "returning the favor" and offering our own life breath to God—as *areshet s'fateinu*, the "offerings of our lips."

God is in charge of the soul. God gives it to us and will take it from us when we die. Our souls live on with God, and while we live, our breath is our connection to God.

QUESTIONS:
1. How do you know that you have a soul?
2. What are things that enlarge your soul?
3. What are things that shrink your soul?

NISIM B'CHOL YOM (198–202). "Praise to You, Adonai our God, Sovereign of the universe, who has given the mind the ability to distinguish day from night." If you translate this more literally, it would be "who has given the rooster understanding to distinguish day from night." Why start with the rooster? Birds were among God's first creations, and the morning gives us the opportunity to experience the order of Creation as if it were the first day of Creation all over again. Not only that, but the cry of the rooster heralds the coming of the morning.

Let's move through some of these blessings. *Pokei-ach ivrim*, "who opens the eyes of the blind": When we were asleep, our eyes were closed, and it was as if we were blind. The first thing we do in the morning is open our eyes. Of course, some people are really blind—

they cannot see, or they have trouble seeing. Helping them is a real mitzvah; that is the mission, for example, of the Jewish Guild for the Blind, where volunteers record books so that blind people can also "read" them. However, there are other kinds of blindness—like the inability to see reality. Some people, when they drive or walk along streets, see people begging for money, but they really don't *see* them. We can only hope that God will open the eyes of those who are blind to those realities. Some people refuse to see injustice. Some family members don't really see other members of their family. Kids who are popular don't always see the kids who are less popular. We all want to be seen.

The great American humanitarian Helen Keller (1880–1968) could not see, hear, or speak. She reportedly taught, "The only thing worse than being blind is having sight but not vision." Everyone needs a vision of how life can be meaningful and joyous and how life can be good for all people.

Malbish arumim, "who clothes the naked": Whenever I get a new garment, I always try to delay wearing it for the first time until Shabbat. It helps make Shabbat even holier for me. This is the blessing that I, and others, say when putting on a new item of clothing for the first time. Yes, I thank God for clothing the naked. But as I say this blessing, I also think about everyone who had a hand in making that piece of clothing—especially because there is a real possibility that some of them, perhaps many of them, are poorly paid, if at all. Some of them live in the developing world or work in terrible conditions in this country. It is possible that some of your most favorite brands of clothing come out of such conditions.

I love these words by the former poet laureate of the United States Robert Pinsky (1940–):

> The back, the yoke, the yardage. Lapped seams,
> The nearly invisible stitches along the collar
> Turned in a sweatshop by Koreans or Malaysians
> Gossiping over tea and noodles on their break
> Or talking money or politics while one fitted
> This armpiece with its overseam to the band.

The poet goes on to remind us that many of our ancestors also worked at sub-survival wages to make clothing. He reminds us of the Triangle Factory fire in New York City (March 25, 1911), which claimed the lives of immigrant clothing workers, many of whom were Jews:

> At the Triangle Factory in nineteen-eleven.
> One hundred and forty-six died in the flames
> On the ninth floor, no hydrants, no fire escapes.

What were these factory workers toiling to create?

> The buttonholes, the sizing, the facing, the characters
> Printed in black on neckband and tail. The shape,
> The label, the labor, the color, the shade. The shirt.[5]

I suggest that when we say the *malbish arumim* blessing, we should feel the clothing on our bodies and think of all those people—most of whom were and are invisible—whose hard work contributed to our not being naked.

She-asani Yisrael, "who has made me a Jew": There is an older version of this prayer that still appears in some prayer books. It thanks God "for not creating me a gentile," and there are also prayers that thank God "for not making me a slave" and "not making me a woman." Liberal Jews have changed these words, turning the negative ideas into positive affirmations. Let us not be grateful for what we are not; let us be proud of what we are. The question, however, remains: Why make it *she-asani Yisrael*, which literally translates as "who has made me Israel," and not *she-asani Y'hudi/Y'hudiyah*, which is literally "who has made me a Jew"? Why are we created, each of us, as Israel, and not as a Jew? The answer is that each of us is Israel/Yisrael—more than we could have ever imagined.

First, each of us is the patriarch Israel/Yisrael, who started life as Jacob. Remember that Jacob pressured his twin brother, Esau, into selling him his birthright in exchange for a bowl of soup (Genesis 25). Remember that Jacob disguised himself as his twin brother to receive the blessing of his dying father, Isaac, who was so blind that he could not recognize which son was before him (Genesis 27). Remember that Jacob dreamed of a ladder of angels (Genesis

28). Remember that Jacob wrestled with a nameless stranger and received the name Yisrael, "the one who struggles with God" (Genesis 32). There is much more to the life of Jacob, but those are the highlights.

Why are we Israel/Yisrael? Within each of us is a person who might take advantage of another person, given the opportunity; a person who has the capability of deception; a young person who dreams of greatness, which the ladder of angels symbolized; a maturing person who wrestles inwardly and outwardly.

Second, each of us is *Am Yisrael*, the Jewish people. Each of us is the story of the Jewish people in miniature:

- The Israelites were slaves in Egypt. Each of us knows what it means to be enslaved to something, to be forced to do something. (You might feel that way about going to school, and when summer vacation comes, it is as if you are getting out of Egypt—at least for a few months.)
- The Israelites crossed the Sea of Reeds and reached freedom. Each of us can understand what it means to be free. You might know people who came from oppressive countries or whose parents or grandparents fled from such countries. You might have Black friends, who really understand the story of the Exodus from Egypt. Years ago, I heard a professor address a group of Jewish and Black people, and he began his speech, "Fellow ex-slaves. . . ."
- The Israelites encountered God at Mount Sinai and received the Ten Commandments. Each of us can stand at our own version Sinai, when we "get" a powerful truth that we had not known before.
- The Israelites built and worshiped the Golden Calf. While we might not bow down to an idol, each of us often have moments when we realize that we are not living up to our own ideals.
- The Israelites traveled through the wilderness in order to reach the Land of Israel. Each of us must engage in our own journey, and we must find our own promised land.

There is an additional layer to this. Each of us is also *M'dinat Yisrael*—the State of Israel:

- The State of Israel has welcomed Jews into the homeland of the Jewish people. Each of us, like the modern State of Israel, knows what it means to welcome people. As Israel brought in those Jews who lived in other countries, we also can extend hospitality (on a much smaller scale).
- The State of Israel has become known as "startup nation," skilled in medical research and technology. More patented inventions have come out of Israel than from almost any other country. You might not be as inventive as Israeli scientists and techies (yet), but perhaps you have devised solutions to things.
- The State of Israel is surrounded by enemies. If you are being victimized by bullies, there is absolutely no reason for you to tolerate that. Report that bullying to responsible adults. Stand up to the bullies. This is what Israel is forced to do too.
- The State of Israel is both deeply admired and deeply hated, and everything in between. We will all go through life with people who love us and, sadly, people who will not love us. You won't always win popularity contests; neither should you want to.
- The anthem of the State of Israel is "Hatikvah," which means "The Hope." Each of us, like the modern State of Israel, knows what it is like to maintain *tikvah*, hope.

We are not *Y'hudi*, not (just) a Jew. We are, in fact, *Yisrael*. Each of us is the Jewish story in miniature.

One last thing. We say these blessings every morning, but they are not just called *b'rachot*, "blessings"; they are also called *nisim*, "miracles." When we say these blessings, we are saying that there are miracles all the time—if we can only open our eyes wide enough to see them.

QUESTIONS:
1. What are some things people are blind to or refuse to see?
2. Have you ever considered where your clothing comes from? Do you know where your clothes are made? How do you think it would feel to say a blessing when you put your clothing on?
3. What characters in the Torah are similar to you?
4. What parts of Jewish history are particularly meaningful to you?
5. What miracles do we encounter every day?

LAASOK/V'HAAREV NA (204). *Laasok/V'haarev Na* shares the commandment "to engage with words of Torah." You would think that a commandment to study Torah would say *v'tzivanu lilmod Torah*, "commanded us to study and learn Torah." Not this one. Here, the commandment is not to study or to learn. Instead, *laasok* means "to make ourselves busy" or "to occupy our time."

That is the whole point. Torah should occupy our time—or at the very least, a part of our time. For what purpose? That we might know God's name. We might call that having a spiritual experience. Torah study is a way into Jewish spirituality.

The blessing shares even more. We need to engage in Torah *lishmah*, "for its own sake." Doing things for their own sake is the supreme religious value in Judaism. In the words of *Avot*, the ethical section of the Mishnah, "Don't be like servants who serve . . . for the sake of receiving a reward" (*Pirkei Avot* 1:3). When we are little kids, we often do things for the reward. We want our parents to approve of what we do (actually, we never really outgrow that). As we grow older, we want our teachers and our peers to approve of what we do (we might someday outgrow that). As we grow older still, we want our bosses, supervisors, and colleagues to approve of what we do (you outgrow that when you retire from your work). Still, the essence of existence is to do things just because, for their own sake.

Let's turn to a very big question. Why get an education in the first place? Many people view education as something you get: getting good grades, getting admitted to a good college, getting a good job, getting a handsome salary, getting access to power or influence. Judaism, though, teaches that a life truly worth living is a life of inquiry and discovery—a life of pursuing knowledge for its own sake. Someone once asked Albert Einstein (Germany and United States, 1879–1955) what it was in the Jewish tradition that made him the proudest to be a Jew. He answered, "The pursuit of knowledge for its own sake."[6] Torah study *lishmah*—not for the sake of glory or money or fame or publishing or grades or even bet mitzvah, but for its own sake—is the ideal.

There is a caveat, though, that is a bit shocking: Even if you don't do things out of a purity of motive, it's still acceptable. For example, there is a discussion in the Talmud about a person who wanted to convert to Judaism because he liked the garments worn by the High Priest. Therefore, he decided that he wanted to become Jewish—just so that he could become the High Priest!

The Rabbis wondered if that would be an acceptable reason to want to join the Jewish people. (Let's leave aside for a moment whether it would even be possible for a Jew-by-choice to become the High Priest; technically, you would have to be descended from Aaron, the brother of Moses, to be High Priest.) They asked, "Should we accept him or not?" (Babylonian Talmud, *Shabbat* 31a).

The great sage Hillel decided that they should accept him. Hillel must have realized that the gentile wanted to convert not out of any purity of motive, but because he liked the clothes. Hillel understood that in the process of learning Torah, the prospective convert would eventually want to be a Jew simply for the sake of wanting to be a Jew.

> When Rav Safra concluded his prayer, he would add, "May it be Your will, Adonai our God, to establish peace in the household above and in the earthly entourage, the Sages, and among the disciples engaged in the study of Your Torah, whether they engage in its study for its own sake or not for its own sake. And all those engaged in Torah study not for its own sake, may it be Your will that they will come to engage in its study for its own sake." (Babylonian Talmud, *B'rachot* 16b–17a)[7]

EILU D'VARIM (206). We have just made a blessing for Torah study, so the next thing in our service is some "Torah" to study. We believe that God is in the way that we study. We also believe that God is in what we do for other people. Our study text teaches both beliefs.

"These are things that are limitless, of which a person enjoys the fruit of the world, while the principal remains in the world-to-come." These words are derived from the Mishnah (*Pei-ah* 1:1), the ancient code of Jewish law, and describe the way Jewish communities are supposed to behave. They list the major obligations that each Jew has toward every other Jew. This text imagines that these actions are investments—not financial investments, but spiritual investments. We do them in this world, but it is as if those actions lie dormant in some kind of cosmic account, and we get the spiritual rewards for them in the world-to-come.

Let's put it differently: You do things in this world but you can never know exactly how powerful your actions are. It is not for you to know. You just do them.

One of these actions is *hachnasat orchim*, "welcoming guests." When I was a teen, I always liked having people "crash" at our house. My late parents were very good about that; we always seemed to have kids in sleeping bags in our living room. Years later, I learned that our role models were Abraham and Sarah, who welcomed three strangers to their tent—strangers who might have been angels—who would announce that Sarah would have a child. A midrash states that Sarah and Abraham's tent was open on all sides, to make sure that they could welcome strangers. This becomes the mitzvah not only of hospitality, but of caring for the those experiencing homelessness. The prophet Isaiah knew that this was a primary Jewish responsibility. He said, "No, this is the fast I desire: To unlock fetters of wickedness, and untie the cords of the yoke" (58:5). A yoke is a wooden frame that forces an animal to carry a burden. Isaiah is using it as a metaphor for oppression. Isaiah continued his message: "To let the oppressed go free; to break off every yoke. It is to share your bread with the hungry, and to take the wretched poor into your home; when you see the naked, to clothe them, and not to ignore your own kin" (58:6–7).

Erica Brown (United States, 1966–), a prominent Jewish educator, shares this memory of another great Jewish educator—the late Bible teacher Professor Nechama Leibowitz (Lithuania and Israel, 1905–77). "Once, in a lecture, Professor Leibowitz said: 'There was never a time when Jews did not take in their homeless. When did Jews stop taking in the homeless? When Jews got wall-to-wall carpeting.' When we had nothing, we were happy to split that nothing with others."[8]

The prayer also talks about *bikur cholim*, "visiting the sick." This is a conscious imitation of God: Just as God visited Abraham while he was in pain after his circumcision, we are obligated to contribute in our own way to healing the sick through our presence. Physical presence is not always possible or appropriate; a phone call, a text, and certainly a prayer can lift the spirits and make us agents of healing other people.

Another value is *l'vayat hameit*, "accompanying the dead for burial." The word "funeral" comes from an old Latin word meaning "death" or "corpse." You would expect that—after all, funerals are about burying the dead. In Judaism, however, there is another term for "funeral"—*l'vayah*, which literally means "accompanying" the dead to the grave. Years ago, I attended a funeral in which all of the mourners walked with the hearse that carried the coffin until it got onto a highway to take the body to its final resting place.

I have often thought that every act in the Jewish life cycle is about accompanying:

- When a child is born there is the *b'rit*, or covenantal ceremony. Traditionally, we reserve a special honor for someone (the *kvater* or *kvaterin*) to accompany (carry) the infant into the ceremony.
- When a child reaches Jewish maturity there is a bet mitzvah. The child chants or reads Torah, accompanied by religious leaders and loved ones who surround the child during the reading. (Ever notice that no one ever stands before a congregation to chant or read Torah alone?)
- When someone gets married, loved ones—often parents—accompany the couple to the chuppah (wedding canopy); loved ones often surround the couple under the chuppah.

The same action happens at a funeral; we accompany the dead to the grave. After the funeral, we accompany the mourners as they go through their journey of grief. The Jew is never alone, whether it is the beginning, middle, or end of the journey.

You might be thinking, "I know that *tzedakah* [righteous giving] is important in Judaism. Why isn't *tzedakah* on this list?" You are right; *tzedakah* is important, and it is not on this list. Why not? Because each of the acts in this list constitute *g'milut chasadim*, "deeds of compassion" or "acts of *chesed*." The word *chesed* is central to Judaism, and yet it is so hard to translate. It means acts of loving-kindness and caring, but so much more than that. As Rabbi Shai Held teaches, "An act of *chesed* is, as Rabbi Yitzhak Hutner [Warsaw and United States, 1906–80] writes, 'the planting of a seed that cannot but bring forth fruit similar to itself.' When someone performs an act of *chesed* for us, 'a seed of *chesed* is planted in our world,' and when both we and the world function 'healthily,' that seed cannot but bring forth more *chesed* in its wake."[9] Or, as someone once put it, when we give *tzedakah*, we give of our money; when we give *chesed*, we give of ourselves.

QUESTIONS:
1. When have you visited the sick? What was it like? What did it do for the sick person? What did it do for you?
2. When have you welcomed strangers? What was it like?
3. Have you attended a funeral? Made a shivah call? What was it like?
4. What acts of *chesed* are the most important to you?

KADDISH D'RABANAN (208). You never know what you might find in your garage. I heard this story from Rabbi David Wolpe (United States, 1958–), who heard it from his own father, the late Rabbi Gerald Wolpe (United States, 1927–2009), who had heard it from another rabbi, which is exactly how these stories come into the world—as tales and texts told by rabbis, teachers, and their disciples. The rabbi who told the story had somehow acquired an old set of Talmud, which he had kept in his garage for many years. There had been a lot of rain, so the rabbi had to move those books. By chance, one of the volumes opened up, and the rabbi found these words scribbled in the margin: "My name is Chaim. I live in this small town in eastern Poland. The Nazis are coming. If this book survives, please start studying here in my memory." By "here," Chaim meant start studying right here—right at this place on the page—and do it in my memory. We can assume that Chaim had died in the Holocaust; when he wrote those words in the margin of the Talmud volume, he knew that death awaited him. And yet, even then, he knew how he wanted his memory to survive—by someone studying the sacred text and doing it in his memory.

Every time we study and every time we pray, we are acting in memory of all those who studied and prayed and those who left their names or whose names were erased by the destruction and obliteration of time.

QUESTIONS:
1. When you have studied something, have you ever felt that you did so because you had an obligation to study it?

> 2. When you have read a book, a poem, or a story or heard a song, have you ever felt the presence of the author or composer?

P'SUKEI D'ZIMRAH—VERSES OF PRAISE

Everything meaningful that we do requires preparation and warm-up—exercise, sports, dancing, playing a musical instrument. Prayer, too!

"What do you do before you pray?" someone once asked an old, pious rabbi. "I pray," she said. "What do you pray?" "I pray that I will be able to pray well." In the words of Rabbi Lawrence Hoffman (Canada and United States, 1942–), "The *P'sukei D'Zimrah* is the 'prayer before the prayer.' It functions as the warm-up for the morning service, a recognition that prayerfulness cannot be summoned on demand."[10]

BARUCH SHE-AMAR (212). Blessed is the One who spoke and the world came to be. Blessed is the One!" This is not only a statement about God or a prayer to God. It is also who God really is! It is actually a name of God—"the One who spoke and the world came to be." Why? Because that was how God created, at the very dawn of Creation: "And God said, 'Let there be light . . . sky . . . water" (Genesis 1). That is how important speech is—it can create worlds.

A little later in the service, we will ask that God "guard my speech from evil and my lips from deception." There is a good reason for this request. In Hebrew, the sin of gossip is called *lashon hara*, "the evil tongue." It is the subject of centuries of moral advice. Jewish sages wrote entire volumes about it. There were Jewish schools in Eastern Europe where the entire curriculum was nothing but the laws of *lashon hara*. The students became as expert in the laws of kosher speech as some were in the laws of kosher slaughter! *Lashon hara* means saying anything bad about anyone, even and especially if it's true. *Lashon hara* means insults, ridicule, and jest. *Lashon hara* means insulting someone's possessions or work or merchandise (which is why my parents taught me to never discuss one store's mer-

chandise in someone else's store). It means commenting on someone's body, money, or medical history. It means saying anything that
might cause another person harm, embarrassment, or displeasure.
"Did you hear what he did?" "Did you hear what she said?" "I heard
that they actually. . . ." "You know, so-and-so is not the best tennis
player/student/babysitter/pianist/teacher/cantor/rabb/educator/
leader. . . ." "I really shouldn't say this, but . . ."

Judaism has an important message about this: Watch what you
say. God created the world through language. As contemporary
Reform Cantor Sarah Grabiner (United Kingdom and Israel, 1991–)
teaches, "Our own words might not have God's power of genesis, but
we know that our speech has the creative potential to inspire move-
ments, build relationships, and transform communities. If even
everyday words are powerful, what might different speech, the kind
of speech that touches on the heart of human existence, be able to
achieve?"[11]

QUESTIONS:
1. What has been your experience with *lashon hara*—either
   speaking it, hearing it, or being the target of it?
2. Do you agree that words can create or destroy worlds?
3. How can we use our language better and with holy
   purpose?

PSALM 92 (214). The first time I ever heard guitar in a Jewish worship service, it blew me away. Many years ago, I attended a Reform
Jewish summer camp—Eisner Camp, in Great Barrington, Massachusetts—for the first time. I was a teen. It was my first week at summer camp. I liked it. Then Friday evening came and, with it, Shabbat
evening services. There were three people playing guitars and leading singing. Everyone was singing along, dancing, and jumping on
the tables in the dining room. The melodies were very cool, and the
whole experience was absolutely thrilling.

This was unlike any Jewish music that I had ever heard in my life.
In my home synagogue, there was an organ and a choir, and we sat

there and listened to the music. No one sang. It was totally passive. Even then, the music was already old.

At that point, I had been playing guitar for several years—mostly folk-rock. When I heard that music at Eisner Camp, it totally changed my life. At that moment, I decided that this was going to be my future. I would learn to play all those songs. I would write my own songs and lead songs at Jewish summer camps and in the Reform youth movement. Years later, when I became a rabbi, I would play guitar in the synagogues I served.

I wasn't alone in my response to this music. Most people loved it. It turns out this was one of the biggest revolutions in American Judaism—we integrated popular culture, even rock music, with what we do Jewishly. This revolution was so successful, in fact, that you probably cannot imagine a Reform Shabbat service without this kind of music. Even if you have never been to Jewish camp, even if your synagogue still uses an organ and a choir, you have probably been exposed to this folk-rock style of Jewish music.

The truth is, playing the "guitar" was not quite as modern and as "cool" as it seemed to have been. It is actually very ancient. Musical instruments have been part of Jewish life almost since the very beginning and certainly were part of the worship in the ancient Temple in Jerusalem. Here are some examples:

- Miriam and the women of Israel played percussion instruments when the Israelites crossed the Sea of Reeds: "Then Miriam the prophet, Aaron's sister, picked up a hand-drum, and all the women went out after her in dance with hand-drums" (Exodus 15:20).
- Some ancient prophets used instruments in their prophesying, using "lyres [a small harp] timbrels, flutes, and harps" (I Samuel 10:5).
- The young David was very talented at playing the harp. When King Saul was depressed, David would play for him to soothe his spirits (I Samuel 16:23).
- When King David brought the Ark of the Covenant into Jerusalem, there was a celebration that included "lyres,

harps, timbrels, sistrums [a kind of rattle], and cymbals"
(II Samuel 6:5).

• When the Babylonians destroyed the First Temple in 586 BCE, they deported the Judeans into exile. Psalm 137 was written during that period of exile:

> By the rivers of Babylon,
> there we sat,
> sat and wept,
> as we thought of Zion.
> There on the poplars
> we hung up our lyres,
> for our captors asked us there for songs,
> our tormentors, for amusement,
> "Sing us one of the songs of Zion."
> How can we sing a song of Adonai
> on alien soil?

There you have it: lyres and harps—the ancient "ancestors" of the guitar.

When I started my career in Miami, Florida, we used a harp in our worship services. Our harp player was an elderly Cuban refugee, who had once been the first harpist in the Havana Philharmonic Orchestra, which had flourished in the years before the Communist revolution in 1959. When she played, I could sometimes see the tears in her eyes. It was as if she knew, like the ancient Temple musicians, what it means to play the harp in exile.

QUESTIONS:

1. Have you had experience with hearing musical instruments in worship services? What do you think of that tradition?

2. Do you play a musical instrument? How do you feel when you play it?

3. The ancient Temple musicians in Psalm 137 are experiencing the feeling of nostalgia. Have you ever felt nostalgia?

ASHREI (215–16). Happy are those who dwell in Your house"—clearly, this psalm is about those who go to God's "oldest" house, the ancient Temple in Jerusalem. We know, however, that house no longer exists. It has been replaced by the synagogue and the home.

The body of this prayer comes from Psalm 145, though it starts with Psalm 84:5—"Happy are those who dwell in Your house; they forever praise You!" The psalm is an acrostic: Every verse begins with a letter of the Hebrew alphabet, in order (though there is no verse that begins with the letter *nun*; more on that later).

Let's talk about happiness. Someone once said that Eskimos have many different words for "snow." This may or may not be true; come to think of it, English has many different words for "frozen precipitation" as well, such as snow, frost, ice, and sleet. Still, if Eskimos have many different words for "snow," then Jews have many different words for "happy."

Many of them show up in the seventh blessing of the wedding ceremony. "Blessed are You, Adonai our God, Ruler of the universe, who creates happiness and joy, groom and bride. Exultation, delight, amusement, and pleasure." There are subtle differences between "delight," "amusement," and "pleasure." Perhaps we go to an "amusement" park, which "delights" us, and that gives us "pleasure." In the context of this wedding blessing, we hope that the couple will find "amusement," "delight," and "pleasure" in each other through loving interactions and encounters.

We can go even deeper than "amusement," "delight," and "pleasure," as good as they might be. As Rabbi Dalia Marx, PhD, teaches:

> Professor Martin Seligman, an American Jewish psychologist (b. 1942) has discerned three types of happiness. The first type is happiness deriving from pleasure and enjoyment. A second type comes from a life of doing and flowing with what is important to that individual (family, work, love, or a hobby), since when we do something we love, we are so invested in it that times goes by unnoticed. The third type is happiness that comes from a life of meaning and purpose, a life of devotion to a cause, working for a higher goal. . . . That is the most profound and enduring of the three and the primary contributor to fulfilment in life.[12]

Professor Seligman was talking about the Hebrew word that begins this psalm, *ashrei*. *Ashrei* means "deeply contented." It is that sense of sitting back and saying, "Wow. My heart is full. I am satisfied."

For many years, I gave a "final examination" to seventh graders in religious school. I asked them, "What is the difference between 'fun' and 'joy'?" They shared all kinds of answers. The best answer I ever heard is this: "When you have 'fun,' it happens, and then it is over. But, when you have 'joy,' it happens, and it lasts forever." May you experience that.

But why is there no verse that starts with *nun*? We can imagine that letter *nun* saying, "What am I—chopped liver?!" So, what happened to *nun* in this psalm? In the Babylonian Talmud (*B'rachot* 4b), Rabbi Yochanan taught that the letter *nun* is the first letter of the Hebrew word *nafal*, "fallen," and they did not want to include the idea that the nation of Israel might fall to its enemies. Why bring a negative thought into such a joyous prayer?

QUESTIONS:
1. How do you define happiness?
2. What are some things that give you deep satisfaction?
3. Can you describe the feelings of those who entered the ancient Temple in Jerusalem? What are your feelings when you enter your own synagogue?
4. Do you agree with the ancient "decision" to omit a verse with the letter *nun*, because *nun* is the first letter of the Hebrew word for "fallen"? How have you resisted negativity?

PSALM 150 (218). The editors of the Hebrew Bible—whoever they were—knew what they were doing.

They made Psalm 150 the last psalm, probably because it is the most complete summary of Biblical Judaism. It asks and answers one question: Where is God?

First, it begins with probably the most famous Hebrew term of all time: *Hal'lu Yah*. This means "praise *Adonai*," and it exists in the

English language as well, as "Hallelujah." Every Sunday morning in churches all over the world, people sing, say, and often shout that Hebrew word. The song "Hallelujah" composed by the late Leonard Cohen (Canada and United States, 1934–2016) is one of the most covered songs in history, with more than three hundred recorded versions. The word "hallelujah" is a gift that the Jewish people gave the world. It is a gift that keeps on giving.

Let's get back to that question—where is God and where do we praise God? The first answer is the ancient Temple in Jerusalem—*b'kodsho*, "in God's holy place." In Biblical times, Jews believed that God either lived in—or (at the very least) visited—the ancient Temple. This means that God is in a building—a sacred building.

Then, the psalm moves immediately to a realm way beyond the ancient Temple, way beyond Jerusalem, and way beyond the earth—all the way into the cosmos. Therefore, God is in the universe. Next, we locate God in what God has done for human beings. In other words, God is in our lives.

Let's return to the idea that God is found in the ancient Temple. We praise God with blasts of the shofar (*teika shofar*, as in the word *t'kiah* that we shout out when we blow the shofar on Rosh HaShanah); with harp and lyre; with timbrel (a small tambourine) and dance; with lute and pipe; with resounding and crashing cymbals. There was an entire orchestra in the ancient Temple, and the ancient Levites were responsible for the music. While the Levites played, people danced in the ancient Temple. Chasidism—the pious, mystical movement of Orthodoxy—brought dancing back to Judaism, after the custom had been hibernating for two thousand years, and now you will see Jews dancing in summer camps and synagogues. Dance is a Jewish thing.

Perhaps your synagogue uses some of the "descendants" of these instruments in its own worship. This is not the case for Orthodox Jews. Orthodox Judaism has frowned upon using musical instruments in the synagogue, for various reasons:

- The Romans destroyed the ancient Temple, and since there had been musical instruments in the ancient Temple, it would be tasteless for Jews to use musical instruments in their worship services.

- A musical instrument might break, and then someone would need to repair it. Some of the actions that would be necessary to repair that instrument are forbidden on Shabbat according to Orthodox Jewish law.
- By the Middle Ages, Christians used musical instruments for worship in their churches. Many Jews wanted to emphasize the differences between Jewish worship and Christian worship; therefore, they did not allow instruments in the synagogue.

To these arguments early Reform Jews in Europe said, "Those restrictions might have been important in the past, but no longer seem to apply. We want beautiful services that will rival the best of what we can hear and experience in opera and theater, and the way to do that is to use musical instruments." (Let me share an aside: The first musical instrument that the early Reform Jews wanted to use was the organ—in particular, the pipe organ. How did they justify that specific instrument? They looked at the *ugav* mentioned in Psalm 150, an instrument that was like a pipe. It was apparently some kind of wind instrument. "Perfect," said the early Reformers. "The pipe organ is the 'descendant' of the ancient *ugav.*" Don't let anyone ever say that Reform Jews aren't creative!) So, where was God in all this? God was in the human striving to be creative.

Let's look at the "last" place where God would be located. The psalm says, *Kol han'shamah t'haleil Yah,* "Let all that breathes praise God." To really understand this, I need to share an important Hebrew word-play. The word for "soul," *n'shamah,* is related to the word for "breath," *n'shimah.* Rabbi Judith Hauptman (United States, 1943–) suggests that we understand this verse in a new way, by looking at the following midrash: Rabbi Levi in the name of Rabbi Chanina taught: "For every single breath that we take we must praise God" (*B'reishit Rabbah* 14).[13] (Years ago, I had a friend who had Orthodox Jewish relatives. He complained to me, "In their house, you can't take a breath without making a blessing!" My response to him:

"Don't you realize that every breath is, in fact, a blessing?")

There is another way to translate *kol han'shamah*. It can also mean "the whole soul." Let the entire soul—not just a piece of the soul, but the whole soul, our entire being—praise God.

This psalm has taken us on quite a journey! God has gone from a sacred building, out and up into the universe, back "down" into our lives through human creativity, and finally into the human soul.

QUESTIONS:
1. Where do you find God's presence most? In the synagogue? In nature? In the heart?
2. What are some of your favorite musical instruments for worship?
3. Do you believe that even breathing is, in its own way, a blessing?
4. When have you felt God in your own soul?

NISHMAT KOL CHAI (219–222). "Let the soul of everything alive bless Your name, Adonai, our God." According to Psalm 150, we bless God in the ancient Temple through musical instruments, through the cosmos, and in the human soul. You didn't think that we would actually stop at human beings, did you? *Nishmat Kol Chai* shares a wild and wonderful idea. Everything that is alive blesses God.

Rabbi Abraham Isaac Kook (Russia and Land of Israel, 1865–1935) was the first Ashkenazic chief rabbi of Israel, even before there was a State of Israel. He was also a mystic and took great pleasure in figuring out the deeper meaning of prayer. He wrote, "All of existence yearns for the source of its life, every plant and every blade of grass, every speck of sand and clump of earth. Everything that reveals life and everything that hides within it life, the small parts of creation and the big, the heavens above and fiery angels, all the details of all being, and the wholeness of it—everything aspires, yearns, longs for the desired wholeness of its supreme, living, holy, pure, powerful source."[14] Everything prays, because everything yearns for God. In fact, there is an ancient Jewish text, *Perek Shirah*, "A Chapter of Song," that actually lists the Biblical verse each aspect of Creation sings: the fields, the waters, the heavens, day, night, sun, moon, and every species of animal, as well! Let everything in Creation praise God.

Let's return to earth and deal with some very human hopes included in this prayer. This prayer says that "Adonai neither slumbers nor sleeps." We hope so! Sleep is a human thing. Psalm 121:1–4 states:

> I turn my eyes to the mountains;
> from where will my help come?
> My help comes from Adonai,
> maker of heaven and earth.
> [God] will not let your foot give way;
> your guardian will not slumber;
> See, the guardian of Israel
> neither slumbers nor sleeps!

And yet, in times of trouble, our ancestors were not so sure that God was actually awake. They thought that God was sleeping and was blind and deaf to our suffering. One example of this comes from Psalm 44:23–25:

> It is for Your sake that we are slain all day long,
> that we are regarded as sheep to be slaughtered.
> Rouse Yourself; why do You sleep, O my Sovereign?
> Awaken, do not reject us forever!
> Why do You hide Your face,
> ignoring our affliction and distress?

The prayer continues by saying, "God awakens the sleeping, arouses those who slumber." This is not only about those who are physically sleeping, but also about those who are spiritually sleeping and cannot wake up to see the beauty of life and the blessings that they have. It is also about those who are morally sleeping—those who see evil happening around them, or starting to happen around them, and do nothing about it.

Another line in the prayer is "God . . . gives speech to the mute." Yes, this is about people who are really mute, who cannot speak. Of course, it goes deeper than that. We pray that God will give speech to those who cannot speak out, who need to protest and are afraid to do so.

The prayer tells us that "God loosens the bonds of captives." These words have new meaning in the shadow of the attack on Israel on October 7, 2023. After that terrible attack, I started to say this prayer every night before sleep: "God, help us free the hostages in Gaza, and give strength, hope, and comfort to their families." Captivity can be understood on many levels. Consider how many people are still slaves, all around the world—slaves to wages that cannot provide for their basic needs, or people who are forced to work in terrible ways.

"God supports the fallen, and strengthens those who are bent over." Or, perhaps, when people who are fallen are able to stand up and those who are bent over are able to straighten up, that outer and inner strength is a sign of the Divine Presence in their lives.

The prayer continues with some of the most beautiful metaphors we have in our prayer book: "Even if our mouths were full of song as the sea, and our tongues full of joy in countless waves, and our lips full of praise as wide as the sky's expanse, and were our eyes to shine like sun and moon; if our hands were spread out like heaven's eagles and our feet swift like young deer . . ." If you ask some people where they think religious devotion is located, they will point to their hearts. They are not wrong, but they are not entirely right either. Welcome to your Jewish anatomy lesson.

The passage correctly states that our praise of God comes from our ability to speak and sing: mouths, tongues, and lips. However, it goes farther and deeper than that. It goes to our eyes. What are we prepared to see? It goes to our hands. What are we prepared to do? It even goes to our feet! In 1965, the late Jewish theologian and social activist Rabbi Abraham Joshua Heschel went to march in Selma, Alabama, for civil rights. His daughter, Dr. Susanna Heschel (United States, 1956–) wrote about her father's experience:

> When my father came back from Selma [in 1965], he wrote in his diary that Dr. King said to him it was the greatest day of his life. My father said the march in Selma felt holy to him. It reminded him of walking with Hasidic rebbes in Europe. He

said, 'I felt my legs were praying.' My father wrote, 'For many of us the march from Selma to Montgomery was about protest and prayer. Legs are not lips and walking is not kneeling. And yet our legs uttered songs. Even without words, our march was worship. I felt my legs were praying.'"[15]

When Jews are involved in the world, every part of our bodies becomes a sacred text.

Still, some people might think that all of this imagery is a little over the top. I don't agree. This prayer is in the "awe" mode, what author Anne Lamott (United States, 1954–), who wrote a book called *Help, Thanks, Wow: The Three Essential Prayers*, would have called "Wow." Think of it this way, in the words of Rabbi Dov Singer:

> I look around me. The world is full of stars and the solar system
> And the wonders of nature
> And technology
> And incredible people.
> Wow.
> It is incredible what is happening here.
> What a wondrous world.
> Praise is the movement of amazement,
> Of awe.
> Opening the eyes to the wonder of creation.
> I pray
> And I sing
> I extol
> And I say
> And my mouth is full of song.
> I am flooded
> My emotions overflow.
> Wow.
> You are worthy of praise.[16]

Our *Nishmat Kol Chai* prayer then continues, "Therefore these limbs which You have formed in us, and this spirit and soul that You have breathed into our nostrils, this tongue which You have set in our mouths, they must acknowledge, bless, praise, and glorify Your name, O our Sovereign." It is true that prayer comes from the heart, passes through the mind, and ultimately comes out of the lips. This prayer acknowledges that in Judaism, the whole body—each and every limb—is involved.

Even though I mentioned this in the acknowledgments, it is worth mentioning again because it is so important. The late Conservative scholar and teacher Dr. Neil Gillman once taught that Judaism is the three *H*'s—the *head*, which is the intellect and involved with learning and teaching; the *heart*, which is spirituality and involved with prayer and worship; and finally, the *hand*, which is activism, *tikkun olam* (repairing the world), and *tikkun haam* (repairing our Jewish people).[17] It is human nature to "major" in one *H*, to "minor" in a second *H*, and not be able to get the third *H* together. He explained that it is okay not to be an expert in all three, because the person sitting next to you or behind you or in front of you in synagogue will have the *H* that you lack. That is the meaning of having a strong, whole Jewish community.

What is your task, as a young Jew?

- Find the *H* you *love*. That is your major.
- Find the *H* you *like*. That is your minor.
- Don't worry about that third *H*. Some other person in your community will love it or like it. Your job is to support that person in their *H* major.

We are all pieces in a big jigsaw puzzle. We see ourselves as those pieces. But God sees us all in our entirety—not only as individual puzzle pieces, but as the picture on the box.

QUESTIONS:
1. Do you believe that everything in Creation praises God? If so, when have you felt that? If not, why not?
2. When have you wished that God would just wake up?
3. When do you think people have been spiritually and morally sleeping and they needed to wake up?
4. When do you think people have been mute—unable to speak—and yet found the courage to speak up?
5. Have you ever felt vulnerable? Did you feel that God would or did help you?

6. What parts of your body are most involved in Judaism?
7. What is your major *H*? Your minor *H*? The *H* you cannot do at all?

YISHTABACH (223). The *Yishtabach* prayer is also called *Birkat HaShir*, "the Blessing of Song," because the ability to sing is a blessing. The Chasidic teacher Zev Wolf of Zhitomir (Ukraine, 18th century) noticed that you can pronounce the letters that make up the Hebrew word for "song" (*shin-yod-reish*) as *sh'yar*, meaning "leftover." Apparently, disciples used to fight for the right to eat the leftovers (*sh'yarim*) that were on the plates of the Chasidic rebbes![18]

Let's talk about leftovers—or, rather, what we eat on the days after Thanksgiving. Leftover turkey is Thanksgiving's unavoidable by-product. By lunch on the Friday after Thanksgiving, it will be turkey casserole. That evening, it will become turkey tetrazzini. On Saturday afternoon, it will become turkey sandwiches. On Sunday afternoon, many of us will munch on leftover drumsticks. And so it goes, until that turkey carcass is completely spent. That turkey carcass is very Jewish. Jews know how to use history's "leftovers." This is the great theme of Jewish history—survival and creativity, even and especially in the midst of tragedy and trial. Let's look at a history of Jewish leftovers.

- An ancient rabbi, Chanina ben Dosa (Land of Israel, first century CE), taught that when Abraham sacrificed the ram in place of his son Isaac, not a single part of that ram went to waste (*Pirkei D'Rabbi Eliezer* 31). Part of the carcass became the coat for Elijah the Prophet. The sinews became the strings of David's harp. One horn became the shofar blown at the Revelation of the Torah at Sinai, and the other will be blown when the Messiah comes. All leftovers.
- In the year 586 BCE, the Babylonians destroyed the First Temple. We had to learn how to sing God's song in a strange land. In exile, Jews created the Torah out of leftover stories, laws, and legends (Nehemiah 8). They used the leftovers of faith.

- In the year 70 CE, the Romans destroyed the Second Temple. The Jews were left without a way of making offerings to God. The ancient Rabbis constructed a Judaism around prayer and worship, commandments and covenant. They rebuilt. They used the leftovers of faith.
- In the year 1492, King Ferdinand and Queen Isabella expelled the Jews from Spain. The Spanish Jewish exiles turned inward. They taught that just as they were in exile, the world itself was in exile. They introduced the idea that whenever we do a mitzvah, we bring the world closer to God. They rebuilt, too, using the leftovers of faith.
- In 1648, the Cossacks destroyed the Jewish communities of Ukraine and Poland. A generation later, Jews learned how to find God in the midst of joy and holy intimacy. Out of the darkness of pogroms, organized acts of violence against Jews, Chasidism was born.
- Out of the ashes of the Holocaust, a people destroyed became a people reborn. Today's Jews are the saving remnant of a people reduced to carcasses on the table of history. That is Zionism and that is Israel today.

There might be a pun between *shir* (song) and *sh'yarim* (leftovers). But, let us make sure that the songs that we offer to God are always the newest, the freshest, and the best—and never the leftovers.

QUESTIONS:
1. What are your favorite Jewish songs? Secular songs?
2. What are your favorite dishes made from leftovers?
3. How can you make sure that the songs that you sing to God are the best, and not the "leftovers"?

CHATZI KADDISH (224). "Exalted and hallowed be God's great name! [Amen!]" You won't really see the word "amen" here in this prayer, but that's okay. It's still there, and we should talk about it. Like "hallelujah," it is one of those words that Judaism has given to the world of prayer and worship. If you ever visit a Black church, you might hear the preacher ask the congregation, "Can I get an 'amen'?" The congregation always gives it! In fact, if you visit any church, you will hear "amen" said throughout the worship service, just as you would in any Jewish synagogue.

Let's look at the word "amen," which actually appears in the Torah. In Numbers 5:22, there is a terrible trial by ordeal for a woman who has been accused of adultery (notice that there is no such similar trial for a man). After the trial, the accused woman must say, "Amen! Amen!" The word also appears in Deuteronomy 27:15–19, where there is a list of blessings and curses that the Israelites will utter on Mount Gerizim and Mount Ebal. This list is a cornerstone of the covenant with God:

> Cursed be anyone who makes a sculptured or molten image, abhorred by the Eternal, a craftsman's handiwork, and sets it up in secret.—And all the people shall respond, Amen. Cursed be the one who insults father or mother.—And all the people shall say, Amen. Cursed be the one who moves a neighbor's landmark.—And all the people shall say, Amen. Cursed be the one who misdirects a blind person underway.—And all the people shall say, Amen. Cursed be the one who subverts the rights of the stranger, the fatherless, and the widow.—And all the people shall say, Amen.

The question remains: What does "amen" mean? It comes from the Hebrew root *alef-mem-nun,* and the word *aman,* which can mean "trust," "steadfastness," "belief," and "faith." For example, the medieval philosopher Maimonides began each of his Thirteen Principles of Faith with the phrase *Ani maamin be-*emunah *sh'leimah . . .*, "I believe with perfect *faith. . . .*" When someone says "amen," it is a way of saying, "I agree," "Yup," "Count me in," or "I wish I had said that!" It is even more important as a response to a prayer or blessing that someone else has said.

We have two sources for this. First, the Babylonian Talmud (*B'rachot* 53b) teaches, "Is that to say that one who recites a blessing is preferable to one who answers 'amen'? Wasn't it taught that Rabbi Yosei says: The reward of the one who answers 'amen' is greater than the reward of the one who recites the blessing?" From this we learn that it is even better to say "amen" to another person's prayer than to have said the original prayer in the first place!

Second, the *Shulchan Aruch* (*Orach Chayim* 215:2), the sixteenth-century classic code of Jewish law, teaches, "If a Jew hears someone say part of a blessing, even if they didn't hear the entire blessing from the beginning to the end and they are not bound by that *b'rachah* [blessing], they still must say: 'Amen.'" To say "amen" to someone else's prayer is very powerful. In some cases, it is enough to simply say "amen" instead of the entire prayer!

When the prayer leader says the first words of the *Chatzi Kaddish*—*Yitgadal v'yitkadash sh'meih raba* ("Exalted and hallowed be God's great name")—what do people in the congregation say? "Amen!" They are saying, "Yes, we agree. Yes, we could have said the same thing." But there is more to it than that, because there is more to "amen" than that. Rabbi Sharon Brous (United States, 1973–) wrote a book about her sacred work as a rabbi and called it *The Amen Effect*. In it, she writes:

> Holding hands at the bedside, as we help usher a beloved from this world, giving them permission to go, promising they'll never be forgotten. Witnessing love-skeptics find their way into one another's hearts and celebrating that sometimes, in life's radical unpredictability, we get love. Locking arms in the center of a downtown intersection, lifting our voices in solidarity and song, weeping, and dreaming of a different future. . . . Crying out from the depths of sorrow, and singing together from that same sorrow. It's in these times that . . . I have learned the power of saying "Amen" to one another's grief and joy, sorrow and celebration with our very presence.[19]

So, when we respond with "amen" to another person's prayer, we are not only saying, "I agree with this prayer," or something like that. We are also saying, "I am present here with you and for you." That is a very big deal.

I want to share two more things about the word "amen" and its root, *aman*. This might seem like a grammar lesson, but it is much more meaningful than that. First, the root of *aman* is used for the

Hebrew word for nursing a child, which is an extremely intimate act of love (Numbers 11:12; Ruth 4:16). Therefore, to say "amen" is to say, "I am in a moment of spiritual intimacy with you."

Second, the root of *aman* is also used for the Hebrew word for art, *omanut*. It takes faith to be an artist. You start the creative work, you may have an idea of where you are going, but you can never really be sure where it will end. Your creative journey might take you in a very different direction. Nevertheless, you have faith that it will work out. It might also take a certain amount of artistry to have faith. To have an artistic sensibility is to see how things fit together, how patterns and colors and textures and materials all interweave with each other. Yes, that is art—and that is also faith.

QUESTIONS:
1. Have you ever said "amen" to another person's prayer or heard someone say "amen" to your prayer?
2. What are some things that you really believe in and are steadfast in?
3. When have you been truly present for another person?
4. Have you ever created a piece of art? Did it take faith to do so?

Act One—What We Believe:
Sh'ma Uvirchoteha—Sh'ma and Its Blessings

After the *Bar'chu*, we get a lesson in basic Jewish beliefs: God creates the world (through the symbolism of darkness, which was present before God created the world, and light, God's first creation); God demonstrates love for the Jewish people through Torah; God redeemed the Jewish people from Egypt (page 49).

BAR'CHU (225)

You already know that the *Bar'chu* is the "call to worship" (page 50), but do you think that it is really that easy? It's not. Rabbi Dov Singer wrote:

The entrance into prayer
Doesn't happen in a single moment.
It needs us to step into it
From the outside in, all the way in.
Entering the holy space is a kind of going inside, step by step,
Gateway upon gateway.
Hence our great teachers built the prayer book
Layer by layer:
There are the initial stages of the prayer that bring me inside,
Preparing, inviting,
And there are pinnacle moments of meeting
That take place only once I am already inside, immersed,
    deeply.
After the peak there is a gradual leave-taking.
Inside our soul there exists a similar pattern of entering, of
    being ready.
This existing pattern within us connects to the way our prayer
    is designed.
Being aware of this inner soul movement of "entering in" can
    aid us in our entrance,
Sensing prayer as dynamic rather than linear,
As a living event, full of movement.[20]

QUESTIONS:
1. What goes through your mind as you prepare to pray?
2. What do you think of the image of the prayer book as
   being built layer upon layer? What else do you know that
   is built in that way?
3. What kinds of situations invite you to pray deeply? When
   do you feel most invited?

YOTZEIR (228)

The *Yotzeir* prayer teaches us that God is *yotzeir or uvorei choshech*,
"Creator of light and darkness." While the master symbol of Creation is light, because that was the first thing that God created, it is
important to remember that God created darkness as well.

My late father was a professional photographer. It was my father's
job in life to look through a lens, see how objects and people were

placed in the lens, capture those images, and then spend time in a darkroom waiting for the image to emerge so that people could see it.

My father never liked color photography. He believed that anyone could create a beautiful color photograph. "Go out to rural Pennsylvania during foliage season," he would say. "Any fool with a camera can take a beautiful picture of that!"

My father taught me that all of the great photographers preferred to work in black and white—Alfred Stieglitz, Alfred Eisenstadt, and Diane Arbus among them. He believed that the true art of photography emerged from the subtle interplay of black and white, light and shadows.

My father never realized that he was teaching me one of the most powerful lessons of life: The true art of life comes from the shadows and from the contrasts between life's light and darkness. Even as a young kid, I came to realize that my father's trade taught him to spend countless hours in the darkroom, with only the pale suggestions of light, in order to create. This taught me another of the most powerful lessons of my life: We spend much of our lives in the darkness, and if you labor with love in the darkness, you can create beauty. Yes, this prayer is about light—but you cannot know light without darkness. Put another way, this prayer is about awakening to the beauty of existence.

Pay attention to the most common vowel sound in this prayer: *Yotzeir or uvorei choshech, oseh shalom uvorei et hakol.* Did you hear it? Rabbi Mitchell Chefitz (United States, 1941–) once pointed out to me that it is the sound of "oh." Oh! Oh, now we see the miracles of the morning!

Light is not only something that you see. Light can be a symbol as well—like the light bulb going off over someone's head in a comic book, symbolizing that they have a new and fresh idea. That is the meaning of the last sentence in the prayer: "Shine a new light upon Zion, that we all may swiftly merit its radiance." Jewish tradition uses the word "Zion" as another name for Jerusalem and for the entire Land of Israel, and it lends itself to the word describing the political movement to restore Jewish sovereignty to the Land of Israel,

Zionism. To love Israel and to be committed to Israel is to bring new light to Zion. Why "light"? Because we bring the light of our ideals, our caring, and even some of our own values to the building of the Jewish state. Jewish history requires nothing less.

QUESTIONS:
1. What is dark within you, and how can you bring it some light?
2. What are the sources of light within you?
3. How can you nurture the light within you?
4. How can you help bring a new light to Zion today? What are some organizations that you can support that would help do that?

EL ADON (314)

If you have ever gone to a Jewish summer camp, like the URJ camps, you have experienced creative services. You might have them at your synagogue as well.

In a creative service, you take the traditional prayers, you think about what they mean, and you write your own creative interpretations. The results can be poems, stories, songs, or dances, because there are many ways to address God and to offer prayer.

Guess what? Jews have been doing "creative worship" for at least fifteen hundred years.

Long ago, there were often many different prayers on a single theme. People knew those prayers and recited them—even before there were handwritten and then printed prayer books. Some of those prayers became "standard," and they were incorporated into "traditional" prayer books.

Those interpretations of traditional themes often included liturgical poems called *piyutim*. Sometimes worshipers recited them along with the "regular" prayers; sometimes they substituted them for the regular prayers. Over the years, many composers have set these *piyutim* to music. In recent years in Israel, there has been a widespread effort to learn those melodies and to write new ones. *Piyut* has become a cool musical style in Israel; several years ago, I went into my favorite music store in Israel, and they had an entire section of *piyut* music that young people were listening to.

El Adon is a *piyut* written by early Jewish mystics. It builds on the theme of the creation of light in the morning. All Creation praises God and God's goodness (*tuvo*), knowledge (*daat*), and understanding (*t'vunah*). The Hebrew text refers to God *hamitga-eh al chayot hakodesh*, "exalted above the holy beings," and sitting on a *merkavah*, a "heavenly chariot," with an entire heavenly army praising God.

Those phrases are left untranslated in our prayer book, probably because they seem too rooted in ancient fantasy. But have no doubt— these images and ideas are how many of our ancestors thought the universe worked.

"You call to the sun and it gives forth light; You set the patterns of the moon." This verse of the prayer reminds us of the Creation story: "God made the two great lights: the greater light to govern the day, and the lesser light to dominate the night and the stars" (Genesis 1:16).

But, wait. If both the sun and the moon are called "the two great lights," why is the moon immediately demoted to "the lesser light"? I learned an ancient legend from Dr. Alyssa M. Gray (United States, 1962–) that explains this seeming contradiction. The moon wondered about its role in giving light: "How is it possible for two kings to use one crown?" God then told the moon to become smaller. This outraged the moon; just because it raised the issue of how it and the sun could share "the light business," why should it shrink itself? God responded that while the sun is visible only during the day, the moon would be visible both day and night. "Yes," replied the moon, "but my light during the day is as insignificant as the light of a candle in the afternoon." God realized the error, and tried to make the moon feel better by establishing Rosh Chodesh (the first day of the lunar month) as a holiday.[21]

I love this whimsical legend because it is fundamentally about questioning fairness and justice. The moon thought that God had insulted her; she protested, and God rewarded her protest by giving her the honor of helping determine the calendar of the Jewish people. In my own expansion of this legend (which first appears in the Babylonian Talmud, *Chulin* 60b), I have taught that God rewarded the moon by allowing it to go through phrases—shrinking and renewing itself every month—just as we all go through phases and just as the Jewish people goes through phases.

Finally, just to make *El Adon* more fun, the author played a little game. As in several other prayers (*Ashrei*, for example), every line of the poem/prayer begins with a different letter of the Hebrew alphabet. That may not have been only a creative amusement for the author; it might have also served as a way for worshipers to remember the lines of the prayer.

QUESTIONS:
1. Have you ever encountered a situation that seemed unfair? What was that situation?
2. Did you challenge anyone in authority about the issue?
3. How was it resolved?
4. What "phases" in life do we go through?
5. What "phases" have the Jewish people gone through in its history?

AHAVAH RABBAH (230)

God loves you. There, I've said it—three little words that Jews rarely hear. But we should hear it more often, because it's right here in our prayer book: *Ahavah rabbah ahavtanu, Adonai Eloheinu,* "How deeply You have loved us, Adonai our God." The sign of that love is the Torah and its laws. This prayer is not the only one that talks about how much God loves us. In *Avot V'Imahot*, we chant that God will bring us redemption for the sake of our ancestors *b'ahavah*, "in love." In the *Kiddush*, we chant that God gives us Shabbat *b'ahavah*, "with love." The list goes on!

Rabbi Shai Held puts it this way: "Judaism is about love. The Jewish tradition tells the story of a God of love who creates us in love and enjoins us, in turn, to live lives of love. We are commanded to love God, the neighbor, the stranger—and all of humanity—and we are told that the highest achievement of which we are capable is to live with compassion. This is considered nothing less than walking in God's own ways."[22]

In other words, the story of Judaism is actually a love story—a romance between the Jews and God. How does that love story unfold?

- Part one: God meets people. That is the period of our Patriarchs and Matriarchs. The Jewish people begins when God, for no apparent reason, fell in love with Abraham and Sarah, Isaac and Rebecca, and Jacob, Leah, and Rachel. That is how the mystics put it.
- Part two: God and people "date." Our Patriarchs and Matriarchs all have conversations with God.
- Part three: During the sojourn in Egypt, God and the Jewish people are out of touch.
- Part four: God hears the cries of the beloved—the ancient Israelites—coming from Egypt.
- Part five: God remembers the love for the Patriarchs and Matriarchs.
- Part six: God and the Jewish people get "married" at Sinai. Jewish tradition says that this happened on Shavuot and that the Torah is like a marriage contract between God and the Jews. It is why some communities today observe Shavuot by writing a *ketubah* (marriage contract) between God and the Jewish people.
- Part seven: Then comes the business with the Golden Calf. This was a big disappointment—a bad day in the marriage.
- Part eight: We endure God's (perhaps petulant or even passive-aggressive) silence. For much of the later parts of the Jewish Bible, God says nothing.
- Part nine: We and God reinvent our relationship over and over again. The Temple is destroyed; the Jews rebuild it; the Romans destroy it again; the Jews figure out new ways of demonstrating their love for God.

Part nine is actually very, very long—and we are still in it. The Jewish romance with God, like many loving relationships, has its good days and its bad days. It has its ups and downs. Sometimes,

God and the Jews seem to be angry with one another. Nevertheless, the relationship endures, and you are part of it.

QUESTIONS:
1. Do you feel God's love? When?
2. Do you ever question God's love?
3. When has the Jewish people experienced God's love the most?
4. What would you want your legacy of a relationship with God to look like?

SH'MA (232–33)

What does the *Sh'ma* mean when it says *Adonai Echad*, "Adonai is One"? The possibilities are almost endless—just like God. It could mean that there is only one God. However, in the ancient Middle East, many nations had multiple gods. The Israelites recognized that. After all, as they crossed the Red Sea/Sea of Reeds, they said, "Who is like You, O God, among the gods that are worshiped?" They acknowledged that many gods existed, but believed that ours—*Adonai*—was the best.

Maybe *Adonai Echad* means that the ancient Israelites had many names for God—or, at least, two names. The Israelites in the Southern Kingdom of Judea might have known God as *Adonai*; in the Northern Kingdom of Israel, they knew God as *Elohim*. Therefore, *Adonai Eloheinu* would have meant: "We call *Adonai* what the northerners call *Elohim*. It is all the same God! God is *Echad!*"

Adonai Echad could mean that there were many various local versions of *Adonai*. In the words of the Biblical scholar Jacob L. Wright (United States, 1973–), "At the beginning, there was more than one YHWH [the ancient four-letter name of God, which we now pronounce as *Adonai*]. Inscriptions refer to 'the YHWH of Samaria' as well as 'the YHWH of Jerusalem' as well as versions of YHWH from various other places. Eventually, the authors of Deuteronomy, in an effort to consolidate a nation from competing centers, would declare that all these versions of YHWH are one and the same: 'Hear

O Israel, YHWH (Adonai) is our God, YHWH (Adonai) is one' (Deuteronomy 6:4)."[23]

Of course, *Adonai Echad* could simply mean that *Adonai* is the only god whom Jews should worship. That seems to be the standard interpretation.

Or is the whole thing a misprint? Hold on a minute: Do I really mean to suggest that the *Sh'ma*, the holiest statement in the entire Torah, is a misprint? In ancient Hebrew, the letter *chet* could sometimes look like the letter *hei*. And the letter *dalet* could sometimes look like the letter *vet*. The Torah text was written by scribes, and they passed their work down from generation to generation. It would have been easy to make a mistake that was preserved. If this happened, instead of *alef-chet-dalet* spelling *echad* (one), the word might have been *alef-hei-vet* to spell *ahav* (love). Rabbi David Sperling, PhD (United States, 1940–), teaches, "Therefore, the real translation should be: Hear O Israel, Adonai our God—love Adonai. You shall love Adonai with all your heart."[24]

This makes perfect sense, if you consider that the words "You shall love Adonai your God" follows the *Sh'ma* both in the Torah and in the worship service itself. If you have to have a typo, make it about love.

As you might imagine, a statement like the *Sh'ma* fills Jewish lore. Here are three of the best *Sh'ma* stories I know.

- The patriarch Jacob is lying on his deathbed. He is afraid. Perhaps this covenant—between him and his God, still in its infancy, that he has sought so hard to fulfill in his own way—will die with him. It is an overwhelming fear. And so, he calls his sons to his bedside. "Do you have any doubts about God?" he asks them. "Perhaps lingering in your mind there is the possibility that you will walk away from this covenant. Reassure me that this is not going to happen. Promise me that this covenant will not die with me." They reply: "Hear, O Israel [for that was one of Jacob's names], just as you have no doubts about God, we have no doubts. *Adonai* is our God. God, alone." Upon hearing those words, Jacob said, softly, "*Baruch shem k'vod malchuto l'olam va-ed.* Blessed is God's glorious majesty forever and ever." Then, and only then, could Jacob die in peace.[25]

- Victor Frankl (Austria-Hungary, 1905–97) was one of the most important psychiatrists and thinkers of our time. He lost his entire family at Auschwitz. And that is not all that he lost. When he entered Auschwitz, the guards took everything from him. They stripped him of his clothing and also took the manuscript of the book that he had been writing, which he had hidden in his clothes. His lifework—gone. Frankl received a new set of clothes, the typical striped uniform that had been previously worn by a prisoner who had died. Days after he put on those clothes, Frankl happened to put his hands into one of the pockets. There, he found a small slip of paper with these words written upon it: "*Sh'ma Yisrael, Adonai Eloheinu, Adonai Echad.*" As Victor Frankl read those words, he knew why this message had been left for him to find. That tattered piece of paper contained holy words, which were the remnants of another prisoner's faith. They were all that Frankl had of that prisoner. This gave Frankl hope and a sense of purpose. After Frankl was released from Auschwitz, Victor Frankl wrote a classic of modern thought called *Man's Search for Meaning* in 1946. To find the tattered words of the *Sh'ma* in the pocket of a uniform at Auschwitz is a message: We must find meaning, even in a concentration camp.[26]

- During World War II, many righteous Christians rescued Jewish children and hid them in Christian monasteries. True, they were safe from the Nazis, but they were far from the faith of their people. After the war, a Jewish man went around Europe, looking for those children. He would visit those monasteries and shout, "*Sh'ma Yisrael. . . .*" If he heard a child completing the sentence—". . . *Adonai Eloheinu, Adonai Echad!*"—he knew that he had found a Jewish child and would be able to claim the child as a Jew and bring them back to the Jewish people.

V'AHAVTA (234)

"Inscribe them on the doorposts of your house and on your gates." This line from the *V'ahavta* explains why Jews have a mezuzah on the doorposts of their homes: Each mezuzah contains a piece of parchment with the Torah passages of the *Sh'ma* and *V'ahavta* (Deuteronomy 6:4–9). The desire to put those words into your home and adorn the place where you live with them is understandable. But why not as a framed piece of art on your living room wall or in your bedroom? Why should it be on the doorpost of the house?

Let's think about the symbolism of the doorpost. The doorpost is an interesting place. First, it is where the outside world meets the inside world, the world of the home. It is where the public meets the private. Second, the mezuzah is typically positioned on the right-hand side of the door at eye level, diagonally pointing into the house at a forty-five-degree angle. It is placed at eye level so that the mezuzah and its words remain part of what we see every day. The reason it is placed at a diagonal slant is a bit more mysterious.

Rashi, the great medieval authority who lived in what is today France, thought that the mezuzah should be vertical. His grandson, Rabbeinu Tam (France, circa 1100–1171), thought it should be horizontal. How did they solve their disagreement? They compromised. That is why to this day the mezuzah is hung diagonally. It is a physical reminder about the art of compromise and the ability to hear and process different opinions.

A midrash expands on this idea: "Rabbi Abahu said in the name of Rabbi Yonatan: Rabbi Akiva had a distinguished disciple, whose name was Rabbi Meir. Even though a reptile is ritually pure, Rabbi Meir could cite forty-nine reasons to prove that the reptile was, in fact, ritually pure. Then, he could cite forty-nine reasons why the reptile was, in fact, ritually impure" (*Midrash T'hillim* 12). Rabbi Meir is not just demonstrating his intellect. This is not just a mental exercise, but instead is a way for Jews to figure out how to live Jewishly and humanly in the world. It means being open to other opinions and to compromise.

QUESTIONS:
1. What are some things that you are willing to compromise on?
2. What are some things that you are unwilling to compromise on?
3. What are some examples of compromise in history?

VAYOMER ADONAI (236)

This paragraph of the *Sh'ma* is often called *Parashat Tzitzit*, "the Portion of the Fringes." It says, "Let them attach a cord of blue to the fringe at each corner." You might be asking yourself, "Haven't we already had a whole thing about the tallit at the beginning of the service?" Yes, but we didn't talk about the tzitzit, the ritual fringes at the four edges of the tallit that symbolize the mitzvot. Many traditional Jews not only wear a large tallit when they pray; they also wear a *tallit katan*, a "miniature tallit," as an undergarment.

Tzitzit are intricately woven together in a kind of sacred macrame. As Rabbi Abraham Millgram (United States, 1901–98) taught, "The numerical value of the word *tzitzit* (fringes) is 600. Each of the fringes contains 8 threads and 5 knots, making a total of 613. This number corresponds to the 613 commandments contained in the Torah."[27] There is also significance about where the tzitzit are supposed to go—on the edge of the garment.

Judaism has a thing about edges. Edges are important. Leviticus 19:9–10 reminds us, "When you reap the harvest of your land, you shall not reap all the way to the edges of your field, or gather the gleanings of your harvest. You shall not pick your vineyard bare, or gather the fallen fruit of your vineyard; you shall leave them for the poor and the stranger: I the Eternal am your God." After reading this, you might think that the edges of the field belong to the poor and the stranger, and you would be right. By leaving them to the poor and the stranger, we are in effect saying, "The edges of my field do not belong to me. They belong to the vulnerable. In a very real sense, they belong to God." This explains why we put tzitzit on the edges of a garment—they remind us of those who live at the "fringes," the edges of society. It is as if wearing the tzitzit means that we become the field. Just as the field belongs to God, so to do we belong to God. The tzitzit remind us of this spiritual truth.

I want to make one last comment about the color of one of the strands of the tzitzit. The color is *t'cheilet*, which we translate as "blue." There is just one problem; we don't know what that blue really looked like.

My "thing" is writing with fountain pens, and my favorite ink color is blue. I have so many variations of blue in my collection that it is getting ridiculous. It is as if I have been searching for the "ideal" blue. It has occurred to me that my search for the "perfect" blue is just a modern, secular version of Judaism's frustrated and frustrating search for the "real" and historically accurate shade of the Biblical *t'cheilet*.

Why don't we know what *t'cheilet* really looked like? For one thing, we just don't know what it was made from. *T'cheilet* comes from a dye that is made from the blood of a certain species of snail called *chilazon* that lived in the Mediterranean Sea. But we are no longer sure what the *chilazon* actually was, so its true identity—and the original source of that mysterious dye—is lost. There are other Jewish things that are lost like this, including the pronunciation of the four-letter name of God. This means trying to make *t'cheilet* from the *chilazon* is a nonstarter. Still, *t'cheilet* must have been a beautiful color. After all, princes and nobles wore garments of *t'cheilet* (Ezekiel 23:6), and it was used for the expensive fabrics in the royal palace of Ahasuerus in Shushan (Esther 1:6).

Some say that *t'cheilet* resembled the color of the sea. Except haven't you noticed that different seas have different colors? Long Island Sound, the Caribbean, the Gulf of Mexico—some of those seas are more gray than anything else. Some say that *t'cheilet* was a sky blue. That's a fair answer, but which sky? Early morning? Afternoon? Dusk? Was *t'cheilet* a "real" blue or a purplish blue? Purple is, after all, the color of royalty.

This is why the real color of *t'cheilet* remains a mystery. There is a small (or not so small) measure of delight in knowing that this is one of those impenetrable mysteries of Jewish history. Like the name of Noah's wife, or the accurate pronunciation of the name of God, or the location of the ten tribes—all mysteries, and all part of the way that we imagine ourselves as Jews.

QUESTIONS:
1. What has been your experience with things or places that are "edgy"?
2. What are your favorite versions of the color blue?

G'ULAH (EMET V'YATZIV AND MI CHAMOCHAH) (238–40)

Here is something that not everyone knows: Each "act" of the worship service must end on a high note. No downers allowed. That is precisely how this act and section of the worship service ends—with the ultimate Biblical high note.

This *G'ulah* prayer tells us that the Israelites are now free from Egyptian slavery, the waters of the Sea of Reeds have parted, and the Israelites have walked through those parted waters. When they got to the shores of the sea, they were still basically an enslaved people. By the time they got to the other side, they were already free people.

Beyond a simple story of slaves becoming a free people, the message here is hope. Hope, as in "HaTikvah," the national anthem of the Jewish people. Hope is an important thing. I think that one of the best ways to know someone is not to know their interests or hobbies (which isn't a bad way either) or where they live or grew up or went to school. No, the best way to know someone is to know what their hopes and dreams are.

For the Jews, the hope and dream are to be free from oppression and that all people will someday be free from oppression. The late Senator Robert Kennedy (1925–68) was one of America's most important political leaders. In June 1966, he visited the University of Cape Town, in South Africa. This was during the terrible period of apartheid, which enforced the separation between Black and white South Africans. Senator Kennedy said, "Each time a person stands up for an ideal, or acts to improve the lot of others, or strikes out against injustice, they send forth a tiny ripple of hope. Those ripples build a current which can sweep down the mightiest walls of oppression and resistance."[28]

QUESTIONS:
1. What are things that you do that send forth a ripple of hope?
2. What are things that others have done that have sent forth ripples of hope?
3. What do you think are the main hopes of Judaism?
4. What do you hope for?

Act Two—What We Need: *T'filah* (242)

We are now at "Act Two—What We Need." This section is *T'filah*, or "Prayer." As I observed earlier, this section on a weekday is much longer. The *T'filah*, or *Amidah*, is shorter on Shabbat because we don't ask God for much on Shabbat. It is supposed to be a day of rest, and even God needs rest! More than that: Shabbat is a day upon which we imagine that the world is perfect, and in a perfect world, we would not need to ask for anything.

At this point in the service, people rise and take three steps forward—as if approaching a monarch.

If you have already studied and prayed the evening service, you will have noticed this strange prayer for prayer—this prayer that asks that God "open my lips." Does this mean I can't open my own lips? Apparently, prayer is a three-step process. First, it starts in the soul. Then it moves to the brain. Next it moves to the lips and then to the ears of everyone else who is praying and perhaps even to God.

For some people, those steps are reversed. For some people, prayer starts in the brain, with how you think about things. Then it moves to the soul, with how you feel. And finally, prayer moves to the lips. Some people believe that the soul is the part of us that is most like

God. Therefore, our prayers really start not within ourselves, but within God. "People may arrange their thoughts, but what they say depends on God" (Proverbs 16:1).

QUESTIONS:
1. When you pray, where do you think the prayer comes from, originally?
2. Do you believe that God hears our prayers?

AVOT V'IMAHOT (244)

A few years ago, Allison (not her real name) became a bat mitzvah. A few months later, I ran into her mother, Debbie (not her real name) at the grocery store. Debbie told me, "Rabbi, I have to tell you: I cannot stop watching the video of Allison's ceremony!"

"That's wonderful," I said. "I am so glad that the day has provided such sweet memories for you."

"Yes, it has," she said. "But to be honest with you, the nice memories thing isn't the whole story. Allison has become a full-blown teenager. She has become, frankly, a royal pain. There are times when I get thoroughly fed up with her. There are times when I think that I am totally going to lose it. That's when I put on the video. I watch it, and I remember how good a kid she really is, and I stop being angry. Until the next time." I laughed.

"That's exactly how God operates as well," I said to her. "You think that we Jews are an easy people? We are like Allison on a really bad day—except, we are worse. God gets totally fed up with us, and then it is as if God puts on the video of all of us standing at Sinai together, and God sighs, and says, 'Wow. I remember how they committed themselves to Me on that day.' On a really bad day, God pulls out the video of how Abraham stood up to God when God wanted to destroy the wicked cities of Sodom and Gomorrah. God looks at the video and says, 'Wow. Abraham was willing to argue with Me—to insist that I not destroy the innocent with the wicked. Good going, Abraham. Oh, all right—I will cut his descendants just a little more slack.'" Debbie laughed, and so did I.

I had just explained one of the most elegant and beautiful teachings in all of Judaism to her—*z'chut Avot V'Imahot*, "the merit of the Patriarchs and Matriarchs of the Jewish people." When the Fathers and Mothers of our people did great and noble things, it is as if God deposited those acts in the Bank of Judaism. Over time, as in any good investment account, those acts accrued interest. Today, we are the inheritors of that bank account.

In Leviticus 26:42, God says, "Then will I remember My covenant with Jacob; I will remember also My covenant with Isaac, and also My covenant with Abraham; and I will remember the land." Why does this verse list Jacob, Isaac, and Abraham in reverse order? A midrash offers an answer. "Why are the Patriarchs mentioned in reverse order? To teach that if the deeds of Jacob do not suffice, the deeds of Isaac will suffice. And if the deeds of Isaac will not suffice, the deeds of Abraham will suffice. The merit of each suffices in itself to suspend the punishment of the world" (*Sifra, B'chukotai*, 8:6–8).[29]

That is because God *zocheir chasdei Avot V'Imahot*—"God remembers the love of our Fathers and Mothers." Their loving deeds are our spiritual bank account. And if we should ever run short of deeds of our own, we get to borrow theirs. That is Judaism: We look back to our ancestors; we look forward to our children.

Back in the 1930s, the Labor Party in Israel was struggling over a crucial question: Should it support partitioning the Land of Israel into a Jewish state and an Arab state (which would have been a Palestinian state) or not? If there was a partition, there would be a Jewish state. But on the other hand, if there was a partition, they would have to give up some of the most precious and sacred parts of the Land of Israel. Favoring partition might lead to peace and would enable them to rescue some of the Jews of Europe, who had nowhere else to go. Rejecting partition might mean giving up part of the Land of Israel forever.

Many people in the Labor Party were torn. The great leader David Ben-Gurion (Poland and Israel, 1886–1973), who would become the first prime minister of the State of Israel, was one of them. He turned to his mentor Yitzchak Tabenkin (Belarus and Israel, 1888–1971), who was one of the elder statesmen of the Labor Party, and he asked him how he should vote. Tabenkin said, "Before I give you my advice, I need to consult with two people. Give me twenty-four hours, and I will tell you what I think you should do." The next day, Tabenkin returned to Ben-Gurion and said, "I think you should vote for partition." Ben-Gurion thanked him for his advice, and then he asked, "With whom did you consult before you made your decision?"

Tabenkin said, "I asked my grandfather, who is no longer alive, and I asked my grandchild who is not yet born. I could only make my decision after I thought about what they would say, and about what would be best in their eyes."[30]

To be a Jew is to consult the Jewish past and to think about the Jewish future.

QUESTIONS:
1. What acts of worthy people from the Jewish past should go into our "account"?
2. In what way have your actions contributed to this account?
3. Have any of your actions deleted from this account?
4. What acts of your parents or grandparents would go into that account?

G'VUROT (246)

As we discussed in the evening service, this prayer traditionally speaks of how, at the end of time, God will resurrect the dead and restore their souls to their bodies (see page 66). Maybe you don't believe in that idea. Many Jews would agree with you; they have trouble with that idea as well. Consider the following idea instead:

Recently, I saw a friend whom I had not seen in about ten years. We had simply been out of touch with each other. Upon seeing me, he said, "*Baruch atah, Adonai, m'chayeih hameitim*. Blessed is Adonai, who revives the dead." A more accurate and graphic translation is, "... who resurrects the dead."

I responded to him by saying, "You remind me of God."

"Why?" he asked me.

"Because I think of you often, but I never see you." We both laughed.

Still, there was something real and powerful in his recitation of that blessing to me. The Babylonian Talmud (*B'rachot* 58b) says that this is the blessing that you must say upon greeting a friend after not having seen that friend for more than twelve months. It is a little confusing though. It is not as if that person had died, God forbid. However, when you have not seen a friend for a year or more (which is the traditional length of saying *Kaddish* for someone who has died), it is as if that friendship has "died" and the person has metaphorically "died" for you. At the very least, that friendship had gone into suspended animation. That is why a reunion is like a miniature resurrection—something or someone once given up for dead (or put on hold) now has new life. Usually after I reunite with someone I have not seen in that long a period of time, the friendship is, indeed, resurrected. It has new life, new meaning—and new love. While it might seem that the relationship died, it had not; it was only asleep.

QUESTIONS:

1. Do you agree that the reunion of friends is like a miniature resurrection?

2. Have you had that kind of separation from someone with whom you had been close? If yes, what was the reunion like?

3. Are there other prayers that you can interpret metaphorically instead of literally? How does understanding prayer as metaphor open up possibilities for you?

K'DUSHAH (248–49)

I cannot imagine any discussion of religion, and certainly Judaism, that does not use the term "holiness," or *k'dushah* in Hebrew. What does "holiness" really mean?

The *K'dushah* is best known for the line *Kadosh, kadosh, kadosh, Adonai Tz'vaot, m'lo chol haaretz k'vodo*, "Holy, holy, holy is Adonai Tz'vaot! God's presence fills the whole earth." This verse is the prophet Isaiah's exclamation of wonder after seeing angelic beings that surround the divine throne (Isaiah 6:3).

Some worshipers go up on their toes as they recite this line, as if they were flying toward the divine throne. Yes, we believe that God is everywhere, but most of us believe that we should always try to ascend higher and higher. (Of course, you have to come down again—off your toes, down to earth, and back to reality.)

This was the sense of holiness as understood by the philosopher Rudolph Otto (Germany, 1869–1937). It was that sense of wonder, of transcendence, of God as entirely other, of fear and trembling—like Dorothy and her friends approaching the Wizard of Oz. It is the way that we feel when we go to holy places. It is a deep and profound sense of "wow" (see page 123). It is about awe and wonder, and the human response to all of it is nothing less than reverence, gratitude, and humility.

Now look at the left-hand side of the page—the parallel reading on page 249. The ancient world already knew a lot about that "wow" sense of holiness. Many ancient peoples encountered their gods that way—in elaborate temples, through sacrifices, and so on. Those were the ritual actions and places that reminded worshipers that they are "down here" and God is "up there."

Then Judaism came up with a revolutionary idea: You don't have to go to a holy place to experience holiness or an intimate sense of God's presence. In fact, when the Babylonians destroyed the Temple in Jerusalem in 586 BCE, you could not have gone there anyway. Judaism changed the paradigm: It was no longer that God was "up there"; God could be "down here" as well. It all depended, however, on the kind of "down here" where God might be.

Look at the start of Leviticus 19 on page 249, which is often called the Holiness Code, from *Parashat K'doshim*. If you think that only priests can be holy, the Holiness Code comes to tell you that God intends these words for the "whole community." The community is not holy yet, but they "shall be holy" if only they do certain things.

What follows is a list of laws that govern individual behavior and the behavior of a society that strives for holiness: revering parents, keeping Shabbat, leaving a corner of the field for the poor (see page 140), not stealing, not acting deceitfully, not defrauding each other, paying workers on time, not insulting the deaf or putting stumbling blocks before the blind, not gossiping, not bearing a grudge, and loving your neighbor as yourself. Rabbi Lauren Berkun (United States, 1972–) taught, "As liberal Jews, we are most comfortable with the ethical dimension of holiness (starting in Leviticus 19 with the Holiness Code). Holiness is about the human aspiration to act in 'godly' ways."[31]

In other words, if you want the same effect as going up on your toes and imagining that you are flying toward God, then watch how you behave with other people. That is what makes you holy. When we engage in acts of social justice and of ethical behavior, it not only gives us the same effect as going up on our toes and imagining that we are flying toward God; this way is actually better. As the Israeli thinker Micah Goodman (1974–) wrote, "God resides in the heavens, but human beings can bring God down to earth—not by means of ritual, but by means of moral conduct. The distance between God and people cannot be bridged by means of religious ritual, but it can be bridged by means of social action."[32]

QUESTIONS:
1. What does holiness mean to you?
2. How can a synagogue infuse more holiness into what it does?
3. Can a society infuse holiness into what it does? How?
4. Which of the acts listed on page 249 of *Mishkan T'filah* have you done?

K'DUSHAT HAYOM (YISM'CHU AND V'SHAMRU) (250)

Many contemporary Jews see Shabbat as a nuisance or a burden. They focus on the many things that traditional Jewish law would forbid you to do, like driving or shopping. There is an aspect of Shabbat that is even more important and that we dare not ignore—the aspect of *oneg*, "enjoyment."

Nowadays, the term *Oneg Shabbat* refers to the refreshments that are served after the Shabbat evening service (the morning equivalent is usually called the *Kiddush*). When I was a kid and we went to synagogue on Friday evening for Shabbat services, I loved the *Oneg Shabbat* more than anything else. I can still taste the chocolate brownies that they served. I also liked that my parents were there with their friends, and sometimes my friends would come as well. We stayed so long that we were often the last people to leave the synagogue—right before the custodian locked the doors. That was our community. It was where we felt at home.

The idea of *Oneg Shabbat* has an interesting history. We know that *Oneg Shabbat* was invented by the great modern Hebrew writer Chayim Nachman Bialik (1873–1934), after he moved to the Land of Israel from Russia in the 1920s. In 1927, he founded the *Oneg Shabbat* Society in Tel Aviv, which sponsored communal gatherings on Shabbat afternoons. There were lectures, Torah study (in the broadest sense of the word, which meant that they included all sacred Jewish literature), communal singing, cantorial music, and refreshments. The idea was so successful that *Oneg Shabbat* societies soon sprung up in other parts of the country and even in the Diaspora.

There were other, sadder, uses of the term *Oneg Shabbat*. During the Holocaust, the people in the Warsaw Ghetto who were prepared to fight the German armies would hold secret meetings on Shabbat. Their leader, Emanuel Ringelblum (1900–1944), created an archive called *Oyneg Shabbos* that told the story of their travails. Years after the destruction of the Warsaw Ghetto in 1943, construction workers in Warsaw found those archives buried in a milk can.

Ringelblum and the Jews in Warsaw knew a very precious aspect of Shabbat—that it is a reminder of the Exodus from Egypt. For them, being in the Warsaw Ghetto was like being in Egypt. On Shabbat, they imagined what it would be like to be free.

There is no doubt that the whole notion of *Oneg Shabbat* is larger than a post–Shabbat service dessert. Let's go back to seeing *Oneg Shabbat*—the enjoyment of Shabbat—as a mitzvah. For a moment, don't think about the restrictions of Shabbat. Instead, think of the opportunities of Shabbat—spending time with friends and family, exploring nature, and so on. I learned about this idea from the contemporary teacher of Jewish mysticism Melilah Hellner-Eshed (Israel, 1958–) who shared this passage from the *Zohar*, the major work of Jewish mysticism: "'Calling it [Shabbat] a delight.' What does 'call' mean? Invite her [Shabbat] as you would invite a guest into your home. Invite her to a table set in an appropriate way; invite her to a home prepared with food and drink, more than other days" (*Zohar* II:47a). Give it a try.

QUESTIONS:
1. What are some aspects of Shabbat that could contribute to your own sense of *oneg*?
2. What do you enjoy about Shabbat?
3. Why do you think that the Jews of the Warsaw Ghetto chose to meet on Shabbat?

AVODAH (252)

Avodah doesn't just translate to "worship." *Avodah* also means "work," and this is mainly how it is used in Modern Hebrew. It is true—prayer and worship are work. It is hard work if we want our prayers to go to the heavens. It is equally hard work if we want our prayers to touch something inside us as well. The late Rabbi Harold Schulweis (United States, 1925–2014) taught:

> Prayer is the search for your individual *neshamah* [soul]. It is the search for the *tzelem Elohim* [the image of God] in you. Prayer is self-discovery. And it's hard. In Rabbinic Hebrew prayer is called "*avodah*," which means work. Why is it so hard? Why is it necessary to search out something that is already in you? First, because the *tzelem*, the *neshamah* in you, in the course of living becomes blotched, blurred, blackened, painted over, distorted, foggy to the point of non-recognition. In Hasidic thinking, this kind of work is called "*arbiten auf zich*," to work on yourself. It is deep, sacred, necessary work.[33]

This prayer says, "... grant us a share in Your Torah." Look at the Hebrew: *v'tein chelkeinu b'Toratecha*, "give us our portion in Your Torah." What could "our portion in Your Torah" possibly mean?

The first possibility is that the Torah that we have is not the only Torah. Some Jewish mystics believe this; they believe that God has a divine Torah on high that belongs only to God and that God alone studies. Within that Torah, there is a portion that is ours alone and that is about each one of us.

The second possibility is also mystical. If you ever look at the Torah scroll, you will notice that there are white spaces between the black letters. What do those spaces mean? We don't know. Perhaps they are another, secret alphabet that only God knows, and they form words that only God can understand. Perhaps in that secret alphabet there are coded messages intended for each of us.

The third possibility focuses on the Torah that we have—the Torah portion you will read from at your bet mitzvah ceremony. Imagine that each of us has a portion in the Torah that "has our name on it." There is a portion of the Torah that came from Sinai that was meant for us, meant to embody us, and meant for us to fulfill. The Baal Shem Tov, the founder of Chasidism (Ukraine, 1700–1760) taught that there are approximately six hundred thousand letters in the Torah and approximately six hundred thousand Jews gathered at the foot of Mount Sinai at the giving of the Torah. Every Jew has a corresponding letter in the Torah. The task of a lifetime is the discovery of that letter and of that story that is for us alone.

V'tein chelkeinu b'Toratecha—"give us our portion in Your Torah." Teach us the Torah that we can do with love.

QUESTIONS:
1. Do you believe that prayer is hard work?
2. When have you prayed and "worked on yourself"?
3. What aspects of the human personality do you think could be transformed by prayer?
4. What story in the Torah is "your" story—a story that speaks specifically to you?
5. What mitzvah is "your" mitzvah—a commandment that has been given to you to fulfill?

HODAAH (256)

The *Hodaah* prayer asks us to remember to be thankful for what we have. Because it is Shabbat, there is little that we ask of God. Shabbat is a time that gives us the opportunity to imagine what life would be like without asking for anything, to have all our needs satisfied. We give thanks for all that we have, for all that we might have, for the ability to give thanks. Rabbi Karyn Kedar (United States, 1957–) wrote:

> Sometimes we see the world
> as if it falls short of what we need.
> There is never enough, there is always something missing.
> The foundation is somehow cracked, leaking goodness.
> When we believe this, we are afraid.
> When we are afraid, we behave badly . . .
> God of all things,
> May I choose to live abundantly.
> And then choose again.
> And again.[34]

Living abundantly means to remember that we really do have enough (most of us, anyway). If we do have enough, we should share it with those who are in need.

There is an additional message in this prayer, hiding in the way it is said. In some synagogues, it is customary for each individual to pray much of the *T'filah* section silently, and then the prayer leader recites the *Chazarat HaSha"tz* (the Prayer Leader's Repetition), by returning to the beginning of the section and repeating it out loud. However, there is also a tradition that even if you say the other prayers in *T'filah* silently, you say *Hodaah* aloud. In fact, I have visited very old synagogues that have the words to this prayer on the wall of the synagogue, so that if someone doesn't have a prayer book or if there are no prayer books, worshipers would at least be able to see this prayer and say it aloud.

Why is there such an emphasis on saying this prayer? Because when it comes to gratitude, we should let our ears hear what our lips are saying. In fact, everyone else should hear it as well, because we are all invested in the attitude of gratitude.

SHALOM (258)

This prayer includes the line "Bless us, our Creator, all of us together, through the light of Your Presence." "All of us together" in Hebrew is *kulanu k'echad*, which literally translates to "all of us as one." Or you could translate it as "all of us as 'the One,'" which means "all of us as God."

Did you know that in many prayer books the first thing that a Jew would typically see, right on the title page, are the words "Behold, I accept upon myself the commandment of 'love your fellow as yourself'"? Before you pray to God—before you pray to "the One"—you need to say to yourself, "My first task is to love my fellow person as I love myself." That is how it flows in the Torah—first we love our neighbor, and only afterward do we come to love God.

The first love that is commanded in the Torah is from Leviticus 19:18, which says "Love your fellow as yourself; I am the Eternal." We tend to think of shalom as world peace, or peace among nations. Let's think of it much more narrowly—making peace with another person.

What happens when we make peace with another person? We experience *or panecha*, "the light of God's Presence." (We find this phrase only in the morning service, because that is when you experience *or*, "light.")

I know a synagogue in suburban New York that has *tzedakah* containers in their lobby so people can leave donations. The synagogue chose to adorn those *tzedakah* containers with a quote from the French Jewish philosopher Emanuel Levinas (1906–95): "We come into the world already obligated by the mere gaze of the other. It is a gaze that demands from us a response." Our societal obligations begin at the moment that we see someone else's face. The mere act of living in community constitutes obligation. When we see the face of another person, that becomes the light of God's Presence.

QUESTIONS:
1. What do you think of the idea that even before we pray to God, we take upon ourselves the commandment to love our fellow human being?
2. What is the difference between loving another person and loving God?
3. How can we make sure that we experience the light of God's Presence when we encounter another person?

T'FILAT HALEV (260)

The *T'filat HaLev* prayer—often called *Elohai N'tzor* from its first words—is the most basic statement of Jewish spirituality. Its author was Mar bar Ravina, a Babylonian sage who lived in the fourth century CE and who had a remarkable reputation for saintliness. It was Mar bar Ravina who, at his son's wedding, broke a plate to startle the celebrating guests out of their revelry and bring them back to reality and sobriety (*Ein Yaakov, B'rachot* 5:2); this story was the origin of the custom of breaking the glass at a Jewish wedding.

Let's talk about the practice of humility by focusing on the Hebrew phrase *v'limkal'lai nafshi tidom, v'nafshi ke-afar lakol tih'yeh*, "Before those who slander me, I will hold my tongue; I will practice humility." The first part—"Before those who slander me, I will hold my tongue"—is perhaps the closest thing that Judaism comes to Zen, the art of absolute equanimity and inner peace. (It is interesting that this hope for inner peace follows the prayer for shalom.) In a way, it is almost like what we used to say as children: "Sticks and stones can break my bones, but names can never hurt me." There is just one problem. I don't think this is true. Names and words *can* hurt.

I once observed a disagreement between two people. One of them said to the other, "If you tell lies about me, I will be forced to tell the truth about you." When you think about it, slander is like the image of the person who opens a pillowcase, watches the feathers fly out into the city, and then tries to gather all the feathers together again—

unsuccessfully. That is the way it is with gossip and slander; you can never make sure that the gossip is "collected" from everyone who heard it, just like you cannot get those feathers back into the pillow.

This is especially true with social media; once something is out there, it is out there forever. A folk saying teaches, "A lie can travel halfway around the world while the truth is putting on its shoes." That is one reason why social media is a challenge, especially for teens. You need to be very careful with it. It is like fire: It can keep you warm, or it can burn you.

Sadly, as an instrument of slander, social media is incomparable. It would take a great deal of inner strength and Zen-like resolve not to go DEFCON 3 on someone who has talked trash about you. You *want* to fight back, but this prayer hopes that you won't.

I am almost okay with that, as a policy about myself. However, if people say terrible things about Israel and Jews, I will always speak up. I will not practice "I will hold my tongue" on them, and you shouldn't stay quiet either. Instead, learn Jewish history, especially about the State of Israel and the history of Zionism. There are many haters out there, so don't hold your tongue. It takes intellect and courage to speak out when you see someone hating on your people, so start cultivating those traits now. If a friend is dissing someone, speak up. Even more so, if your friend is saying ugly things about a group, it is incumbent upon you to speak up.

Let's return to the next part of the prayer. It says, *V'nafshi ke-afar lakol tih'yeh,* which is translated as "I will practice humility" but literally means "May my soul be dust for everyone." Does this mean that we are asking for the ability, the forbearance, and the grace to allow ourselves to be treated like a *shmatta,* a mere rag (as our great-grandparents would have said)? Are we asking for the ability to have our souls treated like dust, like dirt? I am not so sure about that.

It is true that *afar* means "dirt," or "dust." *Afar* can also mean "soil," and it could also mean "earth." If we follow that translation, the prayer does not say "make my soul into dirt," but really "make my soul into *soil.*" What does that mean, though? What is this prayer asking for? It is asking that my soul will become the soil that will fertilize other souls. Make my soul count; make my soul useful; make me fertile ground. This prayer, then, is not really about humility. It's about sustenance.

Every soul has the power to sustain others; every human being has the potential to raise students; every human being can help those in need and be of value beyond the limits of the self. That's why "soil" and "dust" and "earth" appear so prominently in the promises that God makes in the Book of Genesis as the Jewish people is just starting out on its journey. For example, God said to Jacob, *V'hayah zaracha kaafar haaretz*, "Your descendants shall be like the dust of the earth" (Genesis 28:14).

A child once asked, "Does this mean that the Jews would get into people's nostrils and make them sneeze?" Sadly, the idea that Jews are the moral irritants of humanity is an interesting theory of antisemitism. The medieval commentator Rashi, in his commentary on Genesis 28:14, had a better interpretation: Just as it is impossible to count the grains of soil, so, too, it will be impossible to count the Jews. In fact, several Torah books and many generations after Genesis, the non-Jewish prophet Balaam would ask, "Who can count the dust of Jacob, number the dust-cloud of Israel?" (Numbers 23:10).

I think the prayer is saying something different, and something powerful. We, the Jews—and we, each of us—can nourish each other, and we can be the nourishment of the world.

QUESTIONS:
1. Has anyone ever said mean things about you? How have you dealt with it?
2. Has anyone ever said mean things about Israel or the Jews in your presence? How have you dealt with it?
3. How can you "nourish" another person?
4. How can the Jewish people "nourish" the soul of the world?
5. How can you "nourish" the soul of the world?

Act Three—What We Learn:
Seder K'riat HaTorah L'Shabbat—
Reading the Torah on Shabbat (362)

"Act Three—What We Learn" is *Seder K'riat HaTorah L'Shabbat*, the Shabbat Torah reading. The Torah is also read on Mondays, Thursdays, festivals, and Rosh Chodesh (the first day of the Jewish month). Why Mondays and Thursday? One explanation is that those were the days when Jews were most likely to go to market, and therefore they could regularly access the Torah being read in a public place. During this section of the service on Shabbat mornings, we also read the haftarah (a section of the historical and prophetic books of the Hebrew Bible).

I want you to notice something. We often refer to this section as "the Torah service," but it is not exactly a service. It is a *seder*. In Hebrew, *seder* means "order," and the Torah reading has a definite order—like the siddur (prayer book); the Pesach seder, the ritual meal for Passover; and a Tu BiSh'vat seder, the ritual meal for Tu BiSh'vat. So *Seder K'riat HaTorah* really isn't a service within a service. It is a *seder*, an ordered telling of a story.

It's like a musical or an opera in which everything is sung. Perhaps you have been in a musical in your school. Everyone knows what a musical is—a play that includes musical numbers, singing, and often dancing. (I have often wondered why, in real life, people just don't break into song in the middle of a conversation. Apparently, life is not like a musical.) Some musicals include so much music and so little speaking that they almost resemble an opera, which is entirely sung. One famous example of this type of musical is *Hamilton*.

This style pretty much defines *Seder K'riat HaTorah*. Just like a musical or opera has a plot, reading the Torah has a plot. What is this plot? What is going on in this part of the service? Probably more than you think, and far more than I once thought.

I had always thought that *Seder K'riat HaTorah* is the reenactment of the giving of the Torah at Mount Sinai. Then, I realized that nowhere in the traditional Hebrew text of the Torah service is there any mention of the moment at Sinai. Nowhere.

The Torah service mentions two places that are actually the same place: *Y'rushalayim* (Jerusalem) and *Tziyon*. *Tziyon* is Mount Zion, which is where the ancient Temple was located. Jewish literature often uses "Zion" as another name for Jerusalem and for the entire Land of Israel. That was how "Zionism" became the word used to describe the movement to restore Jewish sovereignty to the Land of Israel.

Both of these place names are very special. In 586 BCE, King Nebuchadnezzar of Babylon destroyed the Kingdom of Judah. With it, he destroyed Jerusalem and the Temple, and many Jews were then deported to Babylon. That began the period that we call the Babylonian exile. In the last verses of the Hebrew Bible, we read that King Cyrus of Persia conquered Babylon, and he believed that it was his duty to build God a house (that is, a new Temple) in Jerusalem (II Chronicles 36:22–23). He returned the sacred vessels of the Temple to the Jews and invited the Jews in his kingdom to return to Judea. Many of them did.

Their leaders were Ezra and Nehemiah. Ezra was a scribe and a priest. Nehemiah was the official wine taster for the Persian king. (This was a good job, unless one of the king's enemies poisoned the wine, and then it wasn't a good career move at all.) Ezra and Nehemiah created a Judean state under the dominion of the Persian Empire, and they rebuilt the Temple in Jerusalem. On the first day of the seventh month, which was Rosh HaShanah, the people gathered in front of the Temple in Jerusalem (see Nehemiah 8 for more details). On that day, Ezra read the Torah to the Jewish people for the very first time!

Until then, what we now call the Torah had existed only as fragments—laws, stories, genealogies, and pieces of leftover ancient Middle Eastern mythology. Somehow—we really are not sure how this happened—the scribes of the exiled Jewish community in Babylonia put the Torah together. Their Torah was our Torah in its final form, more or less.

Imagine what it must have felt like when Ezra read that Torah, *the* Torah, for the very first time! You can now understand why the Jewish tradition calls Ezra "the second Moses." However, Ezra not only read the Torah; he interpreted it as well. On that day, Ezra gave the first sermon in history. The Jews who were gathered at the Temple were basically blown away by what they experienced. In response to this amazing moment, they made a list of promises to God and to each other. "We have laid upon ourselves obligations [mitzvot]" (Nehemiah 10:33), including that they would respect the sanctity of the Jewish people, support the ancient Temple through offerings and donations, and primarily "not neglect the House of our God" (Nehemiah 10:40).

At that moment it was as if Ezra and Nehemiah "rebooted" the covenant with God, and the Jews who were present that day "rebooted" the covenant with each other.

That was the first time in Jewish history that the Jews, as a people, publicly renewed the covenant with God that their ancestors had made at Mount Sinai—but it was not the last time. This is actually what is happening during *Seder K'riat HaTorah*. We are not recreating the moment that God revealed the Torah at Mount Sinai; instead, we are recreating the moment when the Jews renewed the covenant with each other. In some ways, that is even better.

In any musical or opera, everyone has a role to play. The same is true for *Seder K'riat HaTorah*.

- The rabbi, cantor, or Torah reader plays the role of Ezra.
- The bimah is the ancient bimah in the Temple in Jerusalem.
- The congregation is the crowd of ancient Judeans.

This musical story is about us—the Jews—and how we tell our own stories. Let's get on with the "show." The ark is opened, and everyone stands.

KABBALAT HATORAH

EIN KAMOCHA (362). Back toward the beginning of the service, we recited a prayer that was a question—more like a rhetorical question. Actually, not a question at all—more like an exclamation: *Mi chamochah ba-eilim, Adonai!* "Who is like You, O God, among the gods that are worshiped?" (The Hebrew phrase ends with an exclamation point; the English translation ends with a question mark. So it is simultaneously an exclamation and a question. Maybe it should be: "Who is like You, O God, among the gods that are worshiped?!") Now comes the (not so long) awaited answer: *Ein kamocha va-elohim Adonai, v'ein k'maasecha,* "There is none like You among the gods, Adonai, and there are no deeds like Yours." As we remove the Torah scroll from the ark, we affirm the uniqueness of God and the past, present, and future rule of God. This means, first and foremost, a world where justice and compassion reign, along with the hope of shalom.

QUESTIONS:
1. In the Bible, God is actively involved with people. After the Biblical period, not so much—if at all. Why do you think God becomes less involved with people after the time of the Bible?
2. The prayer says that "Adonai will give strength to our people." How has God given strength to the Jewish people?
3. The prayer ends with "Adonai will bless our people with peace." What are your hopes for peace?

Av HaRachamim (362). The line "Source of mercy: favor Zion with Your goodness; rebuild the walls of Jerusalem" in *Av HaRachamim* comes from Psalm 51:20, in which the author imagines King David praying to God. He is asking for forgiveness for having committed adultery with Batsheva, who was married to Uriah the Hittite. Moreover, he knows that he will not be able to build the Temple in Jerusalem, because his hands were stained with the blood of his enemies.

Rashi, the medieval commentator, states that this line expresses David's wish that his son Solomon might build the Temple. However, if we consider the idea that the Torah service dramatizes the first reading of the Torah under Ezra and Nehemiah, it is easy to see how this psalm fits into that bigger picture. The walls of Jerusalem symbolize the stability and security of the city; moreover, even as Ezra and Nehemiah were bringing the exiled Judeans back into

Jerusalem, the rebuilding of the walls around the city remained a major issue.

Traditionally, *Ein Kamocha* is sung in a major key, with a triumphant tune (as would befit the opening song of any musical). *Av HaRachamim* is different; the tune suddenly shifts into a minor key, sounding almost mournful. The reason for this is that we often find the phrase *Av harachamim*, "Source of mercy," in prayers that refer to Jewish martyrdom—when Jews gave their lives in order to live as Jews.

Tragically, there has been no shortage of examples of Jewish martyrdom. When Jews face martyrdom, they seek safety—perhaps within the secure walls of a secure Jerusalem.

The melody reminds us of the sadness of the past and the hope for the present and future—that Jerusalem will be secure and Jews will be safe.

QUESTIONS:
1. What are times in Jewish history when a minor key melody would have been appropriate?
2. What does it mean to "rebuild the walls of Jerusalem"? Does that mean safety, security—or something else?

KI MITZIYON (364). The *Ki MiTziyon* prayer says, "For from out of Zion will come the Torah, and the word of Adonai from Jerusalem," because that is where our reenactment is taking place—in Zion, in Jerusalem! However, this prayer is not just talking about we who are standing there; we imagine a day when all the nations will come to Jerusalem to worship. This verse comes from Isaiah 2:2–4, which offers us this vision (see page 73).

QUESTIONS:
1. How do you imagine it would be for all the nations to come to Jerusalem to worship?
2. What do you think would be included in God's instruction to the nations of the world?

S'U SH'ARIM (364). "Lift up your heads, O gates! Lift yourselves up, O ancient doors!" These words are from Psalm 24:9–10. It was first recited when King David brought the original Ark of the Covenant into Jerusalem. Again, the focus is on Jerusalem and not on Mount Sinai.

If you look at the footnote in *Mishkan T'filah*, you will see that this text appears only in Reform liturgy and has appeared in Reform liturgy since its origins in Germany in 1819. Its appearance in this, the most recent liturgy of American Reform Judaism, ties us to our Reform roots. The ancient Sages taught that King Solomon said these words at the dedication of the Temple in Jerusalem. Early Reform Judaism liked to imagine that the local synagogue was the equivalent of the ancient Temple. That is why many synagogues are called "temple" and also why this verse is included in the service. This verse serves not only as a nostalgia piece; it has historical significance that is relevant today. It is important for contemporary Reform Jews to remember that we, too, have a unique tradition and that our tradition is important to us. Just as Sephardic Jews, Middle Eastern Jews, Asian Jews, Chasidic Jews, African Jews, Conservative Jews, and Orthodox Jews have their local ethnic and religious traditions that are unique to them, so do Reform Jews.

QUESTIONS:
1. What traditions of your synagogue are most important to you?
2. What traditions would you want to change?

BARUCH SHENATAN (366). Here it comes—the moment we remember the reading of the Torah in ancient Jerusalem. This leads us right into . . .

SH'MA . . . ECHAD ELOHEINU (366). Wait a minute—we already said the *Sh'ma*. Why say it again in this part of the service? In the fifth century CE, the Persians ruled the Land of Israel. This was the second time of Persian rule; they also ruled the Land of Israel in the sixth century BCE, when Ezra and Nehemiah led the return from exile.

The Persian religion was Zoroastrianism. It is one of the world's oldest religions, dating at least as far back as 500 BCE, and there are still between 110,000 and 120,000 Zoroastrians today, mostly living in India, Iran (where they have been persecuted), and North America. Zoroastrianism believes that there are two gods—a good god of light and an evil god of darkness (think of *Star Wars* and the battle between Darth Vader and Luke Skywalker—who, of course, turn out to be father and son. Sorry for the spoiler!). This is possibly related to why the *Sh'ma* is in the Torah service.

First, including the *Sh'ma* here is an act of identification. Rabbi Judith Hauptman suggests that this repetition might have been triggered by the need to publicly repudiate the basic tenets of other religions (such as Zoroastrianism).[35] Therefore, including the *Sh'ma* here was a way of saying, "We are not Zoroastrians."

Second, including the *Sh'ma* was an act of defiance. In Persia, King Bahram II (who ruled 276–93 CE) actively promoted Zoroastrianism as the state religion and made it his official policy to suppress other religions, including Judaism, Christianity, Buddhism, and Hinduism. There is an ancient tradition that a different Persian king, Yazdegerd, banned the recitation of the *Sh'ma* in the morning service (because of its emphasis on monotheism). That is why it is recited at a later time in the service and perhaps explains how it wound up in *Seder K'riat HaTorah*. In other words, during this period Jews had to "erase," or at least hide, their core beliefs. They moved these beliefs away from "prime time," their central place in the worship service, to "late night," a place later in the service. Presumably, the Persian government might have sent spies into the worship service to see whether the Jews were still affirming their one God, and after they got tired and bored, they didn't stick around until the reading of the Torah! This explanation makes sense—especially when you consider that immediately following the *Sh'ma* here, we say, *Echad Eloheinu*, "Our God is One."

Didn't we already say that a moment ago? Yes, but this reaffirmation is just in case you needed an even more passionate reminder! The truth is, there have always been times when Jews have had to keep their religious identity quiet, and those times still exist today.

You might be interested to learn that our worship service contains other instances of responses to Persian culture. For example, we sometimes refer to God as *Melech malchei ham'lachim*, which our prayer book translates as "Majesty of majesties" but literally translates to "the King of kings of kings." This is because the ancient Persians called their ruler the "king of kings." So, when we say that God is "the King of kings of kings," we are saying that God is above all earthly rulers.

QUESTIONS:
1. When, in Jewish history, have Jews needed to hide their identity?
2. Are there times when you have wanted to hide your Jewish identity? When and where?
3. What does it mean for us to say that God is "Majesty of majesties" or "the King of king of kings"?

HAKAFAH and *L'CHA ADONAI* (366–67).

During the *hakafah*, when we carry the Torah into the congregation, we sing these words: *hag'dulah* (greatness), *hag'vurah* (might), *hatiferet* (splendor), *haneitzach* (triumph), *hahod* (majesty). These words are from I Chronicles 29:11 and refer to King David and the Temple, but there is another aspect to them.

These descriptions also happen to be the names of some of the *s'firot*—the aspects of the divine personality that Jewish mysticism imagines flow into the world. This means there is a lot of symbolism in the act of carrying the Torah into the midst of the congregation. The congregation is not only the congregation; they represent the entire Jewish people and, beyond that, the world. In addition, it is not just the Torah we are bringing to the congregation; it is as if we are carrying the message of Judaism into the world. We are the representatives of a tradition that we hope will transform the world—this is the essence of *tikkun olam*, "repairing the world."

There is more! We cannot see God, of course, but we have symbols for God—those things that are so sacred to us that they are in an entirely different category. Consider the way that Jews treat the

Torah scroll. If someone accidentally drops a Torah scroll (or if people witness a Torah scroll falling to the floor), then there must be a fast (or donations to *tzedakah*).

Consider what happened on Kristallnacht—the "night of broken glass" in November 1938, when the Nazis in Germany and Austria destroyed Jewish homes, businesses, and—most horrifically—synagogues. In fact, the Nazis took particular glee in defacing and destroying Torah scrolls. This is because the Nazis not only wanted to destroy Jews and Judaism (as they would have ultimately wanted to destroy Christianity as well); they wanted to drive God out of the world, because the presence of God represents and demands ethical behavior.

Now you know why we carry the Torah scroll into the congregation and why people will often touch the scroll with their prayer books or tallitot and kiss those ritual objects. The Torah scroll being carried into the congregation represents the presence of God in community. After the *hakafah*, we undress the Torah scroll and prepare it for reading.

> QUESTIONS:
> 1. Do you agree that the Torah scroll represents the presence of God?
> 2. What else represents God's presence for you?
> 3. Do you like the custom of people kissing the scroll?

BIRCHOT HATORAH (368)

The blessing we recite before reading the Torah includes the words "who has chosen us from among the peoples, and given us the Torah." The idea that God chose the Jewish people is central to Judaism. It is also one of the most controversial ideas that Judaism ever developed.

Over the past two thousand years, many Jews have struggled with this idea. Some Jewish thinkers even rejected it. They thought that it was too elitist, that it could give Jews exaggerated ideas about themselves, and that it could even lead to bigotry against non-Jews. What did it originally mean to say that God chose us? Does that mean that we are better than other people and groups?

No. Hardly. To be a chosen people means simply this: God chose Abraham to be a moral force in the world—to be a model for what it could mean to strive for justice and righteousness.

At the very beginning of Jewish history, God said, "Abraham is certain to become a great and populous nation, and through him all the nations of the earth shall be blessed! For I have selected him, so that he may teach his children and those who come after him to keep the way of the Eternal, doing what is right and just, so that the Eternal may fulfill for Abraham all that has been promised him" (Genesis 18:18–19).

Centuries later at Mount Sinai, before the Israelites received the Ten Commandments, God said to Moses, "Thus shall you say to the house of Jacob and declare to the children of Israel: 'You have seen what I did to the Egyptians, how I bore you on eagles' wings and brought you to Me. Now then, if you will obey Me faithfully and keep My covenant, you shall be My treasured possession among all the peoples. Indeed, all the earth is Mine, but you shall be to Me a kingdom of priests and a holy nation'" (Exodus 19:3–6).

What does it mean to be "a kingdom of priests"? What did the priests of ancient Israel do? Among other things, like offering sacrifices, the priests also taught the people. So the role of the Jew in the world would be to teach, to offer advice, to be a role model.

What does it mean to be "a holy nation"? To be holy means to be different, to be set aside. That would also be the role of the Jew in the world—to stand apart and to be different.

This is what it means to be chosen—to bring God's message into the world, be a role model, teach others, and make the world better. No more and certainly no less.

In the blessing we recite after the Torah reading, we say, "Blessed are You . . . who has given us a Torah of truth, implanting within us eternal life." Why do we thank God for giving us the Torah two times? Wouldn't one or the other have been sufficient? What—if any—is the difference between them? Additionally, what does "eternal life" mean—that if we study and learn Torah, we will live forever? The *S'fat Emet*, a major Chasidic commentary on the Torah, says that we need both of those phrases because they mean different things. "'A Torah of truth' refers to the Written Torah."[36] This is the Torah that we find in our Torah scrolls. "'Implanting within us eternal life' refers to the Oral Torah."[37] The Oral Torah is all of the commentaries and expansions on the Written Torah that have emerged in the many centuries since the Torah was first given. The *S'fat Emet* continues to teach that "the *Kadosh Baruch Hu* [Holy Blessed One] wants the children of Israel to expand the Written Torah through their deeds."[38] In other words, when we take the Torah that God gave us, the Written Torah, and expand on it through our learning and our actions—well, that is the essence of what "eternal life" means in Judaism.

There is something else about eternal life I want to share. An ancient collection of Middle Eastern tales called *One Thousand and One Nights* describes a ruler, Shahryar, who decided that he wanted to get rid of his wife, Scheherazade. In order to postpone her fate, she tells him a different story over the course of a thousand and one nights. The king is so intrigued by each story that eventually he abandons his plan and stays married to Scheherazade.

The Jews are the Scheherazade of history. It is almost as if we keep telling our stories, to ourselves and to others, over (get ready) 912,500 nights—approximately 2,500 years multiplied by approximately 365 nights a year! This is our "eternal life"; as long as Jews keep telling their stories, we continue to live and thrive as a people—especially because we keep inventing new stories.

Why have the Jews survived as a people? That was the mystery that the late author Walker Percy (United States, 1916–90) encountered. He wrote, "Why does no one find it remarkable that in most world cities today there are Jews but not one single Hittite [an ancient Middle Eastern people] even though the Hittites had a great flourishing civilization while the Jews nearby were a weak and obscure people? When one meets a Jew in New York or New Orleans or Paris or Melbourne, it is remarkable that no one considers the event remarkable. What are they doing here?"[39] The answer to the question "What are they doing here?" is simple—learning and teaching Torah. That is the key to the continuity of the Jewish people. That is why Torah "implants within us eternal life."

The blessing ends with the words *Baruch atah, Adonai, notein haTorah,* "Blessed are You, Adonai, who gives the Torah." Pay attention to the tense of the verb "gives," which is the present tense. Every time we study Torah, every time we have a new insight into Torah, every time we see something different in a story, a verse, a word, even a letter—it is as if God is giving us the Torah once again.

Some stories get old. Some movies get old. Some songs get old. This story never gets old.

QUESTIONS:
1. In what way does God give (present tense) the Torah?
2. In what way did God give (past tense) the Torah?
3. What stories in the Torah are your favorites?

MI SHEBEIRACH for *ALIYAH* (370)

Can the Torah protect us? It seems to be an odd question, but it also seems to be right there in the blessing for the one who has had an *aliyah* (literally, a "going up" to say a blessing over the Torah): "May [they] merit from the Holy One of Blessing protection, rescue from any trouble or distress, and from any illness, minor or serious."

I struggle with this idea. Over the course of my lifetime and career, I have called many people to say a blessing over the Torah. Many of them, thankfully, have lived long lives. I have called people to the Torah who have lived long into their nineties. They died peacefully and happily, surrounded by their families. They lived relatively healthy lives, until their bodies simply gave out from old age.

But others have not. I have called people to the Torah who have lived long lives but whose lives have been filled with suffering. Some have suffered from cancer, or heart disease, or the indignities of Alzheimer's and dementia. Others have lived shorter lives; they suffered through sad illnesses or, in some cases, died in tragic accidents.

I also have a problem when it comes to being saved "from any trouble or distress." I have called many people to the Torah who have had troubled lives. They had trouble with their parents or their children. They had financial setbacks. They lived through the distress of natural disasters that devastated their homes and their lives.

This might strike you as being odd, but here goes: Not everyone believes everything that is in the siddur. But, often, they still say those words. Why would people say words that they don't believe? Are they not being hypocritical?

If people say things to each other that they don't believe, then, yes—they are being hypocritical and false. If someone says things in public and acts another way in private, then, yes—they are being hypocritical.

I am not sure that saying things in a worship service that you don't believe is being hypocritical. It might be that you would hope to believe those words—that you pray that those words of prayer will be real. That is how it is for me. I want coming up to the Torah to protect people from illness and despair. For now, I don't see it. But, someday . . .

> QUESTIONS:
> 1. Do you believe that people who are called to the Torah for an *aliyah* will be protected from illness and trouble?
> 2. Are there other prayers you do not agree with?
> 3. How do you handle saying a prayer that you might not necessarily agree with?

HAGBAHAH UG'LILAH (370)

One of the good things about Judaism is that anyone, of almost any physical capacity, can participate in it. For one thing, most Jewish ritual objects are rather small and light, like a *grager* for Purim, a Haggadah for Pesach, a shofar for the High Holy Days, or a *lulav* and *etrog* for Sukkot. (Of course, if you are going to construct a sukkah, you need some strength for that. It is also good to be handy with tools. Just saying.)

However, this is the part of Judaism that requires physical strength—to be precise, upper-body strength. We finish the Torah reading, and we call upon someone to lift the Torah (*hagbahah*), who then sits down on a chair while someone else makes sure that the parchment is tightly wound and then dresses the Torah (*g'lilah*). This definitely requires upper-body strength, because the Torah scroll is heavy. The *magbiah* (the one who lifts the Torah) must bend their knees, grab the *atzei chayim* (the handles) of the scroll, and lift the Torah over their head, exposing at least three columns of what the Torah readers have read or chanted to the congregation. Jews have always demonstrated spiritual strength; occasionally, it is a good idea to demonstrate physical strength as well.

When my own sons celebrated becoming *b'nei mitzvah*, it was the congregation's custom for the father to do *hagbahah*. That would have been me. To be honest with you, I was not overly confident in my upper-body strength. Not only that, both of my sons celebrated their ceremonies at the end of summer, which means that their Torah portions were from Deuteronomy. Deuteronomy is, as you know, the last book of the Torah, so most of the parchment would have been on one side of the scroll. This lopsidedness makes it even harder to lift the Torah.

The very last thing in the world that I wanted was to embarrass myself in front of my family and community. "Hey, look at the rabbi! He can't lift the Torah!" So, for several weeks before the ceremony, I went into the empty sanctuary, removed the Torah scroll from the ark, rolled it to the required place, and practiced lifting the Torah. I "pumped Torah." I actually improved my upper-body strength. Hey—some people join a gym; I just lift the Torah. It worked for me, and I was grateful to have the ability to do so, since not everybody does.

QUESTIONS:
1. Why do you think it is important to lift the Torah for the congregation to see it?
2. What kinds of strengths exist besides spiritual and physical strengths? Which kind is your specialty?

V'ZOT HATORAH (370). *V'zot HaTorah* proclaims, "This is the Torah that Moses placed before the people, God's word through the hand of Moses." Really? Did Moses write the Torah? Some Jews have always believed that, yet this statement of faith presents some issues. For example, the Torah ends with the announcement of the death of Moses—his obituary. If Moses wrote the Torah, how did he write his own obituary? More questions: Why are there different names of God in the Torah? Different versions of the same stories? Why is there confusion over the name of the place where the Ten Commandments were given—Sinai or Horeb?

For several centuries, scholars have suspected that originally the Torah consisted of several documents written at different times in Biblical history. At a certain point, ancient scribes edited those documents and created the Torah as we know it today. In other words, great, inspired people wrote the Torah over a period of centuries.

This is called the Documentary Hypothesis, developed by two German scholars, Karl Heinrich Graf and Julius Wellhausen, in the 1800s. They gave "names" to those documents:

- J, where God is called *Adonai*, or *YHVH*, or *JHWH* (the *yod* and *vav* in Hebrew appear as *J* and *W* in German).
- E, where God is called *Elohim*.
- D, the Book of Deuteronomy, and other pieces of the Torah.
- P, the priestly documents, including the Book of Leviticus, other ritual laws, a piece of the story of Creation, and probably most of the genealogical lists of families.
- R, the redactor—the final editor.

Professor Richard Friedman (United States, 1946–) has written several books on this topic; in one of them, all of those sources are actually color-coded![40] Other contemporary scholars, like Rabbi Edward Feld (United States, 1943–), see even more sources within those sources.[41] As feminist scholar Professor Ilana Pardes (Israel, 1956–) has written, "The Bible, as biblical scholarship has taught us, is most likely a patchwork of diverse sources brought together."[42] This applies not only written sources; Professor Pardes notes that the Torah also includes sources that probably originated as oral traditions.

How the Torah was written remains a wonderful and compelling detective story and mystery. Yet, when we lift the scroll and sing the words of this prayer, it doesn't matter what the scholars say. Well, perhaps it does matter in a university setting, when teachers and students gather to analyze the original sources of the Torah. But when we enter the sanctuary, it is as if we "forget" that. Instead, we make a statement of faith and of communal memory. We proclaim that it all comes from Moses.

It also does not it matter if these words are said in a Jewish camp, with campers and counselors wearing shorts and T-shirts, or in a suburban synagogue filled with people wearing more formal clothing. During services, no matter where we are, we are one with all Jews everywhere in the world in all times. The synagogue may be only half full, but every Jew who has ever lived and who ever will live is present. For a few moments, when we stand at the open ark, we are no longer in our synagogue. We are back in Jerusalem with Ezra and Nehemiah. We could go back even further, as if we are standing before Sinai with our ancestors, witnessing the majestic and the awesome.

Our Rabbis once said, "We were sitting and discussing the Torah, going from the Torah to the Prophets, and from the Prophets to the Writings, until the words became as radiant as when they were first imparted at Sinai" (Jerusalem Talmud, *Chagigah* 2:1). Or when they were imparted in Jerusalem by Ezra. That is what can happen whenever we encounter and study the words of Torah.

QUESTIONS:
1. Do you believe that the Torah came directly from God to Moses?
2. If not, what is the meaning behind this statement for you?

MI SHEBEIRACH FOR HEALING (371)

Do prayers for healing work? If we expect prayer to work the way that medicine sometimes works, then the answer is no. What does prayer do, then?

The Talmud says that prayer takes away one-sixtieth of an illness (Babylonian Talmud, *Bava M'tzia* 30b)—in which case, let sixty people come and pray for the person who is sick! That may not work, but there is still great wisdom in this teaching. Relationships matter. People who feel that they are supported by others can begin to feel better—with the help, of course, of modern medicine.

What helps people who are sick? Of course, medical professionals, medication, and surgery. It also turns out that personal presence—being physically present with someone who is sick—has its own power.

However, sometimes I think that perhaps there should be special versions of this prayer for different kinds of healing:

- Healing the feeling of sadness after losing a friendship
- Healing the feeling of emptiness after losing a love
- Healing the disappointment because you did not get the part in the play
- Healing the feeling of humiliation because the coach decided to cut you from the team
- Healing the sense of uprootedness because your parents have told you that you must move.

God, the psalms tell us, is the healer of broken hearts (Psalm 147:3). As it turns out, the presence of God can be quite healing. This is my own prayer for those who need healing:

> *Adonai*, our God, hear our many voices.
> Hear the voices of those who struggle with chronic illness.
> Give them the strength to stand up to the daily pains and
>   discomforts,
> to endure the small and large indignities of living and
>   coping.
> Hear the voices of those whose illnesses are severe and
>   life-threatening.
> Give them the courage to stand up to the monologue of
>   despair.
> When all seems in vain, give them the power of hope.
> Hear the voices of those who are facing their final jour-
>   neys.
> Give them the fortitude to face their fears, and the dark-
>   ness of the unknown,
> even as they walk through the valley of the shadow of
>   death,
> and while there is still the spark of life,

the strength to ennoble and sanctify every day.
Hear the voices of all those in fear, who live with anxiety,
who struggle with demons, both inward and outward.
Give them the light of Your presence,
that they may lift themselves out of the pit of darkness.

Hear the voices of family members—in their own fears,
    born of their love.
Give them the presence to be present for their loved ones,
    to do what they can, to be what they must be.
Hear the voices of physicians and first responders,
    caregivers and medical researchers,
all those who are the artists of healing,
whose knowledge, skill, and compassion are the
    emanations of Your spirit in the world.

QUESTIONS:
1. Have you prayed for someone to heal from an illness? Do
   you think your prayers helped?
2. Some people say that there is a difference between being
   healed and being cured. Do you agree? What might that
   difference be?
3. What are some things besides physical illness that people
   can be healed from?

BIRKAT HAGOMEIL (371)

Over forty years ago, I had a series of surgeries on my eye to repair
a muscle problem. When I was in the hospital, my friends and family prayed for my healing. When I returned to my synagogue community, I was invited to say this prayer—*Birkat HaGomeil*. Or, in
Yiddish, I was invited to *bensch Gomeil*, to say the *Gomeil* prayer of
thanksgiving.

I did this because I had been healed, and it is the custom for one
who is healed to say this prayer. As it turns out, however, this prayer
is not only for someone who has been healed. It is far bigger than
that—so much bigger that it brings us back into American history.

You may have heard American Jews claim that Thanksgiving is
modeled after Sukkot. Sukkot celebrates the harvest, as does Thanks-

giving. Sukkot is about gratitude, as is Thanksgiving. Sukkot carries within it the theme of hospitality, as does Thanksgiving. Therefore, some American Jews have come to believe that Thanksgiving was the American Pilgrim's Sukkot.

Except, it wasn't. First, the Pilgrims did not believe in fixed holidays. In the words of Jonathan Sarna (United States, 1955–), professor of American Jewish history at Brandeis University, "If it was a good season, they would announce a thanksgiving, but it was not Sukkot."[43]

Second, there was a clear, inescapable element of Sukkot that the Pilgrims did not to do—build a sukkah, nor do we have any record of them shaking *lulav* and *etrog*. Finally, the Pilgrims were Christians—Protestants, to be exact. Protestants found great meaning in the Hebrew Bible; however, even as those who sought inspiration in the Bible, they would not have observed any Jewish rituals and certainly would not have observed any Jewish holidays. Not Rosh HaShanah. Not Yom Kippur. Not Shabbat; their main day of worship was Sunday, which they called "the Lord's Day," because their religion taught that Jesus was resurrected from the dead on Easter Sunday. They also would not have observed Sukkot. We can pretty much reject the idea that Thanksgiving was the "American Sukkot."

There is, however, a Jewish connection to Thanksgiving that is far better than the faulty Sukkot linkage. Let us ask ourselves a very simple question: How did the Pilgrims even know that they should give thanks? Was it simply that basic human instinct to express gratitude? I don't think so.

William Bradford—the Pilgrim leader who would later become the governor of Plymouth Colony—had a copy of the Bible on the *Mayflower*. His edition of the Bible had handwritten notes in it, which a Puritan scholar, Henry Ainsworth, had scribbled in the margins. This included a list Ainsworth had written of events that require a prayer of thanksgiving to God. Listed were "the sick, when they are healed; prisoners, when they are released; those that go down to sea, when they are come up to land; and wandering people, when they are come to the inhabited land."[44]

Ainsworth quotes a surprising figure as his authority for this list. Right there, in the margin of his prayer book, we find the following name: Maimonides. Yes, *that* Maimonides—the great Jewish medieval philosopher, physician, statesman, and codifier of Jewish law.

Ainsworth had copied an English version of Maimonides's comprehensive legal code, the *Mishneh Torah*—specifically, the laws of giving thanks. According to Maimonides, who was following a Talmudic tradition (*B'rachot* 54b), "the sick, when they are healed" must recite *Birkat HaGomeil*—as I did; as I have heard many people do.[45] You are sick; you get better—you want to give thanks.

The list includes "prisoners, when they are released." From the 1960s through the 1980s, there were many Russian Jews who were imprisoned in Siberia, for the "crime" of teaching or learning Torah. When they got out of prison, they came to synagogue and recited *Birkat HaGomeil*.

Finally, the list says that the prayer must be recited by "those that go down to sea, when they are come up to land; and wandering people, when they are come to the inhabited land." The Pilgrims, of course, went from sea to land and were a wandering people; that is why they gave thanks. And it was all the "fault" of Maimonides!

I think it is safe to say that the holiday of Thanksgiving is not only quintessentially American, but because of Maimonides's teaching, it *is* quintessentially Jewish.

QUESTIONS:
1. Do you think Thanksgiving is quintessentially Jewish? Why or why not?
2. What are some other occasions that might call for a prayer of thanksgiving?

HAFTARAH (372)

This section of the service is not the "half Torah," despite the fact that many people pronounce it "*haf-TOH-rah*" rather than "*hahf-ta-RAH*." It is not as if the haftarah is only half as important as the Torah reading, though sometimes we treat it that way. In fact, some synagogues have done away with the haftarah altogether.

Every Torah reading has an accompanying haftarah reading. *Haftarah* means "conclusion," because at an earlier point in Jewish history, the worship service actually ended with that reading.

Some scholars believe that the reading of the haftarah originated at a time when non-Jewish authorities outlawed the reading of the Torah, and the Jews read the haftarah sections instead. In fact, in some synagogues, young people who become bet mitzvah read very little Torah and the entire haftarah portion.

The haftarah portions come from *N'vi-im*, "Prophets," the plural of the most important Hebrew term for "prophet," *navi*. These books constitute the second part of the Hebrew Bible, or *Tanach*. The haftarah is either read or chanted directly from a *Tanach* or from a booklet or photocopy.

The ancient Sages chose the haftarah passages because their themes reminded them of the words or stories in the Torah text. Sometimes, they chose haftarot (plural of haftarah) with special themes in honor of a festival or an upcoming festival.

Not all books in the prophetic section of the Hebrew Bible consist of words of prophecy. Several are historical. For example:

- The Book of Joshua tells the story of the conquest and settlement of Israel.
- The Book of Judges speaks of the period of early tribal rulers who rose to power, usually for the purpose of uniting the tribes in war against their enemies—until things fell into chaos again. Some of these leaders were weak. Others are famous: Deborah, the great prophetess and military leader, and Samson, the Biblical strong man.
- The Books of Samuel start with Samuel, the last judge, and then move to the creation of the Israelite monarchy under the first kings, Saul and David (approximately 1000 BCE).
- The Books of Kings tell of the death of King David, the rise of King Solomon, how the Israelite kingdom split into the Northern Kingdom of Israel and the Southern Kingdom of Judah (approximately 900 BCE), and how both kingdoms were ultimately destroyed—Israel by the Assyrians, and

Judah by the Babylonians—and the populations sent into exile.

Then, there are the books that record the words of the prophets, those spokespeople for God whose words fired the Jewish conscience. Their names are immortal: Isaiah, Jeremiah, Ezekiel, Amos, Hosea, Micah, among others. It is a shame that some people treat this section of the service as optional. There are many great lessons in these passages.

The Books of Joshua, Judges, Samuel, and Kings show the people of Israel as being preoccupied with the same sorts of things that would have concerned any ancient (or, for that matter, modern) nation: issues of survival and security. They portray the rulers of ancient Israel as being no better—and certainly no worse—than other ancient or even contemporary rulers. True, they are powerful and heroic, but they are also weak, vulnerable, egotistical, and flawed. The historical material is noteworthy because it portrays the people of Israel as being *potentially* holy—potentially, but not quite yet holy.

On top of that, the prophets were among the greatest and most profound religious teachers in world history. They had keen moral vision, and their words were among the most poetic that any culture have produced. This section of the service contains those stories and those teachings. They are crucial.

BLESSING BEFORE THE HAFTARAH (372). The blessing before the haftarah reading says, "Praise to You, Adonai our God, Sovereign of the universe, who has chosen faithful prophets to speak words of truth . . . and for prophets of truth and righteousness." The late Christian author Frederick Buechner (United States, 1926–2022) commented, "There is no evidence to suggest that anyone ever asked a prophet home for supper more than once."[46] This is because the prophets were tough. They had no patience for injustice, apathy, or hypocrisy. No one escaped their criticisms—not kings, not priests, and not the common people. They taught:

- God commands the Jews to behave decently toward one another. In fact, God cares more about basic ethics and decency than about ritual behavior.
- God chose the Jews not for special privileges, but for special duties to humanity.
- As bad as the Jews sometimes were, there was always the possibility that they would improve their behavior.
- As bad as things might be now, it will not always be that way. Someday, there will be universal justice and peace. Human history is moving forward toward an ultimate conclusion that some call the messianic age—a time of universal peace and prosperity for the Jewish people and for all the people of the world.

The prophets could get very angry with the people that they criticized. They could even get somewhat snarky. God commanded the prophet Jeremiah to stand at the entrance to the ancient Temple in Jerusalem:

> The word that came to Jeremiah from the Eternal: Stand at the gate of the House of the Eternal, and there proclaim this word: Hear the word of the Eternal, all you of Judah who enter these gates to worship the Eternal! Thus said the Eternal of Hosts, the God of Israel: Mend your ways and your actions, and I will let you dwell in this place. Don't put your trust in illusions and say, "The Temple of the Eternal, the Temple of the Eternal, the Temple of the Eternal are these [buildings]." No, if you really mend your ways and your actions; if you execute justice between one party and another; if you do not oppress the stranger, the orphan, and the widow; if you do not shed the blood of the innocent in this place; if you do not follow other gods, to your own hurt—then only will I let you dwell in this place, in the land that I gave to your ancestors for all time. (Jeremiah 7:1–7)

Jeremiah criticized those who thought that it was enough simply to go to the ancient Temple (he might say the same thing about the modern synagogue). Yes, going to the Temple, with all its rituals, was important, but not without ethical and social action—taking care of the most vulnerable in society, safeguarding life, rejecting idolatry.

The prophets combined words of truth with words of righteousness.

> QUESTIONS:
> 1. Some people think that the prophetic tradition has never really disappeared. Do you agree?
> 2. Which historical and contemporary figures remind you of the ancient prophets?

HAFTARAH READING. There was a character on NBC's *Saturday Night Live* called "Debbie Downer," played by the comedian Rachel Dratch (who grew up in a Reform synagogue in the Boston area). No matter the situation, she could always find something negative and pessimistic to say. Judaism, however, does not believe in being "Debbie Downer"—quite the opposite. Even though some Jewish texts are "downers," we cannot finish reading them on a down note. For example, every "act" of the prayer book ends on an up note:

- *Act One—What We Believe* ends with the triumphant crossing of the Sea of Reeds.
- *Act Two—What We Need* ends with a prayer for shalom.
- *Act Three—What We Learn* ensures that no Torah or haftarah reading can end on a negative or pessimistic note, but instead must end with *nechemta*, "words of consolation and comfort."
- *Act Four—What We Hope* ends with *Kaddish*, the prayer that God's kingdom will be realized on earth and that we will achieve all of our sacred ideals.

In this act, Act Three—What We Learn, we see that the prophets could be pretty tough on kings, priests, and people alike, and as we have said, their words are *emet vatzedek*, "truth and justice." However, even though the prophets criticized their contemporaries, they knew that there was always the possibility that the Jews would improve their behavior. As bad as things might be now, it will not always be that way. Someday, there will be universal justice and peace. That is why no haftarah reading can end on a "downer"—they all must end with words of comfort.

QUESTIONS:
1. What brings you comfort when you are feeling sad or upset?
2. What brings you hope when things feel hopeless?

BLESSING AFTER THE HAFTARAH (372). Judaism is filled with "trios"—groups of three. There are the three Patriarchs—Abraham, Isaac, and Jacob. There are three parts of the *Tanakh* (the Hebrew Bible)—Torah, *N'vi-im* (Prophets), and *K'tuvim* (Writings). And don't forget about the three elements of religious life—head, heart, and hand.

The ancient Sages, as well, imagined three essential elements of being Jewish. For example, "Shimon the Just was among the survivors of the Great Assembly. He used to say, 'The world stands on three things: on Torah study, on service [of God], and on kind deeds'" (*Pirkei Avot* 1:2).

The blessing after the haftarah also has its "trio": "For the Torah, for the privilege of worship, for the prophets." This shows how important the prophets are. As Rabbi Abraham Joshua Heschel said, "To us a single act of injustice—cheating in business, exploitation of the poor—is slight; to the prophets, a disaster. To us injustice is injurious to the welfare of the people; to the prophets it is a deathblow to existence; to us, an episode; to them, a catastrophe, a threat to the world."[47] The prophets took the world very seriously. What some people thought was a minor irritation, they thought was a big deal. They were right.

QUESTIONS:
1. Do you agree with Rabbi Heschel's statement?
2. Do you think that all those actions are consequential?
3. What can you do to help fulfill his words?

HACHZARAT HA TORAH (374)

"It is a tree of life for those who hold fast to it, and all its supporters are happy. Its ways are ways of pleasantness, and all its paths are peace. Return us to You, Adonai, and we will return; renew our days as of old." What is the "tree of life" mentioned in this prayer?

That's easy to answer. It is the Torah itself. In fact, that is also what we call the handles on the scroll—the *atzei chayim*, "trees of life."

However, something else is going on here. Let's go all the way back to the beginning when we first encountered the "tree of life"—back to the story of the Garden of Eden, near the very beginning of the Book of Genesis. The Torah teaches:

> To the east, God Eternal planted a garden in Eden, setting the man there whom [God] had formed. Then, out of the soil, God Eternal grew trees alluring to the eye and good for fruit; and in the middle of the garden the Tree of Life and the Tree of All Knowledge. . . . So God Eternal took the man, placing him in the Garden of Eden to work it and keep it. God Eternal then commanded the man, saying, "You may eat all you like of every tree in the garden but of the Tree of Knowledge you may not eat, for the moment you eat of it you shall be doomed to die." (Genesis 2:8–9, 2:15–17)

The Garden of Eden represents an ideal of perfection that existed at the beginning of human history. It contained two trees—the Tree of Life, from which Adam (and later, Eve) could eat, and the Tree of Knowledge, from which they could not eat.

Let's figure out how this applies to the Torah service. At the beginning of the Torah service, we were in Jerusalem with Ezra and Nehemiah, reading the Torah to the people for the first time. The Babylonians had sent the Jewish people into exile, and then they came home again. In other words, Jerusalem symbolizes coming home to a city that represents our ideals.

Now, at the end of the Torah service, we are back in the Garden of Eden, which represents our original home—our ideal home. We see the Tree of Life there.

So, the Torah service begins in Jerusalem—in a place that will *become* ideal. The Torah service ends at the Garden of Eden—in a place that was ideal. However, there is more to this story.

Once upon a time, the Babylonians exiled the Jews from Jerusalem. Once upon a time, God exiled Adam and Eve from the Garden of Eden: "So the Eternal God drove them out of the Garden of

Eden to work the soil from which they had been taken, expelling the humans and stationing cherubim to the east of Eden, and the flaming blade of a flashing sword to guard the way to the Tree of Life" (Genesis 3:23–24).

The Jews came back to Jerusalem, but humanity has not returned to the Garden of Eden.

We want to return! We even say, "Bring us back!" in this part of the service: "Return us to You, Adonai." This idea is strengthened when you consider that the prophet Ezekiel imagined that when the Jews return to the Land of Israel, it will be like the Garden of Eden: "Thus said the Sovereign God: . . . 'I will people your settlements, and the ruined places shall be rebuilt; and the desolate land, after lying waste in the sight of every passerby, shall again be tilled. And it shall be said, *That land, once desolate, has become like the garden of Eden; and the cities, once ruined, desolate, and ravaged, are now populated and fortified*" (Ezekiel 36:33–35).

We all want to go back to the imagined sweetness of the old days. That is why we say, in the final words of the Torah service, *chadeish yameinu k'kedem*, "renew our days as of old." That feeling is called nostalgia.

Oh, if only we could take a time machine, and go back! Make us feel like we are back in Eden—back in the childhood of humanity. We want that sense of newness again. It is like getting a new car. It smells new. We love that smell! We want that smell to stay with us all the time. (In fact, there are sprays that will give you that perpetual new car smell whenever you want it.)

Maybe you feel that way when you take a new computer out of its box or with that new piece of clothing. Nothing feels as good as taking it out of the package or off the hanger for the first time. No matter how many times it goes to the laundry or to the dry cleaners, it never feels brand-new again. (Some people say the same thing about love. They always want to feel the love again—as if for the first time.)

Even as I write these words, I have been going through boxes of old family photographs and arranging to transfer them to a thumb drive, and ultimately, for permanent storage in the cloud. What an experience this has been for me! I actually did something very difficult. I tried to put the photographs in reverse chronological order. First, pictures of me with my grandchildren, then with my sons and their wives, then at various moments in my career. Next are pictures of me with my friends in college and then in elementary school. (Why don't I have many photos from middle school and high school? I guess there are certain things you just want to forget.) After that are the pictures with my younger brother, then us with our late grandparents, and then me as a toddler. Next in line are my late parents, as a young couple, on their wedding day—almost seventy-five years ago, and before that my late mother, as a young woman (she was beautiful), and my late father, at the plane that he flew in during World War II, when he was part of "the greatest generation." Even before that are pictures of my grandfather as a young man before he left Vilna (now Vilnius), in Eastern Europe. Finally, there are pictures of my great-grandparents.

This nostalgic look back into our own history is what the end of the Torah service is saying: Bring us back to Eden. Bring us back to what it was like when everything was all new and fresh and we had all of history before us.

QUESTIONS:
1. In what way is the Torah a tree of life?
2. What moments in your life do you wish that you could revisit?
3. What was sweet about those moments? What was not so sweet?

PRAYERS OF OUR COMMUNITY

PRAYER FOR OUR CONGREGATION (376). The Sages who lived in the time after the destruction of the Temple in Jerusalem longed for its rebuilding. They believed this would occur in messianic times, and they eagerly awaited those times. Therefore, we might be surprised to read the following: "One may not interrupt schoolchildren from studying Torah, even in order to build the Temple" (Babylonian Talmud, *Shabbat* 119b).

That was how important study was to our ancient Rabbis and still is today, and this prayer reminds us of that. That is why the prayer begins "Source of all being, may the children of this community learn these passions from us: love of Torah, devotion in prayer, and support of the needy."

To be honest, Biblical kings were . . . meh. King David was generally good, though he had some major flaws like adultery and murder. King Solomon was good—a little grandiose and egotistical, but he did build the Temple. King Hezekiah was a good king. Some of the others, though, were pretty bad. Consider King Ahaz of ancient Judah. He was a bad king. In fact, the Bible tells us that he made a pilgrimage to the ancient Syrian capital of Damascus, and when he returned to Judah, he worshiped the ancient Syrian gods (II Kings 16:10–13). The name "Ahaz" means "to grab," and that is precisely what Ahaz did. The Talmud recounts, "Why is he called 'the grabber'? For he grabbed synagogues and houses of study, to close them down. Ahaz thought: 'If there are no children who will learn Torah, there will be no adults who will learn Torah. If there are no adults, there are no sages. If there are no sages, there are no prophets. If there are no prophets, there is no Holy Spirit. If there is no Holy Spirit, there are no synagogues and no houses of study. If it were thinkable, the Holy One, would not let the Divine Presence rest over Israel'" (Jerusalem Talmud, *Sanhedrin* 10:2). In reality, no synagogues or houses of study existed in King Ahaz's day, but this text shows how the ancient Sages imagined King Ahaz behaved. They claimed that King Ahaz wanted to drive God out of the Land of Israel by making sure that there would be no children who would learn, which would set the whole nasty cycle in motion.

Our response to King Ahaz's desire is pretty straightforward: Nope. We want people of all ages to learn, and we want God in our midst. To King Ahaz, we say, "Nope. You lose! We will teach our Jewish passion to our children!"

QUESTIONS:
1. Does the Jewish community do enough to support Jewish education and learning?

2. How could it do better?
3. What can you do to support Jewish education and learning?

PRAYER FOR OUR COUNTRY (376). There is a scene in the musical *Fiddler on the Roof* in which some of the Jewish villagers ask the rabbi, "Is there a prayer for the czar [the Russian ruler, who was usually cruel to his Jewish subjects]?" The rabbi thought for a minute and then answered, "May God bless and keep the czar—far away from us!"[48]

In fact, there is a blessing for the czar—or to be more precise, for the governments and the countries in which Jews live. This tradition started with the prophet Jeremiah, who counseled the Jews exiled in Babylon to "seek the peace of the city in which you are in exile and pray to the Eternal in its behalf, for in its prosperity you shall find prosperity" (Jeremiah 29:7). In other words, he was saying, "Get comfortable. We might be here for a while. We might as well make the best of it." Let the record note, however, that Jeremiah speaks only of praying for the city; he says nothing about praying for the city's leaders.

A few centuries after that, the Rabbis taught, "Pray for the welfare of the government, because if not for people's fear of it, we would have swallowed each other alive" (*Pirkei Avot* 3:2). The Rabbis knew that left to their own devices, people would destroy each other, and only a strong government could ward off the forces of societal chaos.

Throughout my life, I have prayed the prayer for the government in many interesting places and times. I have prayed it in in America—for various presidents, some of whom I liked and others whom I did not like. I prayed this prayer in a synagogue in Moscow, at the height of the Soviet oppression of Russian Jews. I heard the worship leaders intoning a prayer asking God "to protect the Soviet Union, the Communist Party, and the Supreme Soviet." I could not tell if there was any irony in their words. Certainly, they knew that there were more than a few KGB (the Soviet secret police) agents sitting in the synagogue among the worshipers. I also said this prayer in a synagogue in London, England. The cantor offered a prayer for "our sovereign Lady, Queen Elizabeth [who has since died] and all the Royal Family, her advisers, and her counselors."

When Jews pray this prayer, we are saying that we hope that those in power and authority use their power and authority wisely. There is no doubt that of all the countries in which Jews have lived, few countries have been as kind and as hospitable to the Jews as the United States of America and Canada. There is nothing wrong—and everything right—with expressing our gratitude for that. That is called *hakarat hatov*, "remembering the good," and it is a mitzvah to do so.

At the same time, patriotism and love of country mean that we want our countries to live up to the highest of values. For Jews, we locate those values not only in the history of the countries in which we live, but also in the words of our tradition. That is why the prayer for our country in *Mishkan T'filah* starts with words of the prophet Isaiah. These words constitute the haftarah reading for Yom Kippur morning. They contain an implicit critique of those countries in which we live—"Why can't our country live up to prophetic ideals?"— and the hope that they will do so. Wherever we live, we want our country to uphold the sacred ideals that the ancient Jewish prophets first brought into the world.

QUESTIONS:
1. What Jewish ideals do you want your country to uphold?
2. What about your country fills you with pride?
3. What would you want to change about your country?
4. What are some ways in which your country has been good to its Jews? What are some ways that it needs improvement?

PRAYER FOR THE STATE OF ISRAEL (377). "Bless the State of Israel which marks the dawning of hope for all who seek peace" (*reishit tz'michat g'ulateinu*). "Seeking peace" is a great and worthy undertaking, but *reishit tz'michat g'ulateinu* means something else. This Hebrew phrase translates literally as "the beginning of the flowering of our redemption." *Tefilat Ha-Adam: An Israeli Reform Siddur for*

Shabbat translates this phrase as "the dawning of our redemption."[49]

What does it mean for the State of Israel to symbolize the redemption of the Jewish people? On one level, it means that the process that started with the redemption from Egypt has come to a full climax with the redemption of the Jewish people from homelessness and powerlessness—the restoration of Jewish sovereignty in the Land of Israel. However, this doesn't answer the question: What does redemption really mean?

Let me tell you the story of two Jews from Ukraine. The first is Shaul Tchernichovsky (1875–1943), one of the greatest poets in modern Jewish literature. Rare is the city in Israel that lacks a street bearing his name. He was born in Russia, and when he was fourteen, his parents sent him to study in Odessa. He became proficient in German, French, English, Greek, and Latin. He knew Shakespeare, Longfellow, and the Greek classics. Eventually, he immigrated to the Land of Israel. However, when he lived in Odessa, Tchernichovsky joined the young Zionist movement, and there he wrote one of his most famous poems—"Tzach'ki," "Laugh." The late singer-songwriter Debbie Friedman (United States, 1951–2011) adapted and sang it with these words:

> Laugh at all my dreams, my dearest;
> Laugh and I repeat anew
> That I still believe in man
> As I still believe in you.
> By the passion of our spirit
> Shall our ancient bonds be shed.
> Let the soul be given freedom,
> Let the body have its bread!
> For my soul is not yet sold
> To the golden calf of scorn
> And I still believe in man
> And the spirit in him born.
> Life and love and strength and action
> In their hearts and blood shall beat,
> And their hopes shall be both heaven
> And the earth beneath our feet.[50]

The second Jew from Ukraine is Naftali Herz Imber, born in 1856. In 1878, he wrote the poem "Tikvateinu," "Our Hope":

> Our hope is not yet lost,
> The ancient hope,
> To return to the land of our ancestors;
> The city where David encamped.
> As long as in his heart within,
> A soul of a Jew still yearns,
> And onward towards the ends of the east,
> His eye still looks towards Zion.
>
> As long as tears from our eyes
> Flow like benevolent rain,
> And throngs of our countrymen
> Still pay homage at the graves of our fathers. . . .
>
> Hear, oh my brothers in the lands of exile,
> The voice of one of our visionaries,
> Who declares that only with the very last Jew,
> Only there is the end of our hope![51]

People fell in love with this poem. Eventually, the lyrics found a melody, perhaps derived from an older Italian, Romanian, or Ukrainian song. It also sounds like Smetana's "Moldau." No one really knows where its melody came from, but in 1933, "HaTikvah" became the anthem of the Zionist movement in 1933. From there, it became the national anthem of Israel and the Jewish people. However, the choice of "HaTivkah" was not a slam dunk. In fact, "Tzach'ki," "Laugh," was a contender!

Let's go back to Naftali Herz Imber. His story is tragic. Although he emigrated to Palestine in 1882, he lived most of his life in poverty. He died of alcoholism in 1909. For much of his life, Imber lived without personal hope. He reserved his hopes for his people and for the soul of his people, the *nefesh Y'hudi*: "*Od lo avdah tikvateinu*, our hope is not yet lost—the hope of two thousand years: to be a free people in our land, the land of Zion and Jerusalem."

That phrase—*od lo avdah tikvateinu*, "our hope is not yet lost"—comes from Ezekiel 37:11, that famous passage in which the prophet sees a valley of dry bones. The cadavers say *avdah tikvateinu*, "our hope is lost." Imber deliberately changed the text because he was trying to communicate something essential: No, our bones are not dried up, and no, our hope is not lost. We will be a free people, in our land, the land of Zion and Jerusalem.

To be honest, I do not know why "HaTikvah" became the national anthem of Israel instead of "Tzach'ki." However, I do know there is an important lesson we can learn from "Tzach'ki," which means "to laugh." The word "laugh" has many meanings, especially in Hebrew. You can laugh at a joke or something that is funny. In Hebrew, the word *tzachak* can also mean "to mock," a sort of derisive laughter. This laughter barely conceals a smirk, a moment of snark. And I believe this is the kind of *tzachak* that Tchernichovsky was writing about in his poem. It is not as if someone's dreams are funny—not yours and not mine. Tchernichovsky seems to be saying, "You might mock my dreams, yet my spirit will be victorious." Even as Jews affirm the centrality of "HaTikvah," the hope, we continue to fight the forces of *tzachak*, the forces of those who mock us and our dreams.

QUESTIONS:
1. In what ways is the State of Israel the dawning of the redemption of the Jewish people?
2. Do you agree with the choice of "HaTikvah" as the national anthem of the Jewish people?
3. What do you think the connection between hope and laughter is?

T'FILAT HADERECH—UPON SETTING FORTH ON A JOURNEY (378). Have you taken a trip lately? You know how it is: You pack, you load up the car, or you go to the train station, the airport, or the pier to take a cruise. You know the feelings, as well: Yes, there is excitement—but perhaps a little bit of nervousness as well. There are always questions of anticipation: Will the car be safe in the parking lot? Will I have enough space to stretch out my legs? Will we get stuck in an endless security line? Will we make the flight or the train or the boat? These are all questions for today rather than the past. Let us also recognize that not everyone can afford to take trips or go on vacations.

Of course, there are other kinds of journeys, like moving from one place to the other. Whether you are moving across country, across town, or even across the street to a new home, there is no question that moving is emotionally disruptive. Moving companies know this; they do their best to convey to their customers that everything is going to be just fine.

This helps us understand why our worship service includes a prayer for a journey. Journeys make us nervous and possibly excited. These are valid human emotions, and one goal of prayer is to help us name and manage those emotions.

I think there is another—perhaps deeper—reason as well. The Torah is a story of journeys.

- The story of humanity started with Adam and Eve's journey away from the Garden of Eden: "So the Eternal God drove them out of the Garden of Eden to work the soil from which they had been taken, expelling the humans and stationing Cherubim to the east of Eden, and the flaming blade of a flashing sword to guard the way to the Tree of Life" (Genesis 3:23–24).
- The story of the Jewish people started when Terah, the father of Abram, took his family out of Ur: "Then Terah took his son Abram and his grandson Lot son of Haran and his daughter-in-law Sarai, and they all left Ur of the Chaldeans to go to the land of Canaan; but they got as far as Haran and settled there" (Genesis 11:31–32).
- Then, Abram and Sarai (who became Abraham and Sarah) made their own journeys out of Haran, to the Land of Israel: "The Eternal One said to Abram, 'Go forth from your land, your birthplace, your father's house, to the land that I will show you'" (Genesis 12:1).
- Two generations later, Jacob made his own journey: "Jacob left Beersheba and set out for Haran. Coming upon a [certain] place, he passed the night there, for the sun was setting" (Genesis 28:10–11).
- Jacob's son, Joseph, made his own journey to find his brothers—who sell him into slavery in Egypt. This ultimately

caused the Jewish people to wind up in Egypt: "When his brothers went to tend their father's flock at Shechem, Israel said to Joseph, 'Surely your brothers are tending the flock at Shechem [by now]. Come, let me send you to them.' He answered, "Here I am!' Israel then said to him, 'Pray go see how your brothers are, and how the flock is doing, and bring me back word.' So he sent him from the valley of Hebron and he came to Shechem" (Genesis 37:12–14).

- Generations later, the Israelites were slaves in Egypt. Moses fled from Egypt after killing the Egyptian taskmaster who had been beating an Israelite slave: "When Pharaoh learned of the matter, he sought to kill Moses; but Moses fled from Pharaoh. He arrived in the land of Midian, and sat down beside a well" (Exodus 2:15).

- Ultimately, the Israelites went free from Egypt: "The Israelites journeyed from Raamses to Succoth, about six hundred thousand fighting men on foot, aside from noncombatants. Moreover, a mixed multitude went up with them, and very much livestock, both flocks and herds. And they baked unleavened cakes of the dough that they had taken out of Egypt, for it was not leavened, since they had been driven out of Egypt and could not delay; nor had they prepared any provisions for themselves" (Exodus 12:37–39).

After that, of course, the Israelites went on their own journey—through the wilderness to the Land of Israel, for forty years of journeying.

We say a prayer for a journey not only because there is an emotional component to a journey, trip, or move. We say a pray for a journey because the journey is an essential part of Jewish memory.

Wherever you go in life, have a good trip.

QUESTIONS:
1. Have you had a trip, journey, or move lately? Where did you go?
2. What emotions or feelings were part of that experience for you?
3. What words of this prayer speak to you?

L'Rosh Chodesh—For the New Month (379). The prayer for Rosh Chodesh asks, "May the new month bring us goodness and blessing," *shet'chadeish aleinu et hachodesh haba (hazeh) l'tovah v'liv'rachah*. A more literal translation of the Hebrew is "God will *renew* us for goodness and blessing in this new month."

There is some wonderful wordplay here, because the Hebrew word for "new" or "renew" is *chadeish*, and the Hebrew word for "month" is *chodesh*. There is a connection between *chadeish*, being new and renewed, and *chodesh*, a month.

When my sons were young, I would take them outside on the night of Purim, point to the full moon, and say to them, "The next time the moon is full will be exactly a month from now, and that will be Pesach." I did this because many (though not all) Jewish festivals take place on the fifteenth day of the Jewish month, which is when the moon is totally round, full, and *shaleim* (complete).

Ever since ancient times, the Jews have paid attention to the moon. It was up to the people themselves, through the procedures of the Sanhedrin—the Jewish supreme court—to witness and report the new moon. The Rabbis considered the moon as the "lesser light"—less intense than the sun (of course, the Rabbis were right, since the light of the moon is actually the reflected light of the sun). There is a lesson here: The Jews might have been "lesser" in numbers and power than other peoples, but we still have our light to share.

As you know, the moon goes through phases, and paying attention to the coming and going of the Jewish months is the best way to understand and see that. At the beginning of a Jewish month, the moon is a sliver. It grows to fullness until the fifteenth day of the month, and then it begins to shrink again. The phases of the moon are predictable: Every month, it is the same thing. Our lives go through phases as well, but unlike the moon, those phases are not predictable: success, disappointment, failure, success again, sadness, happiness, satisfaction, frustration. Ask your parents or your grandparents, or anyone who is substantially older than you are, and they will tell you all about those phases.

An old friend of mine once said, "When I was young, I thought that life would be like Jacob's ladder—that I would climb the rungs of that ladder toward success, and that I would just keep going higher and higher. Now that I am older, I realize that even and especially Jacob's life had its own challenges, downturns, and tragedies." Jacob's life had phases—like the phases of the moon. Your life will have similar phases.

This is true not just of Jacob's life or your life. The life of the Jewish people has had its phases—just like the moon, waxing and waning, ups and downs. It has always been this way:

> The moon begins to shine on the first of Nisan and goes on shining until the fifteenth day, when her disc becomes full. From the fifteenth until the thirtieth day, her light wanes, until on the thirtieth it is not seen at all. So too with Israel: There were fifteen generations from Abraham to Solomon. . . . When Solomon appeared, the moon's disc was full, for it says, "And Solomon sat upon the throne of the Eternal as king" (I Chronicles 29:23). . . . Thus the disc of the moon was at its fullest. From then on, the kings began to diminish in power. (Midrash, *Sh'mot Rabbah* 15:26)

In every society in which Jews have lived, they have gone through phases of success, prosperity, and persecution.

That is why we ask God to "renew us for goodness and blessing in this new month." We know that our lives need blessing and that they also need renewal—just like the moon. We know that our lives will go through phases and that each phase will challenge us, but we pray they will also bring us into something new and potentially wonderful.

QUESTIONS:
1. When have you felt the need for personal renewal?
2. What have you done to make yourself feel better?
3. Have you ever felt that your own life, or the life of your family, is going through phases, like the moon?

HALLEL I (558–59) AND *HALLEL* II (560–69)

It must have been very cool back in Biblical and post-Biblical times when the Temples in Jerusalem existed. Back then, the festivals were a big deal—a very big deal. The term for the festivals—Sukkot, Pesach, and Shavuot—is *Shalosh R'galim,* which I would translate as "the three foot festivals." Jews from all over the Land of Israel and beyond would make a pilgrimage to Jerusalem. There, they would bring their offerings and feel a genuine sense of not only being close to God, but being close to their fellow Jews.

Fun fact: The Hebrew word for "festival" is *chag*—as in the greeting *chag samei-ach,* "may you have a good festival." The Arabic equivalent is the hajj—the pilgrimage to the Muslim holy sites in Mecca, in Saudi Arabia. This, too, is a very big deal—so much so that it is the goal of every Muslim to make that pilgrimage once in their lifetime. Those who do so even get a new "nickname" that they can add to their own name—Hajj, "the one who made the hajj."

Fast-forward to modern times. When contemporary Jews go to Israel, sometimes they feel as if they are making a religious pilgrimage. It is a spiritual journey. That is how I feel when I go.

Now rewind back to ancient times. As we said, people would make pilgrimage to the Temple. When they were there, the Levites would welcome them with song and prayer, and all would recite prayers of thanksgiving for having made the journey. In memory of that journey and time in Jerusalem, we recite or chant the psalms in a special framework called *Hallel.* These psalms are chanted for the *Shalosh R'galim* (Sukkot, Pesach, and Shavuot), and many synagogues also recite them on Yom Haatzma-ut (Israel Independence Day). Today when we recite *Hallel* on the festivals, it is as if we are going back in a time machine to the ancient Temple. It is a journey worth making.

PSALM 113 (561). Psalm 113 proudly proclaims, "God raises the poor from the dust, lifts up the needy from the refuse heap to set them with the great, with the great of God's people. God sets the childless woman among the household as a happy mother of children. Hallelujah." That was how it was—or how it seemed—in Biblical times. God did everything, or almost everything. God fought wars; God brought rain; God did all the blessing and cursing.

That was exactly what the Psalmist thought. If the poor are going to be raised from the dust, then it will be God's job to do it. Lifting the needy from the refuse heap—that's God. If a childless woman is going to have children—also God. In fact, that is how it plays out in the Book of Genesis and in the story of Hannah in I Samuel: If a woman was childless, it was because God had "closed her womb"; if she got pregnant, it must have been because God "opened her womb."

How do we understand these verses today? Rabbi Harold M. Schulweis urged Jews and others to think not about what God does— the actions of God—but instead to focus on what actions are godly:

> To believe in Godliness is to believe in the verbs and adverbs that refer to the activities of divinity. To behave in a Godly fashion is to realize in one's life the attributes of Godliness that are potential in all human and nonhuman energies. . . . The question to be asked of those who seek God is not whether they believe in a noun that cannot be known [God] but whether they believe in the gerunds ["ing" forms of verbs] of Godliness: healing the sick, feeding the hungry, supporting the fallen, pursuing peace, loving the neighbor.[52]

In other words, when we raise the poor from the dust, we are acting in godly ways. When we lift up the needy from the refuse heap (what a powerful image; have you ever seen someone going through garbage cans to find food?), we are acting in godly ways. When we help childless families welcome children through medical intervention, adoption, or surrogacy, we are acting in godly ways. That is worth a heartfelt "Hallelujah!"

QUESTIONS:
1. What are some things that God does in the world?
2. What evidence do we have of divine action in the world?
3. How have you acted in godly ways?

PSALM 114 (562). The author of Psalm 114 wants us to know that the freedom of the Jewish people is miraculous—so much so that even nature participated: "The sea saw them and fled, the Jordan ran backward, mountains skipped like rams, hills like sheep." "Mountains skipping like rams" must have meant an earthquake, though I am not sure about all the other images. What is really going on here?

The psalm starts with the crossing of the Sea of Reeds but quickly goes to the Jordan running backward. When did that happen? Remember that when Moses died, the Israelites were still on the plains of Moab. They had not yet entered the Land of Israel. It would be up to Moses's successor, Joshua, to begin the process of conquering the Land of Israel. In some ways, Joshua is a mirror image of Moses. Just as God parted the Sea of Reeds for Moses and the Israelites, Joshua parted the Jordan:

> [Joshua said,] "When the feet of the priests bearing the Ark of the Eternal, the Sovereign of all the earth, come to rest in the waters of the Jordan, the waters of the Jordan—the water coming from upstream—will be cut off and will stand in a single heap." When the people set out from their encampment to cross the Jordan, the priests bearing the Ark of the Covenant were at the head of the people. Now the Jordan keeps flowing over its entire bed throughout the harvest season. But as soon as the bearers of the Ark reached the Jordan, and the feet of the priests bearing the Ark dipped into the water at its edge, the Jordan, and the feet of the priests bearing the Ark dipped into the water at its edge, the waters coming down from upstream piled up in a single heap a great way off. . . . So the people crossed near Jericho. The priests who bore the Ark of the Eternal's Covenant stood on dry land exactly in the middle of the Jordan, while all Israel crossed over on dry land, until the entire nation had finished crossing the Jordan. (Joshua 3:13–17)

The two stories of water splitting—the splitting of the Sea of Reeds and the splitting of the Jordan River—are somewhat different. In the first story, when the waters of the Sea of Reeds split, God splits the waters but needs encouragement from Moses to make it happen: "Then the Eternal One said to Moses, 'Why do you cry out to Me? Tell the Israelites to go forward. And you lift up your rod and hold out your arm over the sea and split it, so that the Israelites may march into the sea on dry ground'" (Exodus 14:15–16).

In the second story, when the waters of the Jordan River split, God does not make it happen. This time, the priests must walk into the water carrying the Ark of the Covenant; that is the action that will cause the river to split. This is an important difference with an important message: The time for miracles was starting to run out. People must now be partners with God in moving their destiny forward.

QUESTIONS:
1. In what ways is freedom—of the Jews, of any people—miraculous?
2. In what ways is freedom the result of human action?
3. How have you made efforts to work toward human freedom?

PSALM 115 (563). "That's a milk fork, not a meat fork!" How many times have those words been uttered in Jewish homes? The reason is that many Jews keep kosher. One of the traditional rules of keeping kosher is separating milk and meat, which includes not eating meat and dairy products together at the same meal, waiting a period of time between eating meat and dairy, and having two sets of dishes—one for dairy products and one for meat products. In this way, just the mere act of choosing a spoon for a bowl of ice cream becomes a reminder of your Jewish identity.

Another Jewish custom is called *shaatneiz*, which is the prohibition of mixing wool and linen in the same garment. Why would you not mix wool and linen in the same garment? Linen comes from a flax plant. If you want to produce linen, you have to cut down the flax plant. In other words, you have to kill it. Wool comes from a lamb, and while the lamb might be colder after the worker shaves the lamb, at least the animal is still alive.

What do *shaatneiz* and kashrut have in common? They share one of the great facts of Jewish life: There is a realm of life, and there is a realm of death—and the two should not mix.

Meat represents the death of an animal (which is why Judaism would probably prefer us to be vegetarians but will "settle" on meat being slaughtered in a kosher, painless way, with all the blood drained from the meat). On the other hand, milk represents life.

Those things that celebrate life, like Shabbat and the festivals, should not be tainted by death. That is why there are no mourning customs observed on Shabbat or festivals.

This helps us understand Psalm 115 when it says, "The dead cannot praise Adonai, nor any who go down into silence." "Going down into silence" is a Biblical euphemism for descending into Sheol, the dark pit where the dead reside. The text is simply saying that praising God is what the living do, not what the dead do. The philosopher Leon Kass (United States, 1939–) puts it this way:

> You don't have to be Jewish to drink *L'Chaim*, to lift a glass "To Life." Everyone in his right mind believes that life is good and that death is bad. But Jews have always had an unusually keen appreciation of life, and not only because it has been stolen from them so often and so cruelly. The celebration of life—of this life, not the next one—has from the beginning been central to Jewish ethical and religious sensibilities. In the Torah, "Be fruitful and multiply" is God's first blessing and first command. Judaism from its inception rejected child-sacrifice and regarded long life as a fitting divine reward for righteous living.[53]

Life and death. That is the key to understanding Judaism. Judaism is a constant celebration of life.

QUESTIONS:
1. In what ways does Judaism celebrate life?
2. In what ways are you familiar with Jewish traditions that make a clear boundary between life and death?

PSALM 116 (564). I admit to you that it is hard for me to write about Psalm 116. The psalm begins with deep humility and gratitude: "How can I repay Adonai for all God's bounties to me?" Then, it quickly moves from gratitude to sadness and pain: "The death of God's faithful ones is grievous in Adonai's sight." The word that is translated as "grievous" is *yakar*. An even better translation would be "expensive," "costly," "precious," or "dear." That is how my Israeli friends write to me: "Jeff *hayakar*," "Dear Jeff. . . ."

Rashi comments on this phrase from Psalm 116, "The Holy One, blessed be God, showed me that it is a difficult thing and heavy in God's eyes to kill God's pious ones."[54] Let us put ourselves into Rashi's mindset. As we have said, Rashi lived in France-Germany from 1040 to 1105. Actually, there was no such thing as either France or Germany in those days. Rashi lived in the Rhineland, in the region that was on the border of today's France and Germany. To this day, you cannot read either the Bible or the Talmud without encountering his commentary. It is essential reading and learning. Being a commentator on sacred scriptures was not Rashi's full-time job, however. He was a vintner—in the wine business.

I believe this particular verse touched Rashi so deeply because he lived during the Crusades that swept over France and Germany. Officially, the purpose of the Crusades was to liberate the Land of Israel from Muslim rule. Unofficially, however, the purpose of the Crusades was to kill Jews and to destroy Jewish communities throughout Europe, which the Crusaders did as they marched to the Holy Land. Rashi saw that destruction, up close.

That history is what makes his comment so poignant. "The Holy One, blessed be God, showed me that it is a difficult thing and heavy in God's eyes to kill God's pious ones." It is almost outrageous that he could say such a thing.

The ancient Sages taught that divine revelation—God speaking to people—ended with the destruction of the Second Temple. Therefore, counting the years between the destruction and the time of Rashi, it would have been a thousand years since God had spoken to anyone. Yet, Rashi is imagining that God actually communicated with him—that God showed him that it is "difficult" and "heavy" when God's pious ones are killed. "Difficult" and "heavy"—for God. God mourns those deaths.

I write these words several months after October 7. You are reading these words long after that. "October 7" does not even need a description; say the date, and everyone knows what you are talking about. I think this will be true no matter when you are reading this book. It is not outrageous to imagine that God mourns those deaths as well.

PSALM 117 (565). Throughout *Hallel*, we have been praising God and celebrating the unique Jewish connection to God. As we approach the end of *Hallel*, we realize something else: All people can praise God, and all people can be witnesses to God's love for the Jewish people.

When I was eleven years old, my best friend was Ira Handleman (not his real name). Whenever I went to his house, I would meet the old Polish woman who lived with them. Her name was Anya. Anya didn't speak a word of English, and I assumed that she was my friend's grandmother.

"No," he corrected me, "she's the lady who hid my mother in a closet during the war. My mother was so grateful to her that she brought her to the United States with her." I want to make sure you followed that. Anya saved the life of my friend's mother. She was what we call a "righteous among the nations."

Shortly after Ira became bar mitzvah, Mr. Handleman became very successful in the hotel business. The Handleman family decided to make *aliyah* (move to Israel), and we lost touch.

Ten years later, I went to Israel for the first time. Within days of my arrival, I called my old friend's family, and we became reacquainted. Within the first few minutes of our conversation, I jumped to the topic that had been on my mind for years. "And Anya? Whatever became of her?" I asked.

"When we decided to move to Israel," Mrs. Handleman told me, "we offered to buy Anya a house in New York and to support her for the rest of her life. But she said to us, 'Where else could I live? Who else could I live with? You're my family.' And so we brought her with us to Tel Aviv."

Somehow, I knew the answer to the next question even before I asked it. "Is she still alive? She was already so old . . ."

"No, she died just a few years ago."

"Where did you bury her?" I asked.

"Here in Israel. Where else?" I could hear Mrs. Handleman weeping through the phone.

Whenever I think of Anya, and the other righteous among the nations who saved the lives of Jews during the Shoah (Holocaust), I think of what it means for people to bear witness to divine love.

QUESTIONS:

1. Do you think all people can and should praise God? Why or why not?

2. Can you name other people who are considered "righteous among the nations"?

3. Do you think that Jews have a special responsibility to remember those non-Jews who helped save Jewish lives?

PSALM 118 (565–67). Psalm 118 introduces us to three separate groups: "Let Israel declare . . . let the house of Aaron declare . . . let those who fear Adonai declare, 'God's steadfast love is eternal.'" These three distinct groups are: "Israel," the entire Jewish people; "the house of Aaron," the priests, a small part of the Jewish people; and then, "those who fear Adonai." We are clear about who the entire Jewish people are. Less clear, perhaps, is who the priests are, though their role was central and crucial in the ancient Temple. But who are "those who fear Adonai"?

We can find our answer by looking at the Hebrew. The Hebrew word *yirei* is translated here as "fear," as in "to be afraid." However, we can also translate *yirei* as "awe"—"those who are in awe" or "those who revere."

Who were those people who "feared God"? The great Biblical commentator called Radak (Rabbi David Kimchi, France, 1160–1235) thought that they were Israelites of great piety and wisdom. Rashi thought that they were converts to Judaism. Others, including Abraham Ibn Ezra, who lived in the 1100s, thought that this referred to righteous gentiles.[55] History can teach us about the identity of those *yirei Elohim*. In post-Biblical times, there were entire synagogues in the Diaspora that were filled with *yirei Elohim*, "God-fearers." They were not officially Jewish, but they were monotheists, learned Torah, and observed some Jewish customs.

In 1976, archaeologists in Turkey uncovered a pillar from ancient Greek times that contained numerous Jewish names. It also listed a number of non-Jews who were honorary members of the Jewish community. They worshiped the one God of the Jews, which—when you consider Greek culture, where people worshiped multiple gods—was truly a rebellious act.

Throughout history, there have been spiritual descendants of those "God-fearers." There were various groups during the Protestant Reformation who maintained some Jewish customs. There were groups like the Russian Subbotniki who observed the Sabbath. In recent years, people who are descended from Conversos—Jews who were forced to convert during the Spanish Inquisition—have adopted Jewish customs and are seeking to return to Judaism. With just that small mention in *Hallel—yirei Adonai*, "those who fear Adonai"—we recognize that there have always been those among us who, while not formally Jewish, affirm and respect Judaism.

You might even have some of them in your family.

QUESTIONS:
1. Do you know any non-Jews who are "God-fearers"— whom you might call "honorary Jews"?
2. What is Reform Judaism's history regarding non-Jews who live in the midst of the Jewish community?
3. Are there ways that we can better welcome "God-fearers"?

PSALM 118:19–29 (567–68). I was never any good at building stuff. When I was a kid, I used to like making model airplanes and cars. Sometimes, I was so impatient to finish the model that I would leave stuff out. After all, if the model looked good from the outside, what difference did it make? Turns out, it makes a big difference!

There was the time in shop class when I had an assignment to build a scale model of a house out of heavy cardboard. My house looked great. I invented my own modern design. However, when I handed it in to the teacher, he looked at it and said, "Jeff, this is very nice. I have one question for you: Where is the door?" It was true: I had designed a great house, but I forgot to build a door.

This brings us to that wonderful, mysterious sentence in this psalm: "The stone that the builders rejected has become the chief cornerstone." What did that originally mean? It might have been about construction and the rebuilding of the Temple, when the Judeans returned from exile. Or it might have been something deeper.

Several medieval commentators believed that the "stone that the builders rejected" referred to the Jews. Rashi understood it as "a people that was humble among the peoples."[56] Ibn Ezra went further and said, "The peoples of the world insulted the Jews, but in the end the Jews overcame them."[57]

I understand it to mean that the Jews are one of the "building blocks" of civilization. There were other "builders" as well—the ancient Egyptians, the ancient Greeks, and the ancient Romans—and they rejected the Jews. This aligns with the words of Rabbi Samson Raphael Hirsch (Germany, 1808–88), a modern commentator, who said, "The architects who labored in behalf of the supposed welfare of the nations did not even think that they could include Israel as one building block among all the other stones. Thus they scornfully left Israel to lie by the wayside, and now it is precisely Israel that has become the chief cornerstone of the edifice of man's salvation."[58]

This is especially true in the United States. The founders of the Republic saw their story as a Jewish story. They saw themselves as ancient Israelites, King George III of Great Britain as Pharaoh, the Atlantic Ocean as the Sea of Reeds, and their new land as another Land of Israel. That is why there are so many Biblical place names in New England and the Middle Atlantic states: Salem, Massachusetts; Bethel, Connecticut; New Canaan, Connecticut; Bethlehem, Pennsylvania (and New Hampshire); Jericho, New York—all the way south to Rehoboth Beach, Delaware, which shares its name with Rehovot, Israel, and is a reference to Genesis 26:22. In fact, the United States is unique in this way. There are almost no Biblical place names in Europe. As the author Thomas Cahill (United States, 1940–2022) wrote, "We can hardly get up in the morning or cross the street without being Jewish. We dream Jewish dreams and hope Jewish hopes. Most of our best words, in fact—new, adventure, surprise, unique, individual, person, vocation, time, history, future, freedom, progress, spirit, faith, hope, justice—are the gifts of the Jews."[59] The haters might have rejected the Jews, but let there be no doubt: The Jews are the cornerstone of the temple of the world.

We can deepen our understanding of this even more by looking at our own lives—at our own building blocks, the things that make us uniquely us. A contemporary teacher wrote, "We are the 'builders' of our own lives. How often do we reject, or ignore, our own building-blocks! How many things we have done that seemed trivial, almost unnoticed, at the time, but that turn out to be terribly important, to us and to others, as we look back."[60]

QUESTIONS:
1. What elements of Judaism do you think are essential to the world?
2. What elements of Judaism do you think that the world still has not figured out?
3. What are some elements of your own life that you might have once rejected or ignored?

Y'HALAL'LUCHA—CLOSING BLESSING (569). The closing blessing for *Hallel* proudly proclaims, "All Your works shall praise You, Adonai our God." *All* Your works—not just Jews; not just human beings; not just animals. Not just the grass, trees, and flowers. Not just the mountains, seas, and rivers. Everything.

The Hebrew poet Micah Joseph Berdichevsky (Ukraine and Germany, 1865–1921) wrote:

> It is not we alone who pray;
> all things pray.
> All things pour forth their souls.
> The heavens pray, the earth prays,
> every creature and every living thing prays.[61]

You might not believe this. You might not believe that everything prays, because you might believe that in order to pray, you need both a mind and a soul (not to mention a mouth, but there is such a thing as silent prayer). In fact, I am not so sure that I believe this. Still, I think it would be good to be able to believe this—that all of Creation yearns for God and wants to be close to God. I certainly do. Maybe you do too.

QUESTIONS:
1. Do you believe that all things pray?
2. What are some prayers that different things might pray?

Act Four—What We Hope

As the service approaches its end, we turn toward the future and a summary of Jewish hopes. We pray *Aleinu* and *Kaddish*. Someday, everyone will understand that God is One. Someday, there will be perfection and peace, God's sovereignty on earth.

ALEINU (586–91)

"We therefore hope in You, Adonai our God. May we soon behold the glory of Your might: sweeping away the false gods of the earth that idolatry be utterly destroyed; perfecting the world under the rule of God [*l'takein olam b'malchut Shaddai*]" (page 588).

The *Aleinu* prayer is expressing the hope that someday idolatry will disappear. Idolatry does not only mean worshiping "false gods of the earth." Idolatry means treating as ultimately important and holy something that is not important and holy in itself. Some people turn their nation into a "god" (the Nazis did that). Some kids make popularity, or good grades, or fancy bet mitzvah gifts, into "gods." Some parents might do this too!

Aleinu foresees the end of history, and it hopes for a good end of that history. That good end of history is what we call the time of the Messiah, when idolatry disappears. For that reason, *Aleinu* ends with the ancient hope: *Bayom hahu yih'yeh Adonai echad ushmo echad*, "On that [Messianic] day, Adonai will be one, and God's name will be one." On that day, everyone will know that there is only one God.

QUESTIONS:
1. What "idols" do you worship?
2. What "idols" do you see others worshiping?
3. What are you doing to bring the day when the world will reflect divine unity?

KADDISH YATOM (598)

There have been so many losses, and therefore, there have been so many occasions for *Kaddish*. One of the greatest modern Hebrew writers was Shmuel Yosef ("Shai") Agnon (Polish Galicia and Israel, 1887–1970). Already in 1947, a year before the creation of the State of Israel, he composed a prayer that people would say at military funerals as an introduction to the Mourner's *Kaddish*:

> When a king of flesh and blood goes to war against his enemies, he sends his soldiers to kill and to be killed. He may love his soldiers or he may not love them. He may have regard for them or he may not have regard for them.
>
> Even if he has regard for them, however, he regards them as dead, for the angel of death is close upon the heels of a man who goes to war, and accompanies him to kill him. When he is cut down and slain by an arrow or a sword or any of the other instruments of destruction, another man is put in his place.
>
> The king does not feel that someone is missing. After all, the nations are many and their troops are many. If one of them is killed, the king has many replacements.
>
> But our [Ruler], Holy One, Blessed Be [God], wants life and loves peace and pursues peace and loves [God's] people Israel. [God] chose us, and not because we are a large nation, for we are one of the smallest of nations. We are few, and owing to the love with which [God] loves us, each one of us is, for [God], an entire legion. [God] does not have many replacements for us.
>
> If one of us is missing, then the [Ruler's] forces are diminished, with the consequence that [God's] kingdom is weakened, as it were.
>
> One of [God's] legions is gone and [God's] greatness is lessened. For this reason, it is our custom to recite the kaddish when a Jew dies.[62]

You might disagree with some of the ideas in this prayer. You might disagree with the idea of God as "ruler," or "king," as it says in the original Hebrew. You might also disagree with the idea that Israeli soldiers fight in "God's army." I encourage you to read a bit deeper. There is much wisdom here.

First, Agnon is saying something simple and sad. It is the way of war that soldiers will die in battle. This is a basic truth about the world. Second, Agnon is saying that human rulers (or presidents, or prime ministers) send soldiers into battle, and if they are killed, then they simply send in reinforcements. It is sad, but the war must go on. However, God is not that way. God loves us as individuals. Therefore, when someone is killed, it is sad for God.

Agnon goes even further and claims that the death of an individual *weakens* God. What does that mean—that a human death weakens God? It means that it is not only that we need God. God also needs us. It is not only that we need to pray to God—to show gratitude, to feel connected to God, other Jews, the world, all humanity, and the universe. It is also that God needs our prayers—because God also mourns for the dead!

This might be a confusing thing to say. After all, couldn't God have stopped the killing?

Sadly, no. Personally, I do not believe that God is all-powerful. I believe that when God created human beings, God created them with free will—the ability to make their own choices. God wants us to choose good, but it doesn't always work out that way. Sadly and tragically, many people choose to do evil, and that evil can have lethal results.

This brings us back to the opening words of *Kaddish*: "Exalted and hallowed be God's great name," *Yitgadal v'yitkadash sh'mei raba*. I don't think we should translate *yitgadal* as "exalted." The Hebrew root of *yitgadal* is *gadal*, which means "magnified," "big," "large," and even "grow."

I would translate *Yitgadal v'yitkadash sh'mei raba* as "Magnified and hallowed be God's great name." My own interpretation is that whenever a death occurs, one of the letters of God's four-letter name drops off. When we say *Kaddish* and praise God even in the midst of pain and loss, it is an act of heroism and bravery. It is a way of saying, "I still have faith in God." When we do that, it is as if our prayer restores that fallen letter to God's great name. God's name becomes larger. It is magnified.

I want to share one more thing about Agnon's introduction to *Kaddish*. When Agnon wrote these words, things were not going well around him. In his book *Kaddish*, Leon Wieseltier (United States, 1952–) writes:

> [Agnon] was writing in Jerusalem when the city was under fire, and so he turns to address the harsh historical circumstances. "If this is what we pray and what we say for every individual who dies, how much more shall we pray it and say it for our brothers and our sisters, the lovely and pleasant and dear children of Zion who were slain for the land of Israel, whose blood was spilled for the honor of [God's] blessed Name, for [God's] people and [God's] land and [God's] heritage! Indeed, everyone who dwells in the land of Israel is one of the legions of . . . the Holy One, Blessed Be [God]. . . . When one of them is killed, [God] is bereft of others to put in his place. And so my brothers in the house of Israel, all of you who mourn in this mourning, let us direct our hearts to . . . Heaven, the [God] of Israel and its Redeemer, and pray for ourselves and for [God], as it were: 'Magnified and sanctified may [God's] great Name be . . .'"[63]

It is, finally, at this moment that I address the horrors that occurred on October 7, 2023. By the time you read this, much time will have passed since that day. It is as if I am writing a memo to my future reader. I believe that we will always remember that day because it changed Jewish history. We will always remember "our brothers and our sisters, the lovely and pleasant and dear children of Zion who were slain for the land of Israel, whose blood was spilled for the honor of [God's] blessed Name, for [God's] people and [God's] land and [God's] heritage!" Whenever I say *Kaddish*, they—and all those Jews who died because they were Jews—are with me.

QUESTIONS:

1. What do you think of the image of God as a ruler who sends soldiers into battle?
2. What troubles you about that image?
3. Do you believe that God is all-powerful?

Conclusion

Far too many young people view bet mitzvah as both a performance and a graduation. Sadly, that is what it has often become: a performance—like a piano recital, where you get to play what you have learned, and everyone politely applauds (of course, there is the additional nice party afterward, which might not happen at a piano recital); and a graduation—far too many young people see bet mitzvah as the end of their Jewish studies and Jewish involvement. Luckily, many young people will "find" Judaism again when they go to college, but all too often there are several years where teens are AWOL from Jewish life, which means that the prayers they have so faithfully learned will fall silent on their lips.

Here is my hope for you: Hang in there. You might not be able to attend worship services regularly. I get it—when young people are in their teens, life has a way of getting crowded and complicated with various school, extracurricular, and social commitments taking up so much time. Still, I hope that the lessons you have learned here will remain with you in the coming years. Those questions at the end of every prayer are not just questions about a particular prayer; they are questions about life, and the prayers in the Jewish tradition have a way of letting us engage in those questions.

I end with one of my favorite stories. Reb Naftali Zvi of Ropshitz (Polish Galicia, 1760–1827) was a great Chasidic teacher. One night, he found himself unable to sleep, and so he took a walk in his village. There, he met the night watchman. "Who do you work for?" Reb Naftali asked.

"I work for the village. I make sure that the streets are safe, and that the citizens are secure." Then, the watchman turned to Reb Naftali, and asked him, "And who do you work for?"

Reb Naftali thought for a few minutes and then said, "I am not sure. But, if you come work for me, I will more than double your salary."

"Really?" said the watchman, clearly interested in the career move. "What would my duties be?"

"All you would have to do," replied Reb Naftali, "is walk with me and, every once in a while, ask me that question: 'Who do you work for?'"

Reb Naftali knew that he worked for God. He just needed the night watchman to remind him of that fact.[64]

Remember that the ancient Jewish word for "worship" is *avodah*, which also means "work." Worship is work—hard work, in fact. It is a skill, like dance or theater or writing or sports. It takes a lifetime to develop that skill. It is a skill you can master—you have already started to do so.

Like Reb Naftali, when you pray and do that hard work, you will realize something amazing, something special, something that will change your life. You will realize that you work for God.

Good luck, and blessings on your journey.

Notes

Unless otherwise indicated, all translations of Torah are from The Torah: A Modern Commentary, *rev. ed. by W. Gunther Plaut (CCAR Press, 2005). Other Biblical translations are from* The JPS Tanakh: Gender Sensitive Edition *(Jewish Publication Society, 2023). Quotes from Pirkei Avot are from* Pirkei Avot: A Social Justice Commentary *by Shmuly Yanklowitz (CCAR Press, 2018).*

INTRODUCTION
1. *Fiddler on the Roof,* directed by Norman Jewison, written by Joseph Stein (1971).
2. Many of these terms for God appear in Steven M. Brown's book *Higher and Higher: Making Jewish Prayer Part of Us* (Rowman & Littlefield/ United Synagogue of Conservative Judaism, 1980).
3. Melilah Helner-Eshed, lecture, Shalom Hartman Institute, Jerusalem, Israel, July 2012.
4. Dov Singer, *Prepare My Prayer: Recipes to Awaken the Soul*, ed. Reut Brosh, trans. Leah Hartman (Maggid, 2020), 105. © 2020 Maggid Books. Used with the permission of Koren Publishers Jerusalem Ltd. and the Toby Press LLC.

MAARIV—EVENING SERVICE
1. Translation adapted from the William Davidson digital edition of the *Koren Noé Talmud*, with commentary by Adin Even-Israel Stein-saltz. License: CC-BY-NC, https://creativecommons.org/licenses/ by-nc/4.0/, found on Sefaria (sefaria.org).
2. Translation adapted from the William Davidson digital edition of the *Koren Noé Talmud.*
3. Hillel Zeitlin, *Gaguim L'Yofi* [Longings for beauty], ed. Yonatan Meir and Levi Bartov (Blima Books, 2022), 25.
4. "The Lord," track 1 on Paul Simon, *Seven Psalms*, 2023.
5. "The Declaration of the Establishment of the State of Israel," Jewish Virtual Library, https://www.jewishvirtuallibrary.org/the-declaration-of-the-establishment-of-the-state-of-israel.
6. "Jewish Mysticism—and Kushner Offers a Way to Try It on for Size," *Jewish News of Northern California*, February 27, 2004, https:// jweekly.com/2004/02/27/jewish-mysticism-kushner-offers-a-way-to-try-it-on-for-size/.

7. Ellen Frankel, "A Woman's Voice," in *My People's Prayer Book*, vol. 8, *Kabbalat Shabbat*, ed. Lawrence Hoffman (Jewish Lights, 2013), 88.

8. Undated, untitled lecture by Lawrence Kushner, quoting Jonathan Omer-Man.

9. Aryeh Lev Stollman, *The Far Euphrates* (Riverhead Books, 1997), 137.

10. "Roll into Dark," by Noam Katz, track 5 on *A Drum in Hand*, Riot Drum Studio, 2009. Lyrics by Noam Katz © 2009. Used by permission.

11. Reuven Kimelman (untitled lecture, CLAL conference, 1983).

12. Shai Held, *Judaism Is About Love: Recovering the Heart of Jewish Life* (Farrar, Straus and Giroux, 2024), 85.

13. Amos Oz and Fania Oz-Salzberger, *Jews and Words* (Yale University Press, 2012), 8.

14. Translation adapted from the William Davidson digital edition of the *Koren Noé Talmud*.

15. *Hakhsharat HaAvrekhim* 7:3, translated by Betzalel Edwards (Sefaria, 2022). License: CC-BY, https://creativecommons.org/licenses/by/3.0/, found on Sefaria (sefaria.org).

16. Lawrence Kushner, *Honey from the Rock: An Easy Intrduction to Jewish Mysticism* (Jewish Lights, 1999), 126.

17. Blu Greenberg, *How to Run a Traditional Jewish Household* (Simon & Schuster, 1983), 26.

18. Abraham Joshua Heschel, *The Sabbath* (Farrar, Straus and Giroux, 1951), 67. Quoted in *Mishkan T'filah: A Reform Siddur* (CCAR Press, 2007), 163.

19. Richard Brooks, dir., *Cat on a Hot Tin Roof* (Metro-Goldwyn-Mayer, 1958).

20. Vilna Gaon, *Sefer Alim Li'Trufah*, as quoted by Dan Epstein in "Taanit Dibbur" Sefaria study sheet, https://www.sefaria.org/sheets/265017.2?lang=bi&with=all&lang2=en.

21. André Neher, *The Exile of the Word: From the Silence of the Bible to the Silence of Auschwitz* (Jewish Publication Society, 1981), 14.

22. *Etz Hayim: Torah and Commentary*, ed. David L. Lieber (Jewish Publication Society, 2001), 323.

23. As quoted in Nehama Leibowitz, *Studies in Bereshit* (World Zionist Organization, 1981), 134.

24. *Sheiltot D'Rav Achai Gaon* 145:2, found on Sefaria (sefaria.org).

25. *Siddur Lev Shalem: For Shabbat and Festivals*, ed. Edward Feld (Rabbinical Assembly, 2016), 56.

26. Marvin Lowenthal, *Henrietta Szold: Life and Letters* (Viking Press, 1942), 92.

27. *Mishkan HaNefesh: Machzor for the Days of Awe; Yom Kippur* (CCAR Press, 2015), 598.

SHACHARIT—MORNING SERVICE

1. Sandy Eisenberg Sasso, *God's Paintbrush: The Anniversary Edition* (Jewish Lights, 2004).
2. Translations of the Mishnah are from the William Davidson digital edition of the *Koren Noé Talmud*.
3. Translations of the Babylonian Talmud are from the William Davidson digital edition of the *Koren Noé Talmud*.
4. Dalia Marx, *From Time to Time: Journeys in the Jewish Calendar* (CCAR Press, 2024), 178–79.
5. Robert Pinksy, "Shirt," in *The Want Bone* (Ecco Press, 1990), 53–54. © 1990 by Robert Pinsky. Used by permission of HarperCollins Publishers.
6. Albert Einstein, *The World as I See It* (Book Tree, 2007), 90.
7. Translation adapted from the William Davidson digital edition of the *Koren Noé Talmud*.
8. Erica Brown, *Seder Talk: The Conversational Haggada* (Koren, 2015), Kindle.
9. Held, *Judaism Is About Love*, 47.
10. Lawrence Hoffman, ed., *My People's Prayer Book: Traditional Prayers, Modern Commentary*, vol. 3, *P'sukei D'Zimrah (Morning Psalms)* (Jewish Lights, 1999), 5.
11. Sarah Grabiner, in Hoffman, *My People's Prayer Book*, vol. 3, 120.
12. Marx, *From Time to Time*, 149.
13. Judith Hauptman, in Hoffman, *My People's Prayer Book*, vol. 3, 144.
14. Avraham Yitzhak HaKohen Kook, *Olat Re'iya, Inyenei Tefilla* 7, quoted in Singer, *Prepare My Prayer*, 110.
15. Susannah Heschel, "Following in My Father's Footsteps: Selma 40 Years Later," in "Praying with My Legs," WeRepair.org, https://werepair.org/wp-content/uploads/2022/01/Praying-With-My-Legs.pdf.
16. Singer, *Prepare My Prayer*, 51.
17. Neil Gillman, untitled lecture, CAJE Conference, Hofstra University, August 2004.
18. Lawrence Kushner and Nehemia Polen, *Filling Words with Light: Hasidic and Mystical Reflections on Jewish Prayer* (Jewish Lights, 2004), 43.
19. Sharon Brous, *The Amen Effect: Ancient Wisdom to Mend Our Broken Hearts and World* (Avery, 2024), xiii.
20. Singer, *Prepare My Prayer*, 17.
21. Lawrence A. Hoffman, ed., *My People's Prayer Book: Traditional Prayer, Modern Commentaries*, vol. 10, *Shabbat Morning: Shacharit and Musaf (Morning and Additional Services)* (Jewish Lights, 2007), 83–85.

22. Held, *Judaism Is About Love*, 3.

23. Jacob L. Wright, *Why the Bible Began: An Alternative History of Scripture and Its Origins* (Cambridge University Press, 2023), 85.

24. David Sperling, quoted in Eugene Borowitz, *Ehad: The Many Meanings of God Is One* (Sh'ma, 1988), 85.

25. Adapted from *B'reishit Rabbah* 98:3.

26. As found in Viktor E. Frankl, *Man's Search for Meaning* (Beacon Press, 2006), 115.

27. Abraham Millgram, "The Tallit: Spiritual Significance," My Jewish Learning, https://www.myjewishlearning.com/article/the-tallit-spiritual-significance/.

28. Robert F. Kennedy, "Day of Affirmation." University of Cape Town Centre for Curating the Archive, https://doi.org/https://humanities.uct.ac.za/cca/projects-archive-and-curatorship-arc-visual-university/robert-f-kennedy-speech-university-capetown-south-africa-day-affirmation-6-june-1966. Accessed January 16, 2025.

29. Translation of *Sifra* by Shraga Silverstein (license: CC-BY, https://creativecommons.org/licenses/by/3.0/), found on Sefaria (sefaria.org).

30. Marc Angel, "A Covenant for All Generations: Thoughts for *Nitsavim-Vayelekh*, September 20, 2014," Institute for Jewish Ideas and Ideals, https://www.jewishideas.org/ covenant-all-generations-thoughts-nitsavim-vayelekh-september- 20-2014.

31. Lauren Berkun, untitled lecture, Shalom Hartman Institute, Jerusalem, Israel, July, 2023.

32. Micah Goodman, *The Last Words of Moses* (Maggid, 2023), Kindle.

33. Harold M. Schulweis, "The Individual in the Jew," sermon, Valley Beth Shalom, 1994, https://www.vbs.org/worship/meet-our-clergy/rabbi-harold-schulweis/sermons/individual-jew. Used by permission of the Harold M. Schulweis Institute.

34. Karyn D. Kedar, "God of All Things," in *Amen: Seeking Presence with Prayer, Poetry, and Mindfulness Practice* (CCAR Press, 202), 61.

35. Judith Hauptman, in Lawrence Hoffman, *My People's Prayer Book: Traditional Prayers, Modern Commentary*, vol. 4, *Seder K'riat HaTorah (The Torah Service)* (Jewish Lights, 1999), 83.

36. Yehudah Leib Alter of Ger, *S'fat Emet, K'doshim* 2, in translation of *S'fat Emet* by Dan Levy, found on Sefaria (sefaria.org).

37. Yehudah Leib Alter of Ger, *S'fat Emet, K'doshim* 2. S

38. Yehudah Leib Alter of Ger, *S'fat Emet, Shavuot* 2, in Sefaria Community Translation of *S'fat Emet*, found on Sefaria (sefaria.org).

39. Walker Percy, *The Message in the Bottle: How Queer Man Is, How Queer Language Is, and What One Has to Do with the Other* (Farrar, Straus and Giroux, 1984), 6.

40. See Richard Elliot Friedman, *Who Wrote the Bible?* (Simon & Schuster, 2019) and *The Bible with Sources Revealed* (Harper Collins, 2005).

41. See Edward Feld, *The Book of Revolutions: The Battles of Priests, Prophets, and Kings That Birthed the Torah* (Jewish Publication Society, 2023).

42. Ilana Pardes, *The Biography of Ancient Israel: National Narratives in the Bible* (University of California Press, 2000), Kindle.

43. Robert Gluck, "Did Sukkot Help Shape Thanksgiving?," Jewish News Syndicate, September 18, 2013, https://www.jns.org/did-sukkot-help-shape-thanksgiving/.

44. Moshe Sokolow, "Thanksgiving: A Jewish Holiday After All," Jewish Ideas Daily, November 23, 2011, http://www.jewishideasdaily.com/1011/features/thanksgiving-a-jewish-holiday-after-all/.

45. Maimonides, *Mishneh Torah, Hilchot B'rachot* 10:8.

46. Frederick Buechner, *Wishful Thinking: A Seeker's ABC, Revised and Expanded* (HarperCollins, 1993), 89.

47. Abraham Joshua Heschel, *The Prophets: An Introduction* (Harper Torchbooks, 1962), 4.

48. *Fiddler on the Roof.*

49. *Tefilat Ha-Adam: An Israeli Reform Siddur for Shabbat*, ed. Dalia Marx and Alona Lisitsa, trans. Levi Weiman-Kelman and Efrat Rotem (Maram and IMPJ, 2022), 263.

50. Debbie Friedman, vocalist, "Laugh at All My Dreams," music by Debbie Friedman, text by Maurice Samuel, interpretation of "Sach'ki, Sach'ki" by Saul Chernokovsky, track 12 on *Ani Ma-Amin*, 1976.

51. Dalia Marx, "*Tikvateinu*: The Poem That Inspired Israel's National Anthem, Hatikva," TheTorah.com, https://www.thetorah.com/article/tikvatenu-the-poem-that-inspired-israels-national-anthem-hatikva.

52. "To Believe in Goodness," from Edward Feinstein, *In Pursuit of Godliness and a Living Judaism: The Life and Thought of Rabbi Harold M. Schulweis* (Jewish Lights, 2020), 151. Used by permission of the Harold M. Schulweis Institute.

53. Leon R. Kass, "L'chaim and Its Limits: Why Not Immortality?," *First Things*, May 2001, https://www.firstthings.com/article/2001/05/lchaim-and-its-limits-why-not-immortality.

54. Translation adapted from *The Judaica Press Complete Tanach with Rashi*, trans. A. J. Rosenberg.

55. Shimon Bakon, "Who Were the 'Fearers of the Lord' (*Yir'ei Hashem*) in Psalms?," *Jewish Bible Quarterly*, https://jbqnew.jewishbible.org/assets/Uploads/424/jbq_424_bakonyireihashem.pdf.

56. Translation from *The Judaica Press Complete Tanach with Rashi*, trans. A. J. Rosenberg.

57. Author's translation.
58. Samson Raphael Hirsch, trans. and commentary, *The Hirsch Psalms* (Feldheim, 1966), 319.
59. Thomas Cahill, *The Gifts of the Jews: How a Tribe of Desert Nomads Changed the Way Everyone Thinks and Feels* (Random House, 1998), 257.
60. Arthur Green, *Well of Living Insight: Comments on the Siddur* (Paraclete Press, 2023), 264.
61. Micah Joseph Bertichev, "It Is Not We Alone," in *Likrat Shabbat: Worship, Study and Song for Shabbat and Festival Services and for the Home*, ed. and trans. Rabbi Sidney Greenberg (Hartmore House, 1973, 1975), 13.
62. Quoted from *The Orange Peel and Other Satires* by S.Y. Agnon (The Toby Press, 2015), © 2015 The Toby Press LLC, as found in Leon Wieseltier, *Kaddish* (Knopf, 1998), 23.
63. Quoted from *The Orange Peel and Other Satires* by S.Y. Agnon, 23.
64. Nelly Altenburger, "Stories About Prayer," Adath Israel, Rabbi's Blog, October 24, 2020, https://adathisraelct.org/2020/10/stories-about-prayer.

About the Author

RABBI JEFFREY SALKIN is one of American Judaism's most prolific and most quoted rabbis. His colleagues have described him as "courageous," "always relevant," and "one of American Judaism's true public intellectuals."

For more than forty years, Rabbi Salkin served as a congregational rabbi in Reform synagogues and served in various leadership roles within the Reform Movement. He is the co-founder of Wisdom Without Walls, an online salon for Jewish ideas, which engages Jews and prominent thought leaders in conversations about American Judaism post–October 7. He is a well-known speaker who has shared his ideas nationally and internationally.

He is the author of twelve books, including the best-selling *Putting God on the Guest List: How to Reclaim the Spiritual Meaning of Your Child's Bar or Bat Mitzvah.* His column "Martini Judaism: For Those Who Want to Be Shaken and Stirred," published by the Religion News Service, won a Wilbur Award from the Religion Communicators Council for best religion column of the year, as well as two previous awards. "Martini Judaism" is also an award-winning podcast, available through Spotify, Google, and Audible.

Rabbi Salkin's essays have appeared in *The Washington Post, Commentary, Wall Street Journal, Huffington Post, Tablet, Mosaic, Forward,* and *JTA.* He has discussed the American political scene on CNN and the BBC. He has contributed numerous articles to scholarly journals. His books have inspired conversations on such subjects as American Jewish identity, Israel, gender, and Jewish culture, and he has written three Torah commentaries. He delivered the keynote on religion and spirituality at the world-famous Chautauqua Institution, as well as participating in interreligious dialogues in international forums.

For more than forty years, Rabbi Salkin served congregations in New York, Florida, Pennsylvania, and Georgia, and has served as visiting rabbi at Beit Warshawa, the progressive congregation in Warsaw, Poland. He currently lives in Montclair, New Jersey, and his hobbies are playing guitar, biking, and consuming coffee.